SAVING DINNER

SAVING DINNER

The Menus, Recipes, and Shopping Lists to Bring Your Family Back to the Table

LEANNE ELY

BALLANTINE BOOKS · New York

2009 Ballantine Books Trade Paperback Edition

Copyright © 2003, 2009 by Leanne Ely

Published in the United States by Ballantine Books, an imprint of The Random House Publishing Group, a division of Random House, Inc., New York.

BALLANTINE and colophon are registered trademarks of Random House, Inc.

Originally published in hardcover and in a different form in the United States by Ballantine Books, an imprint of the Random House Publishing Group, a division of Random House, Inc., in 2003.

Library of Congress Cataloging-in-Publication Data

Ely, Leanne.
    Saving dinner : the menus, recipes, and shopping lists to bring your family back to the table / Leanne Ely.
        p. cm.
ISBN 978-0-345-51629-9
    1. Cookery.   2. Dinners and dining.   I. Title.

    TX714.E457 2003
    641.5'4—dc21

                                                                    2003052133

Printed in the United States of America

www.ballantinebooks.com

9 8 7 6 5

This book is lovingly dedicated to my dear friend Marla Cilley, whose friendship and encouragement go beyond books, business, and success. Thank you, Marla, for everything.

A LETTER TO MY READERS

Dear Friends,

Thank you for coming back for a second helping of the original *Saving Dinner*. My publisher and I believe this second edition is significant because it reflects not only the ongoing importance of the family dinner table but also our changing times via the new section in the book on Freezer Dinner Kits.

You'll read more about Freezer Dinner Kits in the book, but let me just say this at the get-go: I believe so strongly in families eating together at the dinner table and wanted yet another way to help families get there. And after having survived all-day cooking-and-freezing scenarios myself (cook all day, then eat twice-cooked, reheated food for a month) back in the 1990s, I knew I didn't want to go there again. I liked the *idea* of those franchise meal-assembly places, but the ingredients badly needed some nutritional CPR. Add in the whole time element of using those franchise places—the night or Saturday away from the family, the drive there, the hours cooking in a commercial kitchen, the drive home with the fruit of your labor—plus the hundreds of dollars using those places cost, and it all seemed like too much. Sadly, a lot of those places are starting to close now.

We knew we could do it better nutritionally, for a whole lot less money, and give you back your time by giving you the ability to do it in the comfort and familiarity of your own kitchen. The entire staff at SavingDinner.com worked to bring this concept into reality. From the first testing of recipes to writing out all the instructions, our first Mega Menu-Mailer (twenty recipes) was born over three years ago. We've since switched up the concept a little, tightened up the instructions, and made it even simpler than it was originally—you'll read more about that in what we affectionately call the Freezer Meals chapter in this book.

Without further ado, I invite you into my kitchen to sit down and relax. Let me get you a cup of comfort and check out my new (and improved!) *Saving Dinner*. You're going to love how easy it is to save dinner at your house!

Love,
Leanne

CONTENTS

ACKNOWLEDGMENTS

Oh my gosh, this is gonna take awhile. Go put on some tea and put your feet up.

I have to start with my agent, Michelle Tessler, whose representation went way beyond all my wildest expectations. A phenomenal job, Michelle—thank you.

God bless Maureen O'neal, the original editor on *Saving Dinner*, who truly believed in this book from the beginning. However, my biggest thanks now goes to my current editor (and *Saving Dinner* believer), Christina Duffy, who has now been working on *Saving Dinner* books for years. I am truly grateful.

My second "editor," my mom. Her editorial assistance, encouragement, and ability to stifle her gasps as I ask for yet another editorial favor has been beyond great—what can I say? You're the best—thanks, Mom!

And then there are the countless women who stand behind this book.

The subscribers to my Menu-Mailer, who clamored for this book to happen in the first place. To Sandy, a Menu-Mailerette who took on the grocery lists for me in the Spring section—thank you for your help!

The FlyBabies on Marla's FlyLady e-mail list, who made Menu-Mailer what it is today—I so appreciate you all—thank you.

The Swap Sisters, who helped with the grocery lists—Cyndy, Vicki, Carol, Kathleen, and Tami—another round of thanks!

And a huge thanks to my own family for putting up with me during the writing of yet another book—you guys are the best!

INTRODUCTION

"Dinner! Come to the table!"

Do you remember your mom hollering those same words when you were a kid? Do you remember running toward those familiar smells and rushing to take your place at the table?

The family dinner table is a place of communion and fellowship, and a means of reconnecting with those we care about the most. Over a simple family meal, important stuff happens. Relationships are realigned, the news of the day is exchanged, and coming events are discussed. More important, memories are made for both adults and children. One day, your child will look back with fondness on all those dinners around the family table. One day, you will look back wistfully, actually missing the chaos of trying to get everyone to the table while the meal was still hot!

Unfortunately, today's family dinner table is all but missing from the home. We have sacrificed our family table for all manner of activities, and, way too often, our meals are situated around the blue glow of the family television. Conversation is limited to pass the salt and stony silence prevails while the blare of TV fills the room.

But that's not the only problem. Actually making the meals is a big issue, too. Women are busy, exhausted, and overwhelmed with responsibility. Mom works hard at the job or at home all day and then takes on another job schlepping kids to lessons, rehearsals, and practices. Making the weekly menu to post on the refrigerator has become a relic of the past—who has the time? And going to the grocery store is something that happens several times a week, because there is no plan and a list hasn't been made. Grocery shopping usually entails buying overpriced, processed convenience foods. Or worse, showing up at the grocery store with a couple of cranky kids right after work to get something quick. Or even worse, skipping the whole thing and driving through for fast food. The result: guilt over the money spent and the nutrition lost, and a strong sense that somehow, because of all this, the family is suffering and missing out.

Saving Dinner is the younger "sister" of Menu-Mailer, my online menu service (*www.menumailer.net*). Menu-Mailer was born out of a strong desire to help bring back the family dinner table. As the Food for Thought columnist for FlyLady.net, I help Marla Cilley (the FlyLady) with all things pertinent to food and its preparation. Marla regularly challenges the ladies on her list to clutter-bust their homes, but this time was taking on a bigger, two-week decluttering challenge—what Marla calls the Super Fling Boogie. So we put our heads together to come up with an idea to help the ladies with dinner. Marla thought a week's worth of recipes would really help because the ladies wouldn't have to think about dinner. I agreed and said it would be even better with a grocery list—that's the hard part. We sent out the first menu with the grocery list and the ladies went crazy! The second week, we did it again, and by then there was a frenzy—they wanted the menus and the grocery list on a regular basis. I was reticent due to the amount of work involved—I would do only recipes that met the following criteria: (1) healthy, (2) easy to prepare, and (3) something I'd actually eat! A lightbulb went off in my head. Menu-Mailer was born and became a paid subscription service, with the website soon following.

And while *Saving Dinner* meets all the criteria of a Menu-Mailer, its being in book form gives me an opportunity to offer a lot more information, important how-to's and what for's, equipping you to confidently answer that all-important question, "What's for dinner?"

The ladies who use my service and read my books are kindred spirits. They are women who, like me, need real-life solutions—not another "make-it-quick" dinner book. *Saving Dinner* is a quantum leap beyond a mere book—it's a real tool that offers reliable help to get you beyond frustrated and guilty, to being a champion in the kitchen.

It is in that spirit that I offer *Saving Dinner* as my contribution to your family. I can promise you this—the book you hold in your hands right now will make dinner happen if you use it—the family fellowship part is up to you.

Remember this—menus aren't just for restaurants. They deserve a special place of honor in every family's home. You now have what you need—let's get busy.

HOW TO USE THIS BOOK

Saving Dinner is designed to give you everything you need to do dinner. The recipes, serving suggestions, and, most important, categorized shopping lists are all contained within this book. And while you can't take the lists out of the book, you can go to the Saving Dinner website (savingdinner.com) and print out the appropriate list if that's more convenient than taking the book to the store.

Serving Suggestions are asterisked on the grocery lists because I don't want you to feel roped in by any of my recommendations. I tell my subscribers on Menu-Mailer that I want to give you freedom from kitchen bondage, not make your life harder. So if the Serving Suggestions turn your key, use them. If they don't, ignore them—it's not hard to do because the grocery list has them marked so they can be easily skipped.

I would also suggest you read the recipes before you hit the grocery store each week with the list. It helps to know what your menu is about before you head out the door. That five minutes of reading through the menu and recipes may help you make a quick decision if your store is out of something or if you would prefer a substitute. You can't do that if you don't know what you're shopping for!

This book is chock full of sidebars . . . read them! There is a ton of information to help you take full advantage of these menus and to make the recipes your own. As I was writing these recipes out, I would think of something else that would empower you in the kitchen, so I made a sidebar out of it. The more you know, the faster you're able to do the recipes and shopping. That's a good thing!

When appropriate, I have added Do Ahead Tips to help make dinner easier the next day (e.g., soaking the beans, precooking turkey or chicken for a salad, etc.); however, there all kinds of things you can do the day before if you so desire. I kept it basic, you might want to do more—it's totally up to you. You also can move days around if you want—just remember that the Do Ahead Tips may no longer be appropriate if you do.

If you do want to make substitutions (due to allergies, preferences, etc.) on some of the grocery items, feel free! For instance, I've had subscribers e-mail me to say that my chicken recipes work great for pork, too! So, even though all of the work of planning a menu has already been done for you, the Serving Suggestions have been written out and planned based on the season, and the grocery list has been categorized, that doesn't mean that's it. You most certainly can make changes, and I encourage it. *Saving Dinner* may be the most important cookbook you ever own because of the empowerment it offers you in the kitchen and with your family. However, you still need to make it your own, and there certainly is room for you to do that.

FALL

As the weather starts to change, the welcome relief from the heat begins to take hold and paint the leaves of the trees autumnal colors. With crisp fall weather, warm comfort foods begin to play into these coming weeks. The rich, glorious flavors of fall are showcased in this first set of menus with rich stews, thick soups, and recipes featuring delicious winter squashes.

❦ Week One

DAY ONE: Apple Chicken
DAY TWO: Roast Beef Picante
DAY THREE: Beany Burritos
DAY FOUR: Moroccan Fish Tangine
DAY FIVE: Italian Turkey Meat Loaf
DAY SIX: Crock Pea Soup

SHOPPING LIST

MEAT
6 boneless, skinless chicken breast halves
1½ pounds boneless sirloin roast
6 whitefish fillets
½ package Italian turkey sausages
½ pound ground turkey
1 ham bone

CONDIMENTS
vegetable oil
olive oil
cider vinegar
dry white wine
Worcestershire sauce

PRODUCE
1 lime
2–3 lemons
4 Granny Smith apples
3 pounds onions (keep on hand)
garlic (you'll need 7 cloves)
3 tomatoes
2 bell peppers

1 bunch carrots
celery (you'll need 1 stalk)
1 small jalapeño pepper
1 small bunch parsley
1 bunch cilantro
1 bunch green onions
**russet potatoes (1 meal)
**butternut squash (2 meals)
**broccoli (2 meals)
**kale (2 meals)
**spinach (I like baby spinach) (2 meals)
**baby carrots (2 meals)
**sweet potatoes (1 meal)
**2–3 heads lettuce (*not* Iceberg)

CANNED GOODS

1 28-ounce jar spaghetti sauce
1 14-ounce can chicken broth
1 14-ounce can beef broth
1 jar salsa (your favorite)
1 small can tomato puree (you'll need 3 tablespoons)
1 14½-ounce can diced tomatoes with Italian herbs
1 15-ounce can pinto beans
1 15-ounce can black beans

SPICES

1 envelope taco seasoning (low sodium is a good option)
paprika
ground cumin
bay leaves
thyme

DAIRY/DAIRY CASE

eggs (you'll need 1)
Parmesan cheese (you'll need ⅓ cup, grated)
**sour cream (I use low fat)

DRY GOODS
brown sugar (you'll need ⅓ cup)
sugar (you'll need 2 teaspoons)
cornstarch (you'll need 4 tablespoons)
oats (you'll need ½ cup)
flour (you'll need ⅓ cup)
1 pound split peas
**brown rice (2 meals)
**pasta (1 meal)

BAKERY
6 flour tortillas (whole wheat, if available)
**whole-grain rolls (1 meal)

APPLE CHICKEN

Serves 6

1¼ teaspoons vegetable oil
6 boneless, skinless chicken breast halves, cut into ½-inch cubes
4 Granny Smith apples, cored and sliced into ½-inch wedges
¾ cup dry white wine
¾ cup chicken broth
⅓ cup brown sugar
¼ cup cider vinegar
3 tablespoons cornstarch
2 tablespoons Worcestershire sauce
½ teaspoon salt
1 teaspoon black pepper

Heat oil in a large nonstick skillet. Add chicken and brown on all sides. Add apple slices, sauté 3 minutes, stirring occasionally. Add ½ the wine and chicken broth, reduce heat, cover, and simmer 10 minutes. Mix remaining wine and broth together with remaining ingredients;

add to skillet. Cook over medium heat, stirring constantly until sauce thickens.

PER SERVING:
161 Calories; 2g Fat (15.5% calories from fat); 7g Protein; 24g Carbohydrate; 2g Dietary Fiber; 16mg Cholesterol; 246mg Sodium. Exchanges: ½ Grain (Starch); 1 Lean Meat; ½ Fruit; 0 Fat; ½ Other Carbohydrates.

SERVING SUGGESTIONS: Baked potatoes, baked butternut squash, and steamed broccoli.

ROAST BEEF PICANTE

Serves 6 (with leftovers)

½ cup finely chopped onion
¼ cup water
3 tablespoons lime juice
2 large cloves garlic, pressed
1 tablespoon olive oil
½ small jalapeño pepper, finely minced
½ teaspoon thyme, divided
Salt and pepper to taste
1½ pounds boneless sirloin roast
1 cup beef broth
2 teaspoons sugar
1 tablespoon cornstarch
2 tablespoons parsley, chopped

For marinade, combine onion, water, lime juice, garlic, olive oil, jalapeño pepper, ¼ teaspoon of the thyme, salt, and pepper. Place beef in a plastic bag. Pour marinade over meat, seal bag, and refrigerate 6–8 hours.

Remove meat from marinade, reserving marinade. Place meat on a rack in a roasting pan.

Preheat oven to 350 degrees F. Roast for 40–50 minutes or until desired doneness. Remove meat from pan; cover with foil. Let stand 10 minutes.

Meanwhile strain remaining marinade. Deglaze pan with ½ cup of the beef broth; pour into a small saucepan. Add the strained marinade, sugar, and remaining ¼ teaspoon thyme to saucepan. Combine remaining broth with cornstarch; add to saucepan. Cook and stir until thickened and bubbly. Cook and stir 1 minute more. Stir in parsley. Slice meat to serve; serve with sauce.

PER SERVING:
181 Calories; 7g Fat (36.8% calories from fat); 22g Protein; 6g Carbohydrate; trace Dietary Fiber; 51mg Cholesterol; 346mg Sodium. Exchanges: 0 Grain (Starch); 3 Lean Meat; ½ Vegetable; 0 Fruit; ½ Fat; 0 Other Carbohydrates.

SERVING SUGGESTIONS: Brown rice, steamed kale, baked sweet potatoes, and a salad. Remember, you want to use the leftover beef tomorrow night (but leftovers are not absolutely necessary).

A SALAD (side) BAR

I can't help but push the nutritional envelope hard when it comes to making salads. If you're at all following the Serving Suggestions in the book (and I really hope you are!), you will notice the abundant suggestions for salad to be served with nearly all the recipes. The reasons for all this green boils down to the fact that we eat entirely too many cooked foods and rarely eat anything raw. A salad gives your body the alimentary opportunity to tackle a raw food and get those important enzymes, vitamins, and minerals so readily available from uncooked produce.

But in order to avail yourself of these nutrient-rich possibilities, it is necessary to understand what constitutes healthy when it comes to salad making. A pale hunk of Iceberg lettuce with a goopy ladle of blue cheese dressing doesn't cut it. And yet so many people think because they've eaten this "salad," they're giving their bodies the nutrition it needs. Not true!

A good rule of thumb for evaluating a good salad should be **color**. Color is a great indicator of what's ahead: good nutrition or near-empty calories. **The more vibrant the color, the healthier it is.**

Let's go back to that Iceberg lettuce salad. It's pale green and white. The Iceberg lettuce's value is mostly the water it carries. Fiber is minimal and nutrition almost nonexistent. The blue cheese is dripping with all kinds of fat so that X's that off the list immediately. Let's do a salad makeover, shall we?

First of all, you need to choose **green**. Green like spinach, salad bowl (Butter or Bibb), or romaine lettuces—all wonderful examples of what green should look like. The color is there and so is the nutrition.

Look for **red**. Tomatoes come to mind. Vine ripened and full of vitamin C, tomatoes also contain the important phytochemical lycopene that helps fight cancer.

Orange or **yellow**? How about some colorful bell pepper or (when in season) summer squash? Carrots are fantastic sources for beta-carotene, a pre-vitamin for vitamin A. Beta-carotene has so many important functions, but the best part about beta-carotene is that it will convert into only as much vitamin A as the body needs, so there's no worry about taking in too much. You know what happens if you have too much beta-carotene? You turn orange! My son was orange for the first and second years of his life—he *loved* sweet potatoes.

This is all common-sense nutrition here, but the point is to get you thinking next time you're meandering your way through the produce section at the grocery store. Think in vivid, living color—you *need* the nutrition!

BEANY BURRITOS

Serves 6

1 tablespoon olive oil
1 onion, chopped
1½ cups leftover beef, chopped
1 package taco seasoning mix (low sodium, if available)
1 can black beans, rinsed and drained
1 can pinto beans, rinsed and drained
6 flour tortillas (whole wheat, if available)
Chopped green onions, salsa (your favorite jarred variety), sour cream, and chopped cilantro

In a skillet, heat oil over medium heat and sauté onion till translucent. Add leftover chopped beef, taco seasoning, and both cans of beans; stir till well heated through.

Warm tortillas and fill with bean beef mixture. Garnish as you like it!

PER SERVING:
317 Calories; 3g Fat (9.5% calories from fat); 26g Protein; 46g Carbohydrate; 14g Dietary Fiber; 34mg Cholesterol; 429mg Sodium. Exchanges: 2½ Grain (Starch); 2½ Lean Meat; ½ Vegetable; 0 Other Carbohydrates.

SERVING SUGGESTIONS: A big spinach salad and a bowl of baby carrots ought to do the trick!

MOROCCAN FISH TANGINE

Serves 6

3 garlic cloves
3 tablespoons ground cumin
3 tablespoons paprika
3 tablespoons tomato puree
6 tablespoons lemon juice
6 whitefish fillets
3 tomatoes, sliced
2 bell peppers, seeded and thinly sliced
Salt and ground black pepper to taste
Chopped cilantro

Whole-wheat tortillas have a better flavor and texture than white flour tortillas, and if you have a choice at the grocery store, give these whole-grain alternatives a try. Also check the package for lard or shortening—you definitely want vegetable oil instead (much healthier).

Corn tortillas are corn tortillas, although some brands are better than others. You'll have to try different brands to see which one you like best. Here in California, we have every brand known to man and then some. Choices become smaller and smaller the farther east you go.

One more thing: Remember that you have incredible power as a consumer. Tell the dairy manager guy (or whoever is in charge of the department at the grocery store that carries the tortillas) what you want. If you want whole-wheat tortillas, ask for them. You will be surprised at how accommodating supermarkets are becoming. The competition for your grocery dollar is stiff. If the market you're frequenting now won't yield to your requests, find one that will.

In a medium bowl, mix together the garlic, cumin, paprika, tomato puree, and lemon juice. Place the fish in a 9 × 13–inch pan and spread this mixture over the fish; cover and chill for about 30 minutes to let the flavors penetrate the fish.

Preheat the oven to 400 degrees F.

Arrange half of the tomatoes and peppers in a baking dish. Cover with the fish, in one layer, and then arrange the remaining tomatoes and peppers on top. Salt and pepper to taste. Cover the baking dish with foil and bake for about 20 minutes, until the fish flakes easily with a fork. Sprinkle with chopped cilantro and serve.

PER SERVING:
54 Calories; 1g Fat (19.1% calories from fat); 2g Protein; 11g Carbohydrate; 3g Dietary Fiber; 0mg Cholesterol; 44mg Sodium. Exchanges: 0 Grain (Starch); 0 Lean Meat; 1 Vegetable; 0 Fruit; 0 Fat.

SERVING SUGGESTIONS: Steamed kale, brown rice, and a green salad. Pass the baby carrots around the table, too!

ITALIAN TURKEY MEAT LOAF

Serves 6

1 large egg
½ 14½-ounce can diced tomatoes with Italian herbs, undrained
½ cup finely chopped onion
⅓ cup minced fresh parsley
½ cup oats
⅓ cup grated Parmesan cheese
Salt and pepper to taste
½ package Italian turkey sausages (removed from casings; about 4 sausages)
½ pound ground turkey
⅓ cup spaghetti sauce

Preheat oven to 375 degrees F.

In a large bowl, beat the egg and stir in tomatoes, onion, parsley, oats, Parmesan cheese, salt, and pepper. Then mix in by hand the Italian sausage and ground turkey just until blended. Make into a large meat loaf on a baking sheet (like a jelly roll pan), patting to remove any air spaces. Bake for one hour. Top with spaghetti sauce and continue baking 15–30 minutes. Let stand 10 minutes before serving.

PER SERVING:
259 Calories; 12g Fat (41.8% calories from fat); 20g Protein; 19g Carbohydrate; 4g Dietary Fiber; 96mg Cholesterol; 888mg Sodium. Exchanges: ½ Grain (Starch); 2 Lean Meat; 2½ Vegetable; 1 Fat.

SERVING SUGGESTIONS: Pasta, steamed broccoli, and baked butternut squash.

CROCK PEA SOUP

Serves 12 (freezes well)

1 pound split peas, rinsed
1 ham bone, optional
1 onion, chopped
2 carrots, peeled and sliced
1 stalk celery, chopped
2 cloves garlic, pressed
1 bay leaf
1½ quarts water (use chicken broth if not using ham bone)
Salt and pepper to taste

Put all ingredients except the salt and pepper into a Crock-Pot. Cover and cook on high for 4–5 hours or low for 8–10 hours, or until peas are very soft. Before serving, remove bone and bay leaf. Salt and pepper to taste.

PER SERVING:
161 Calories; 2g Fat (11.2% calories from fat); 11g Protein; 25g Carbohydrate; 10g Dietary Fiber; 9mg Cholesterol; 22mg Sodium. Exchanges: 1½ Grain (Starch); 1 Lean Meat; ½ Vegetable; 0 Fat.

SERVING SUGGESTIONS: A spinach salad and some whole-grain rolls.

❧ Week Two

DAY ONE: Chicken and Rice Chowder
DAY TWO: Asian Orange Salmon
DAY THREE: Baked Rigatoni
DAY FOUR: Stuffed Quesadillas
DAY FIVE: Red Beans and Rice
DAY SIX: Crock Beef Sandwiches

SHOPPING LIST

MEAT

6 boneless, skinless chicken breast halves
6 salmon fillets
½ pound extra-lean ground beef
1 pound kielbasa (low fat, if available)
3 pounds sirloin tip roast (you can use a cheaper cut, but fat
    count will be higher)

CONDIMENTS

olive oil
soy sauce
barbecue sauce

PRODUCE

1–2 lemons
tomatoes (you'll use 1 cup chopped)
3 pounds onions (keep on hand)
1 head garlic
1 bunch celery (you'll need 1 stalk)
1 bunch green onions
1 bell pepper
1 bunch cilantro
**russet potatoes (1 meal)
**coleslaw (1 meal)
**kale (1 meal)
**spinach (I like baby spinach) (2 meals)

**baby carrots (2 meals)
**2–3 heads lettuce (*not* Iceberg) (1 meal)

CANNED GOODS
1 28-ounce jar spaghetti sauce
3 14-ounce cans chicken broth (you'll use 4½ cups)
1 jar salsa (your favorite)
2 15-ounce cans red beans

SPICES
thyme
cayenne pepper
rosemary
bay leaves

DAIRY/DAIRY CASE
low-fat milk (you'll use 1½ cups)
orange juice (you'll use ½ cup)
1 cup non-fat cottage cheese
1 cup part-skim-milk mozzarella cheese, shredded
¼ cup Romano cheese, grated
6 ounces low-fat Jack cheese, shredded
1 8-ounce container low-fat sour cream

DRY GOODS
brown sugar (you'll need ½ cup)
brown rice (you'll need 3½ cups)
oats (you'll need 1 cup)
1 pound rigatoni
flour

BAKERY
12 flour tortillas
whole-wheat hamburger buns (1 meal)
**whole-grain rolls (1 meal)

CHICKEN AND RICE CHOWDER

Serves 6

4½ cups chicken broth, canned or homemade
½ cup water
3 boneless, skinless chicken breasts, cooked and chopped
2 teaspoons thyme
Salt and pepper to taste
½ cup brown rice
1 tablespoon olive oil
4 cloves garlic, pressed
1 large onion, chopped
2 carrots, chopped
1 stalk celery, chopped
3 tablespoons flour
1½ cups 1% low-fat milk

In a large saucepan, bring chicken broth and water to a boil and add the chicken. Add thyme and season with salt and pepper; add rice and reduce heat.

In a skillet, heat olive oil over medium-high heat. Add garlic, onion, carrots, and celery; cook until onions are translucent. Add flour to the mix and combine well. Add this mixture to the broth mixture in the saucepan.

Stir milk into everything and continue to simmer, stirring occasionally, until thickened, about 20–30 minutes.

PER SERVING:
298 Carlories; 6g Fat (18.5% calories from fat); 35g Protein; 24g Carbohydrate; 2g Dietary Fiber; 71mg Cholesterol; 697mg Sodium. Exchanges: 1 Grain (Starch); 4 Lean Meat; 1 Vegetable; 0 Non-Fat Milk; ½ Fat.

SERVING SUGGESTIONS: A big green salad and some whole-grain rolls would top this meal off nicely.

ASIAN ORANGE SALMON

Serves 6

½ *cup orange juice*
½ *cup soy sauce*
½ *cup brown sugar*
½ *cup green onions, chopped*
3 *tablespoons lemon juice*
3 *cloves garlic, pressed*
6 *salmon fillets*

In a large plastic, zipper-topped bag, combine first six ingredients and mix well. Add fish and marinate in fridge for an hour, turning bag occasionally. Go make your salad, call your mom, or fold a load of wash while you wait.

Preheat broiler.

Transfer marinade to a bowl. Place salmon on broiler pan and cook about 4–6 minutes on each side (depending on the thickness of your fish and your broiler—I'd watch it pretty carefully). Baste fish with marinade every time you check on it. When fish flakes when tested with a fork, it's done.

PER SERVING:
271 Calories; 6g Fat (20.1% calories from fat); 36g Protein; 18g Carbohydrate; 1g Dietary Fiber; 88mg Cholesterol; 1492mg Sodium. Exchanges: 5 Lean Meat; ½ Vegetable; 0 Fruit; 1 Other Carbohydrates.

SERVING SUGGESTIONS: Baked potatoes, steamed kale, and steamed baby carrots are perfect side dishes.

BAKED RIGATONI

Serves 6

½ *pound extra-lean ground beef*
1 *cup oats*
1 *jar spaghetti sauce*
1 *cup non-fat cottage cheese*
3 *cups rigatoni, cooked*

1 cup part-skim-milk mozzarella cheese, shredded
¼ cup Romano cheese, grated

Preheat oven to 350 degrees F.

In a skillet, cook beef until browned and crumbled. Drain grease and blot beef well with paper towels (with this step the fat grams will be lower than what shows up in the nutritional info below). Add oats to beef and stir well to incorporate.

Add spaghetti sauce, cottage cheese, and rigatoni to the beef and mix well. In a 11 × 7–inch casserole dish, add your rigatoni mixture and top with mozzarella and Romano cheeses. Bake for 20–30 minutes or until hot and cheese is melted.

PER SERVING:
372 Calories; 14g Fat (34.4% calories from fat); 25g Protein; 36g Carbohydrate; 3g Dietary Fiber; 43mg Cholesterol; 488mg Sodium. Exchanges: 2 Grain (Starch); 2½ Lean Meat; 1½ vegetable; 1½ Fat.

SERVING SUGGESTION: Serve with a spinach salad, and you're set.

STUFFED QUESADILLAS

Serves 6

1 tablespoon olive oil
1 onion, chopped
3 skinless, boneless chicken breasts, cut in 1-inch strips
Salt and pepper to taste
12 flour tortillas
6 ounces low-fat Jack cheese, shredded
Salsa (your favorite jarred variety)
Cilantro, chopped
Low-fat sour cream

In a skillet, heat the olive oil over medium-high heat. Add onion and chicken, salt and pepper to taste, and sauté till chicken is thoroughly cooked. Remove chicken and onions and set aside.

In that same skillet, heat a flour tortilla. Spread a little cheese on the bottom, top with a portion of the chicken and onions, top with a little more cheese and another tortilla. Once it's cooked on the one side, flip it over to continue cooking.

Cut quesadilla into quarters and serve with salsa, chopped cilantro, and sour cream.

PER SERVING:
686 Calories; 16g Fat (21.4% calories from fat); 47g Protein; 85g Carbohydrate; 5g Dietary Fiber; 74mg Cholesterol; 1126mg Sodium. Exchanges: 5½ Grain (Starch); 4½ Lean Meat; ½ Vegetable; 2½ Fat.

SERVING SUGGESTION: A spinach salad will round this off nicely.

DO AHEAD TIP: Cook rice for Red Beans and Rice tomorrow.

RED BEANS AND RICE

Serves 6

1 pound kielbasa, cut into ¼-inch-thick slices
1 onion, chopped
2 cloves garlic, pressed
1 bell pepper, chopped
2 cans red beans, drained
1 cup tomatoes, chopped
½ teaspoon thyme
¼ teaspoon cayenne pepper, optional
Salt and pepper to taste
3 cups brown rice, cooked

In a skillet over medium-low heat, cook sliced sausage for about 2 minutes. Add onion, garlic, and bell pepper, and sauté till veggies are tender. Add beans and tomatoes with their juice. Season with thyme, cayenne (optional), and salt and pepper to taste. Serve over rice.

PER SERVING:
569 Calories; 22g Fat (34.6% calories from fat); 27g Protein; 66g Carbohydrate; 18g Dietary Fiber; 51mg Cholesterol; 834mg Sodium. Exchanges: 4 Grain (Starch); 2½ Lean Meat; 1 Vegetable; 3 Fat.

**NUTRITION NOTE: Buy low-fat kielbasa if available to substantially lower fat grams.

SERVING SUGGESTION: A big green salad.

CROCK BEEF SANDWICHES

Serves 6

3 pounds sirloin tip roast, trimmed
3 cloves garlic, pressed
2 teaspoons rosemary, crumbled
1 bay leaf, snapped in half
¾ cup soy sauce
1½ cups water
barbecue sauce

Put everything in your Crock-Pot and set on low to cook for 6 hours or until meat is tender.

Shred beef with two forks and serve on whole-wheat hamburger buns with a bottle of barbecue sauce.

PER SERVING:
318 Calories; 10g Fat (29.7% calories from fat); 50g Protein; 4g Carbohydrate; trace Dietary Fiber; 136mg Cholesterol; 2200mg Sodium. Exchanges: 0 Grain (Starch); 7 Lean Meat; 1 Vegetable; 0 Fat.

SERVING SUGGESTIONS: Coleslaw and a bowl of baby carrots.

**NUTRITION NOTE: You can use a cheaper cut of beef, but the fat grams will skyrocket. Using a trimmed roast like this will keep it lean and probably make for some terrific leftovers!

SEASONED WITH SALT

🍂 You will notice in a lot of my recipes, I say "salt and pepper to taste." There is a reason for this—not because I'm trying to frustrate you! Salt should be added slowly and, depending on the recipes, in steps. That's how the pros do it and it makes sense—this is how to get the best taste and make sure you don't oversalt. The reason to salt anything is to bring out the flavor of food—not mask it.

But salt is salt is salt . . . right? Not necessarily. There are big differences in types of salt—kosher salt, sea salt, and regular table salt. You may want to rethink your salt shaker.

Kosher salt is coarse and free of any additives. The taste is lighter, less salty than regular table salt, and it's a good choice for cooking. As a matter of fact, in a poll of fifty top U.S. chefs, 86 percent preferred cooking with kosher salt than with any other kind.

Sea salt is made from evaporated seawater and contains the extra minerals found in the seawater itself. La Baleine (French for whale) is the brand of sea salt most readily available in supermarkets. It comes in a blue container with a whale on the label. It's pricier than table salt for sure, but it will last awhile.

Table salt is pure sodium chloride with a small amount of chemical substance that stops it from clunking together and keeps it free flowing. Believe it or not, table salt often has dextrose (a sugar) added to stabilize it—who knew?

❧ Week Three

DAY ONE: Chicken and Artichoke Casserole
DAY TWO: Texas One Dish
DAY THREE: Halibut Marengo
DAY FOUR: Smashing Pumpkin Soup
DAY FIVE: Great Greek Pasta
DAY SIX: Crock Frijoles

SHOPPING LIST

MEAT
9 boneless, skinless chicken breast halves
1 pound extra-lean ground beef
6 halibut (or other white fish) steaks
3 turkey bacon slices

CONDIMENTS
olive oil
hot pepper sauce

PRODUCE
1–2 lemons
3 pounds onions (keep on hand)
1 head garlic
1½ cups mushrooms
2 tomatoes
2 green bell peppers
1 small red pepper
1 small red onion
1 bunch green onions
2 chipotle peppers, optional
**russet potatoes (1 meal)
**butternut squash (1 meal)
**broccoli (1 meal)
**kale (1 meal)
**cilantro (1 meal)
**spinach (I like baby spinach) (2 meals)

**baby carrots (1 meal)
**sweet potatoes (1 meal)
**2–3 heads lettuce (*not* Iceberg)

CANNED GOODS
1 jar marinated artichoke hearts
6 14-ounce cans chicken broth
tomato puree (you'll need 1½ cups)
1 14½-ounce can diced tomatoes
pumpkin puree (you'll need 2 cups)

SPICES
chili powder
garlic powder
cumin
thyme
nutmeg
curry powder
oregano
cayenne pepper
salt
ground black pepper

DAIRY/DAIRY CASE
butter (you'll need 4 tablespoons)
low-fat milk (you'll need 2 cups)
½ cup Feta cheese
**low-fat Cheddar cheese, grated (6 ounces)

DRY GOODS
1 pound rigatoni
1 pound dry pinto beans
oats (you'll need 1 cup)
flour
brown rice (2 meals)

BAKERY
**whole-grain rolls (1 meal)

CHICKEN AND ARTICHOKE CASSEROLE

Serves 6

6 boneless, skinless chicken breast halves, cut in 1-inch strips
4 tablespoons butter
2 cloves garlic, pressed
1 cup mushrooms, sliced
1 jar marinated artichoke hearts, drained
2 tablespoons flour
1 can chicken broth

Preheat oven to 350 degrees F.

In a skillet over medium heat, brown chicken lightly in 2 tablespoons butter, add the garlic and mushrooms, and keep cooking till chicken mixture is smelling very garlicky.

In a baking dish, add the browned chicken mixture. Place the artichoke hearts atop the chicken.

In the skillet, melt remaining butter and add the flour, whisking to blend (no lumps!). Add broth and cook until thickened, then pour over chicken mixture.

Bake 30–45 minutes.

PER SERVING:
352 Calories; 11g Fat (29.6% calories from fat); 56g Protein; 3g Carbohydrate; trace Dietary Fiber; 158mg Cholesterol; 374mg Sodium. Exchanges: 0 Grain (Starch); 7½ Lean Meat; 0 Vegetable; 1½ Fat.

SERVING SUGGESTIONS: Steamed kale, baked butternut squash, and brown rice.

TEXAS ONE DISH

Serves 6

1 pound extra-lean ground beef
2 onions, chopped
1 bell pepper, chopped
1 cup oats
1 can diced tomatoes, with juice

½ cup brown rice
1 teaspoon chili powder
1 teaspoon garlic powder
1 teaspoon cumin
1 teaspoon salt
Pepper to taste

Preheat oven to 350 degrees F.

In a large skillet, sauté beef and onions over medium-high heat. When onions begin to look translucent, add bell pepper. Continue cooking till beef is browned completely. Drain grease well and blot with paper towels to reduce fat grams on this recipe. Add oats, stirring well to incorporate.

Add remaining ingredients, stirring well to completely mix. Transfer to a 2-quart baking dish. Bake for 45 minutes or until rice is tender.

PER SERVING:
316 Calories; 15g Fat (41.4% calories from fat); 19g Protein; 28g Carbohydrate; 3g Dietary Fiber; 52mg Cholesterol; 415mg Sodium. Exchanges: 1½ Grain (Starch); 2 Lean Meat; 1 Vegetable; 1½ Fat.

SERVING SUGGESTIONS: Baked sweet potatoes and spinach salad would be perfect.

HALIBUT MARENGO

Serves 6

6 halibut steaks (or another mild fish that's available to you)
Salt and pepper to taste
1 medium tomato, diced
1 tablespoon olive oil
½ cup sliced fresh mushrooms
½ cup onions, chopped
2 tablespoons lemon juice
½ teaspoon thyme, pressed

Preheat oven to 350 degrees F.

Sprinkle halibut with salt and pepper and place in shallow baking dish. Spoon tomato over halibut.

In a skillet, heat oil and sauté mushrooms and onions till soft, then add lemon juice, thyme, salt and pepper; mix well. Spoon over halibut. Bake for 20–30 minutes or until fish flakes.

PER SERVING:
157 Calories; 5g Fat (29.3% calories from fat); 24g Protein; 3g Carbohydrate; 1g Dietary Fiber; 36mg Cholesterol; 64mg Sodium. Exchanges: 0 Grain (Starch); 3½ Lean Meat; ½ Vegetable; 0 Fruit; ½ Fat.

SERVING SUGGESTIONS: Baked potatoes, steamed broccoli, and a big green salad.

SMASHING PUMPKIN SOUP

Serves 6

1 tablespoon olive oil
1 onion, chopped
4 cups chicken broth
2 cups pumpkin puree
¾ cup green onions, chopped
⅛ teaspoon nutmeg
½ teaspoon curry powder
Salt and pepper to taste
2 cups milk

In a soup pot, heat oil over medium high heat and sauté onion. Cook till very soft and add remaining ingredients, except milk. Cook uncovered for 15 minutes. Add milk and continue to cook (but not boil—it will break) for another 5 minutes. Salt and pepper to taste.

PER SERVING:
131 Calories; 6g Fat (41.3% calories from fat); 7g Protein; 13g Carbohydrate; 3g Dietary Fiber; 11mg Cholesterol; 553mg Sodium. Exchanges: 0 Grain (Starch); ½ Lean Meat; 1½ Vegetable; ½ Non-Fat Milk; 1 Fat.

SERVING SUGGESTIONS: A huge spinach salad and whole-grain rolls are all you need.

GREAT GREEK PASTA

1 pound rigatoni, uncooked
1 tablespoon olive oil
2 cloves garlic, pressed
1 small red onion, chopped
3 boneless, skinless chicken breasts, cut into bite-size pieces
1 large tomato, chopped
½ cup Feta cheese, crumbled
2 tablespoons lemon juice
2 teaspoons oregano
Salt and pepper to taste

In a large pot, bring water to boil for pasta. Cook till al dente; drain and set aside.

While pasta is cooking, in a large skillet heat olive oil over medium-high heat. Add garlic and onion, and sauté till translucent but not brown. Add chicken and cook until chicken is done, about 5 minutes.

Reduce heat to medium low and add tomato, Feta, lemon juice, and oregano. Add pasta. Stir until completely heated through, salt and pepper to taste, and serve.

PER SERVING:
482 Calories; 8g Fat (14.7% calories from fat); 39g Protein; 61g Carbohydrate; 3g Dietary Fiber; 80mg Cholesterol; 224mg Sodium. Exchanges: 4 Grain (Starch); 4 Lean Meat; ½ Vegetable; 0 Fruit; 1 Fat.

SERVING SUGGESTIONS: A green salad and some baby carrots ought to do it. This is rich and wonderful!

DO AHEAD TIP: Soak beans for tomorrow's meal.

Serves 6

BEAN THERE, DONE THAT

Being the quintessential cheap eat and nutritional wunderkind that beans are, nothing beats a big batch o' beans. They are easy to prepare and virtually foolproof to make, especially when you employ these tips:

- The Presoak. After your beans have soaked overnight, give them a rinse and put fresh water in the pot for cooking. Some people may complain that you're soaking away some of the nutrition, but honestly, you're eliminating a lot of musicality of beans by doing this—if you follow my meaning.

- The Salting. Wait until your beans are completely tender before adding salt. Salt can make the tenderizing process not happen.

- The Water. If you have hard water, your beans may not soften. Use bottled water if that's the case. You can add some baking soda, too (1 teaspoon per quart).

- The Age. Old beans mean tough beans. Make sure you buy your beans fresh and that they're from a market with a good turnover. Otherwise, those beans may stay as hard as granite—even if you diligently apply all these fine steps. Beans are beans, but old beans are rocks.

3 turkey bacon slices
½ small green bell pepper
½ small red bell pepper
1 small onion, chopped
3 cloves garlic, pressed
5 cups chicken broth
1½ cups tomato puree
2 pureed chipotle peppers, optional
½ tablespoon cayenne
Salt and pepper to taste
Hot pepper sauce to taste
1 pound pinto beans

In a large skillet, cook off the turkey bacon. Then add green and red bell pepper and chopped onion; sauté 5 minutes. Add garlic, chicken broth, tomato puree, chipotle peppers, cayenne, salt, pepper, and hot pepper sauce to taste; add beans. Transfer everything to a Crock-Pot and cook on low 8 hours. When beans are tender, salt to taste.

PER SERVING:
327 Calories; 3g Fat (7.2% calories from fat); 19g Protein; 57g Carbohydrate; 20g Dietary Fiber; 6mg Cholesterol; 2261mg Sodium. Exchanges: 3 Grain (Starch); 1 Lean Meat; 1½ Vegetable; 0 Fat.

SERVING SUGGESTIONS: Serve on a bed of brown rice; top with a little grated, low-fat Cheddar cheese and a liberal sprinkling of chopped cilantro. A salad will round things out nicely.

🍁 Week Four

DAY ONE: Parmesan Drumsticks
DAY TWO: Cube Steaks with Blue Cheese
DAY THREE: Mustard Glazed Salmon
DAY FOUR: Cream of Cauliflower Soup
DAY FIVE: Chicken Stroganoff
DAY SIX: Really Easy Mixed Bean Chili

SHOPPING LIST

MEAT
12 chicken drumsticks, skinless
5 boneless, skinless chicken breast halves
6 cube steaks
6 salmon fillets

CONDIMENTS
olive oil
honey mustard

PRODUCE
1 small red onion
3 pounds onions (keep on hand)
1 head garlic
1–2 bunches green onions (you'll need ¼ cup and 5 green
   onions)
½ pound mushrooms
1 sweet potato
**russet potatoes (1 meal)
**acorn squash (1 meal)
**broccoli (2 meals)
**banana squash (1 meal)
**spinach (I like baby spinach) (1 meal)
**baby carrots (1 meal)
**green beans (1 meal)
**sweet potatoes (1 meal)
**2–3 heads lettuce (*not* Iceberg)

FROZEN FOODS
1 10-ounce bag cauliflower
1 10-ounce bag whole-kernel corn

CANNED GOODS
chicken broth (you'll need 1½ quarts)
1 jar salsa (your favorite)
1 14½-ounce can diced tomatoes (you'll need ½ can)
1 15-ounce can pinto beans
1 15-ounce can black beans

SPICES
1 envelope taco seasoning (low sodium, if available)
paprika
oregano

DAIRY/DAIRY CASE
butter (I keep 1 pound unsalted on hand in the freezer)
Parmesan cheese (you'll need 1 cup, grated)
6 tablespoons blue cheese crumbles
low-fat milk (you'll need 1½ cups)
½ cup low-fat sour cream

DRY GOODS
flour (you'll need 2 tablespoons)
1 pound egg noodles, yolk-free
**brown rice (2 meals)

BAKERY
**whole-grain rolls (1 meal)
**corn muffins (1 meal)

PARMESAN DRUMSTICKS

Serves 6

1 cup Parmesan cheese
3 teaspoons oregano
2 teaspoons paprika
Salt and pepper to taste
¼ cup butter
1 tablespoon olive oil
12 chicken drumsticks, no skin

Preheat oven to 350 degrees F.

In a bowl, combine Parmesan cheese, oregano, paprika, and salt and pepper to taste.

Line shallow baking pan with foil.

In a small frying pan, melt butter and oil together. Dip each drumstick in the butter mixture, then in the cheese mixture, and place on the foil-lined pan.

Bake drumsticks for one hour or until chicken is completely cooked.

PER SERVING:
262 Calories; 18g Fat (61.3% calories from fat); 24g Protein; 1g Carbohydrate; trace Dietary Fiber; 90mg Cholesterol; 386mg Sodium. Exchanges: 0 Grain (Starch); 3½ Lean Meat; 2½ Fat.

SERVING SUGGESTIONS: Serve with baked sweet potatoes, steamed broccoli, and brown rice.

CUBE STEAKS WITH BLUE CHEESE

Serves 6

6 cube steaks
Salt and pepper to taste
6 tablespoons crumbled blue cheese
¼ cup red onion, finely chopped

Preheat broiler.

Meanwhile, in a skillet, brown cube steaks to your liking, salt and pepper to taste. Blot grease off meat (fat grams will be lower than what shows up in the nutritional info below).

Place beef on a broiler pan and top each steak with blue cheese and red onion. Stick under the broiler to melt, then serve.

PER SERVING:
238 Calories; 16g Fat (60.9% calories from fat); 22g Protein; 1g Carbohydrate; trace Dietary Fiber; 70mg Cholesterol; 172mg Sodium. Exchanges: 3 Lean Meat; 0 Vegetable; 1 Fat.

SERVING SUGGESTIONS: Baked potatoes, baked banana squash, steamed spinach.

MUSTARD GLAZED SALMON

Serves 6

> *6 salmon fillets*
> *6 tablespoons honey mustard*
> *¼ cup green onions, finely chopped*

Preheat oven to 350 degrees F.

In a shallow baking dish, place your fish and top with honey mustard (1 tablespoon per fillet).

Bake for 15 minutes or longer, depending on the thickness of the fish and when fish flakes easily with a fork. Top with chopped green onions before serving.

PER SERVING:
213 Calories; 7g Fat (30.4% calories from fat); 35g Protein; 1g Carbohydrate; trace Dietary Fiber; 88mg Cholesterol; 319mg Sodium. Exchanges: 0 Grain (Starch); 5 Lean Meat; 0 Vegetable; 0 Fat.

SERVING SUGGESTIONS: Brown rice, baked acorn squash, and steamed broccoli round this off nicely.

CREAM OF CAULIFLOWER SOUP

Serves 6

3 tablespoons butter
1 small onion, chopped
2 tablespoons flour
1½ quarts chicken broth
1 10-ounce package frozen cauliflower
1½ cups milk
Salt and pepper to taste

In a soup pot, melt butter and add onion. Cook till onion is translucent. Add flour and incorporate, making sure flour isn't lumpy before adding chicken broth. Add broth and bring to a boil.

Add cauliflower to broth and simmer until cauliflower is tender, about 10 minutes.

Transfer cauliflower to a blender and puree (use a slotted spoon). Add back to the soup pot. Mix well and add milk; add salt and pepper to taste. Heat to a very low simmer, but do not boil, or soup will break.

PER SERVING:
148 Calories; 9g Fat (56.3% calories from fat); 8g Protein; 8g Carbohydrate; 1g Dietary Fiber; 24mg Cholesterol; 858mg Sodium. Exchanges: 0 Grain (Starch); ½ Lean Meat; ½ Vegetable; 0 Non-Fat Milk; 1½ Fat.

SERVING SUGGESTIONS: A big green salad and some whole-grain rolls will do the trick.

Serves 6

3 tablespoons butter
4 cloves garlic, pressed
5 boneless, skinless chicken breast halves, cut into thin strips
5 green onions, minced
½ pound mushrooms, sliced
½ can diced tomatoes, drained
1 pound egg noodles
½ cup low-fat sour cream
Salt and pepper to taste

In a skillet, over medium-high heat, melt butter. Add garlic and sauté quickly (don't let it brown). Add chicken, green onions, mushrooms, and tomatoes and cook until chicken is cooked, stirring frequently.

Meanwhile, you should have your water on to boil. Cook pasta according to package directions and drain.

Reheat chicken mixture if necessary to get it hot. Add sour cream to the skillet, and salt and pepper to taste. Spoon chicken over pasta and serve.

PER SERVING:
673 Calories; 11g Fat (14.8% calories from fat); 64g Protein; 86g Carbohydrate; 5g Dietary Fiber; 111mg Cholesterol; 219mg Sodium. Exchanges: 5½ Grain (Starch); 5 Lean Meat; 1 Vegetable; 2 Fat; 0 Other Carbohydrates.

SERVING SUGGESTIONS: Steamed baby carrots and some green beans would work.

REALLY EASY MIXED BEAN CHILI

Serves 6

> *1 can pinto beans, rinsed and drained*
> *1 can black beans, rinsed and drained*
> *1 package taco seasoning mix*
> *1 jar salsa (your favorite)*
> *1 10-ounce package frozen corn*
> *1 sweet potato, cubed*

Dump everything into a Crock-Pot, set on low, and cook for 6–8 hours. Mix well before serving.

PER SERVING:
283 Calories; 1g Fat (3.4% calories from fat); 15g Protein; 55g Carbohydrate; 15g Dietary Fiber; 0mg Cholesterol; 584mg Sodium. Exchanges: 3 Grain (Starch); ½ Lean Meat; ½ Vegetable; 0 Other Carbohydrates.

SERVING SUGGESTIONS: Serve with a big green salad and some corn muffins (homemade or store bought).

❧ Week Five

DAY ONE: Asian Honey Chicken
DAY TWO: Perfect Pot Roast
DAY THREE: Oven-Fried Fish
DAY FOUR: Baked Macaroni and Three Cheese
DAY FIVE: Turkey Piccata
DAY SIX: Crockery Beanery

SHOPPING LIST

MEAT
6 boneless, skinless chicken breast halves
2 pounds beef chuck
6 fish fillets
6 turkey breast cutlets

CONDIMENTS
sesame oil (you'll need ⅛ cup)
olive oil
vegetable oil
honey (you'll need ¼ cup)
soy sauce (low sodium, if available)
**mayonnaise (1 meal)

PRODUCE
3 pounds onions (keep on hand)
1 head garlic
1 small green bell pepper
1 small red bell pepper
1 bunch carrots (you'll need 6)
1 bunch celery (you'll need 1 stalk)
1 pound red potatoes
1 bunch green onions (you'll need 5)
2 lemons
**russet potatoes (1 meal)
**butternut squash (1 meal)
**broccoli (1 meal)

**coleslaw (1 meal)
**kale (1 meal)
**spinach (I like baby spinach) (1 meal)
**baby carrots (1 meal)
**sweet potatoes (1 meal)

CANNED GOODS

1 small jar capers
1 14½-ounce can tomato puree
1 28-ounce can diced tomatoes
1 28-ounce jar spaghetti sauce
1 15-ounce can kidney beans
1 15-ounce can black beans
1 15-ounce can baked beans
1 15-ounce can corn

SPICES

thyme
chili powder
oregano
cumin

DAIRY/DAIRY CASE

butter
6 ounces Provolone cheese
6 ounces low-fat mozzarella cheese
1 wedge Parmesan cheese (you'll need ½ cup grated)
**Romano cheese

DRY GOODS

1 cup Italian bread crumbs, pressed
1 package ziti pasta
flour
**brown rice (1 meal)
**pasta (1 meal)

BAKERY

**corn muffins (1 meal)

ASIAN HONEY CHICKEN

Serves 6

⅛ cup sesame oil
¼ cup honey
¼ cup low-sodium soy sauce
3 cloves garlic, pressed
6 boneless, skinless chicken breast halves, sliced in strips
1 tablespoon vegetable oil
5 green onions, minced
½ green bell pepper, diced
½ red bell pepper, diced
2 small carrots, grated

In a large zipper-topped plastic bag, mix together oil, honey, soy sauce, and garlic. Add chicken and marinate for 8 hours or so. (Do this right after breakfast—it will take you two minutes.)

Heat vegetable oil in a wok or large skillet over medium-high heat. Sauté chicken till nearly cooked; add the remaining ingredients, and keep cooking till veggies are tender and chicken is cooked thoroughly.

PER SERVING:
378 Calories; 8g Fat (18.5% calories from fat); 56g Protein; 19g Carbohydrate; 2g Dietary Fiber; 137mg Cholesterol; 566mg Sodium. Exchanges: 7½ Lean Meat; 1½ Vegetable; 1 Fat; 1 Other Carbohydrates.

SERVING SUGGESTION: Serve with brown rice and you're set!

PERFECT POT ROAST

Serves 6

1 tablespoon olive oil
2 pounds beef chuck, trimmed of fat
Salt and pepper to taste
2 medium onions, sliced
4 carrots, diagonally sliced

1 stalk celery, sliced
1 pound red potatoes, cut in half
2 teaspoons thyme
1 28-ounce can diced tomatoes

Preheat oven to 350 degrees F.

In a large Dutch oven, over medium heat, add oil and when hot, add beef to brown. Salt and pepper all sides of beef. Remove beef when browned and add all sliced veggies. Stir for just a minute, add thyme and a little more salt and pepper, pull out and set aside.

Return meat to the Dutch oven, throw veggies on top, add diced tomatoes and a little water (about ¼ cup). Cover and bake at least 1 hour.

PER SERVING:
438 Calories; 26g Fat (54.0% calories from fat); 27g Protein; 24g Carbohydrate; 4g Dietary Fiber; 87mg Cholesterol; 107mg Sodium. Exchanges: 1 Grain (Starch); 3½ Lean Meat; 2 Vegetable; 3 Fat.

SERVING SUGGESTIONS: Steamed kale and baked sweet potatoes, and you're ready!

OVEN-FRIED FISH

Serves 6

4 tablespoons butter
1 cup Italian bread crumbs, crushed
½ cup Parmesan cheese, grated
Salt and pepper to taste
6 fish fillets

Preheat oven to 375 degrees F.

In a saucepan, melt butter and spread on the bottom of a 13 × 9–inch baking dish.

To crush Italian bread crumbs, place in a plastic bag and use a rolling pin to flatten. Pour contents onto a pie pan. Add cheese and salt and pepper, and blend well.

SOMETHING FISHY

🍁 If you're wondering why the fish is rarely specified (salmon would be an exception) in these recipes, it's because fish is tough to dictate. There are too many possibilities for problems. For some, it's a regional, availability thing; for others, the choice is based on affordability; for still others, it's the convenience factor—there are bags of frozen generic white fish that can be picked up at the market. And to be perfectly honest, I really don't want to field e-mails from people asking me what grouper is or what to do because they can't find halibut. I know there are a lot of distinctions that might make one fish a little more preferable over another when you're making certain recipes, but I don't want to go there. I have enough on my plate, and so do you.

All fish, whether it's fresh, frozen, freshwater, or from the ocean, will work in these recipes, period. That's all you need to know. This isn't some foodie book that's promising you your own Emeril-like experience. This is real-life cooking—so let's get on with it already.

Dip the fish first in the butter then into the crumbs. Place the fish in the baking dish when coated.

Bake fish for 15–20 minutes or until fish flakes with a fork.

PER SERVING:
361 Calories; 12g Fat (30.1% calories from fat); 47g Protein; 14g Carbohydrate; 1g Dietary Fiber; 125mg Cholesterol; 857mg Sodium. Exchanges: 1 Grain (Starch); 6 Lean Meat; 2 Fat.

SERVING SUGGESTIONS: Baked potatoes, coleslaw, and a bowl of baby carrots.

BAKED MACARONI AND THREE CHEESE

Serves 6

¾ pound ziti pasta, cooked
1 jar spaghetti sauce, your favorite
1 cup low-fat sour cream
6 ounces Provolone cheese, thinly sliced
6 ounces low-fat mozzarella cheese, shredded
½ cup Romano cheese, grated

Preheat oven to 350 degrees F. Lightly grease a 9 × 13–inch baking pan.

In a large mixing bowl, toss together the pasta, spaghetti sauce, and sour cream. Mix together the Provolone, the mozzarella, and the Romano cheeses and set aside. Now layer half the pasta mixture into the baking dish and sprinkle half the cheese mixture on the pasta. Layer remaining pasta on top and then the rest of the cheese. Bake for 30 minutes or until bubbly. Don't let the cheese brown.

PER SERVING:
519 Calories; 20g Fat (34.6% calories from fat); 28g Protein; 56g Carbohydrate; 3g Dietary Fiber; 53mg Cholesterol; 765mg Sodium. Exchanges: 3 Grain (Starch); 2½ Lean Meat; 1½ Vegetable; 2½ Fat; ½ Other Carbohydrates.

SERVING SUGGESTIONS: Serve with a large salad and some baby carrots.

TURKEY PICCATA

Serves 6

2 tablespoons butter
1 tablespoon olive oil
6 turkey breast cutlets
2 tablespoons flour
2 lemons, juiced
1 tablespoon capers

In a skillet, melt half the butter and all of the oil together. Dredge turkey in flour and sauté turkey till done. Remove and keep warm.

In the skillet, whisk in the lemon juice and scrape up the browned bits off the bottom of the pan. Add remaining butter, whisking to incorporate. Add capers and return turkey to skillet; turn to coat. Serve, spooning sauce and capers over the top.

PER SERVING:
147 Calories; 7g Fat (42.7% calories from fat); 18g Protein; 4g Carbohydrate; trace Dietary Fiber; 55mg Cholesterol; 213mg Sodium. Exchanges: 0 Grain (Starch); 2½ Lean Meat; 0 Fruit; 1 Fat; 0 Other Carbohydrates.

SERVING SUGGESTIONS: Serve with pasta topped with a little Romano cheese, steamed broccoli, and baked butternut squash.

CROCKERY BEANERY

1 can black beans, drained
1 can kidney beans, drained
1 can baked beans
1 can tomato puree
1 can corn, drained
1 onion, chopped
2 cloves garlic, pressed
1 tablespoon chili powder
1 tablespoon oregano
1 tablespoon cumin

In a slow cooker, combine everything and cook on low for at least 6 hours.

PER SERVING:
224 Calories; 1g Fat (4.8% calories from fat); 14g Protein; 43g Carbohydrate; 13g Dietary Fiber; 0mg Cholesterol; 270mg Sodium. Exchanges: 2½ Grain (Starch); ½ Lean Meat; ½ Vegetable; 0 Fat.

SERVING SUGGESTIONS: Serve with corn muffins and a big spinach salad.

🍁 Week Six

DAY ONE: Chicken Pepper Skillet
DAY TWO: Cheeseburger Casserole
DAY THREE: Hoppin' John Soup
DAY FOUR: Honey Dijon Fish
DAY FIVE: Mexican Turkey Hash
DAY SIX: Crock Chicken and Autumn Vegetables

SHOPPING LIST

MEAT
5 boneless, skinless chicken breast halves
¾ pound extra-lean ground beef
½ pound kielbasa
6 fish fillets
1 pound ground turkey
6 skinless chicken thighs

CONDIMENTS
olive oil
Dijon mustard
rice vinegar
honey
white wine, optional
1 jar salsa (your favorite, you'll need ½ cup)

PRODUCE
3 pounds onions (keep on hand)
1 head garlic
1 red bell pepper
1 bunch carrots
1 bell pepper
3 russet potatoes (**additional potatoes for 1 meal if you
    follow Serving Suggestions)
2 turnips
**butternut squash (1 meal)
**broccoli (1 meal)

**kale (1 meal)
**spinach (I like baby spinach) (2 meals)
**winter squash (1 meal)
**sweet potatoes (1 meal)
**2–3 heads lettuce (*not* Iceberg)

FROZEN FOODS
2 cups tricolored bell pepper (or substitute other frozen bell peppers)

CANNED GOODS
5 14-ounce cans chicken broth
2 15-ounce cans black-eyed peas
1 15-ounce can navy beans
1 15-ounce can diced tomatoes
1 jar salsa (your favorite)

SPICES
basil
thyme
garlic powder
cayenne pepper
cumin
tarragon

DAIRY/DAIRY CASE
butter
Romano cheese, grated (you'll need 3 tablespoons)
1 bag low-fat Cheddar cheese, grated (you'll need 1 cup)
1 8-ounce container half and half

DRY GOODS
12 ounces fettuccine
8 ounces spinach egg noodles
oats (you'll need 1 cup)

flour (you'll need ⅓ cup)
brown rice (you'll need 1 cup)

BAKERY
**corn muffins (1 meal)
**corn tortillas (1 meal)

CHICKEN PEPPER SKILLET

Serves 6

2 tablespoons olive oil
5 boneless, skinless chicken breast halves, cut in inch strips
1 large onion, chopped
3 cloves garlic, pressed
Salt and pepper to taste
2 cups frozen, tricolored bell peppers
12 ounces fettuccine
2 teaspoons basil
3 tablespoons Romano cheese, grated

In a skillet, heat oil over medium-high heat and add chicken, onions, and garlic. Salt and pepper chicken to taste and cook until chicken is browned. Add frozen bell peppers, turn heat to low, and let simmer until chicken is finished cooking.

Meanwhile, cook the pasta according to package directions. Drain and toss into the chicken mixture. Add basil and toss again. Serve with a sprinkling of Romano cheese on top.

PER SERVING:
504 Calories; 9g Fat (16.3% calories from fat); 55g Protein; 48g Carbohydrate; 3g Dietary Fiber; 118mg Cholesterol; 176mg Sodium. Exchanges: 3 Grain (Starch); 6½ Lean Meat; 1 Vegetable; 1 Fat.

SERVING SUGGESTION: A big green salad, and you're set!

CHEESEBURGER CASSEROLE

Serves 6

¾ pound extra-lean ground beef
1 cup oats
1 onion, chopped
1 red bell pepper
1 large carrot, grated
1 15-ounce can diced tomatoes, undrained
1 teaspoon thyme
1 teaspoon garlic powder
Salt and pepper to taste
8 ounces spinach egg noodles
1 cup low-fat Cheddar cheese

Preheat oven to 350 degrees F.

In a skillet over medium-high heat, brown beef till crumbled and cooked. Drain grease and blot well with paper towels (with this step fat grams will be lower than what shows up in the nutrition info below). Stir in oats till well combined.

Increase the heat and add onion, bell pepper, and carrot and cook for 5 minutes. Add tomatoes, thyme, garlic powder, and salt and pepper to taste.

Meanwhile, cook the noodles according to package directions, drain, and set aside. Toss together meat mixture and noodles; pour into a baking dish and top with cheese. Bake until cheese is hot and melty, about 15 minutes.

PER SERVING:
381 Calories; 14g Fat (32.6% calories from fat); 24g Protein; 40g Carbohydrate; 5g Dietary Fiber; 79mg Cholesterol; 188mg Sodium. Exchanges: 2½ Grain (Starch); 2 Lean Meat; ½ Vegetable; 1 Fat.

SERVING SUGGESTIONS: Baked sweet potatoes and a spinach salad would be perfect.

DO AHEAD TIP: Cook rice for tomorrow's Hoppin' John Soup.

❧ I don't believe in soup being served as a first course—unless, of course, you have a butler. I am a busy mom, and, for me, time is at a premium each and every night. I need good, quick recipes that are healthy and tasty and won't wreck the family budget. That's why I include a soup recipe once a week during this season's menus. But we're not talking wimpy, watery, lightweight stuff. We're talking Soup with a capital S. Good, old-fashioned, stick-to-your ribs Soup.

Here are a few hints to make your soup, souper!

- Stock. Using water instead of stock will make a great soup recipe mediocre at best. You will make watery, yucky, no-good soups that no one will eat. Stock is what gives your soup flavor and body. You gotta have stock—homemade or canned. No stock, no soup.
- Sauté your veggies. Not all soup recipes tell you to do this (and even some of my Crock-Pot soup recipes won't), but I have noticed that when the veggies are sautéed a bit, the flavors of the soup and the vegetables themselves are immensely improved.
- Salt and pepper to *your* taste. When you make soup, you have to taste it. Noth-

HOPPIN' JOHN SOUP

Serves 6

1 tablespoon olive oil
1 onion, chopped
½ pound kielbasa, chopped
2 cans black-eyed peas, drained
1 can navy beans, drained
1 cup brown rice, cooked
2 cans chicken broth
1 teaspoon garlic powder
½ teaspoon cayenne pepper, optional
⅓ teaspoon thyme
Salt and pepper to taste

In a soup pot, heat oil over medium-high heat. Add onion and cook till translucent. Add kielbasa, peas, beans, rice, broth and seasoning. Stir well to blend and heat. Mash beans slightly to help thicken soup (use the back of your spoon or a potato masher). Serve when hot.

PER SERVING:
499 Calories; 14g Fat (25.7% calories from fat); 29g Protein; 65g Carbohydrate; 15g Dietary Fiber; 25mg Cholesterol; 676mg Sodium. Exchanges: 4 Grain (Starch); 2½ Lean Meat; ½ Vegetable; 2 Fat.

SERVING SUGGESTIONS: Serve with corn muffins (homemade or store bought) and a big green salad.

ing grinds me the wrong way more than to have a recipe tell you to measure the pepper. Forget it! Taste your soup and add it according to your particular taste.

• Correct the seasoning. After your soup has been cooking for a while, chances are good the thyme will have lost its initial punch or the garlic may have dissipated somewhat. You can correct that by going back toward the end of the cooking, tasting your soup, and adding a bit more if you think it needs it—even if the recipe doesn't say to do this, do it anyway. Your soup will be better for it.

HONEY DIJON FISH

Serves 6

> 3 tablespoons Dijon mustard
> 3 tablespoons rice vinegar
> 3 tablespoons honey
> 6 fish fillets

Preheat the broiler.

In a small bowl, combine mustard, vinegar, and honey. Place fish on broiler pan and brush one side of fish with mustard mixture. Broil for 3–5 minutes. Turn fish over, reapply mustard mixture, and broil again for 3–5 minutes or until fish flakes easily with a fork.

PER SERVING:
228 Calories; 2g Fat (7.6% calories from fat); 42g Protein; 10g Carbohydrate; trace Dietary Fiber; 99mg Cholesterol; 219mg Sodium. Exchanges: 5½ Lean Meat; 0 Fat; ½ Other Carbohydrates.

SERVING SUGGESTIONS: Serve with baked potatoes, steamed broccoli, and baked winter squash.

DO AHEAD TIP: Bake 3 extra potatoes for tomorrow night's dinner.

MEXICAN TURKEY HASH

Serves 6

> 2 tablespoons olive oil
> 1 onion, chopped
> 1 bell pepper, chopped
> 3 cloves garlic, pressed
> 1 teaspoon cumin
> ½ cup salsa (your favorite)
> 3 baked potatoes, peeled and chopped into ¼-inch pieces
> 1 pound ground turkey
> Salt and pepper to taste
> 2 cans chicken broth

In a skillet over medium-high heat, heat the oil. Add the onion, bell pepper, garlic, and cumin. Cook for about 3 minutes, till veggies are soft but not brown. Add salsa and potatoes and stir till well blended. Add turkey and continue cooking. Season with salt and pepper.

When turkey is fully cooked, add broth and simmer for 5 minutes, until everything is nice and hot.

PER SERVING:
293 Calories; 11g Fat (35.2% calories from fat); 18g Protein; 30g Carbohydrate; 3g Dietary Fiber; 60mg Cholesterol; 429mg Sodium. Exchanges: 1½ Grain (Starch); 2 Lean Meat; 1 Vegetable; 1 Fat.

SERVING SUGGESTIONS: Spinach salad, warmed corn tortillas, and additional salsa, if desired.

CROCK CHICKEN AND AUTUMN VEGETABLES

Serves 6

1 tablespoon olive oil
6 skinless chicken thighs
Salt and pepper to taste
2 onions, chopped
2 turnips, cut in ½-inch slices
2 carrots, cut in ½-inch slices
1 teaspoon tarragon
1 can chicken broth
½ cup white wine, optional
2 tablespoons butter
2 tablespoons flour
1 cup half and half

In a large skillet, heat oil over medium-high heat. Cook chicken until browned, about 3 minutes. Remove from skillet; salt and pepper to your taste.

Reduce the heat and add the onion to the skillet and cook for two minutes. Add remaining veggies and tarragon, tossing well to mix, but don't cook. Place vegetables in the Crock-Pot, then layer chicken on top. Pour in the chicken broth and wine.

Cook on low for 5–6 hours. When chicken is cooked, remove chicken and veggies; keep warm.

In a saucepan, melt better over low heat. Add flour and whisk together till well blended (no lumps!). Cook for a minute but don't brown. Add cooking liquid and bring to a boil to simmer for a minute. Add half and half and bring up to a low simmer and cook until thickened, about 5 minutes. To serve, pour the sauce over the vegetables and chicken.

PER SERVING:
254 Calories; 14g Fat (51.5% calories from fat); 17g Protein; 12g Carbohydrate; 2g Dietary Fiber; 82mg Cholesterol; 280mg Sodium. Exchanges: 0 Grain (Starch); 2 Lean Meat; 1½ Vegetable; 0 Non-Fat Milk; 2 Fat.

SERVING SUGGESTIONS: Serve with baked butternut squash and steamed kale, and you're good to go.

❧ Week Seven

DAY ONE: Beef Fajitas
DAY TWO: Chicken Balsamic
DAY THREE: Baked Tomato Basil Fish
DAY FOUR: Apple Turkey Burgers
DAY FIVE: Curried Chicken and Rice Soup
DAY SIX: Crock Lentil Stew

SHOPPING LIST

MEAT
9 boneless, skinless chicken breast halves
1 pound flank steak
6 fish fillets
1½ pounds ground turkey

CONDIMENTS
vegetable oil
olive oil
rice vinegar
balsamic vinegar
lemon juice
red wine, optional

PRODUCE
3 pounds onions (keep on hand)
1 head garlic
1 small green bell pepper
1 small red bell pepper
1 lemon
2 limes
1 bunch cilantro
3 plum tomatoes
1 bunch carrots
1 bunch celery
**kale (1 meal)
**baby red potatoes (1 meal)

**baby carrots (2 meals)
**broccoli (1 meal)
**spinach (I like baby spinach) (1 meal)
**winter squash (1 meal)
**2–3 heads lettuce (*not* Iceberg; use color as your guide, the
    darker the green, the better) (3 meals)
**anything else you'd like in your salads (3 meals)

CANNED GOODS
1 small jar chunky applesauce (you need ¼ cup)
5 14-ounce cans chicken broth
1 15-ounce can stewed tomatoes
1 5-ounce can tomato paste
1 14½-ounce can Italian tomatoes
**applesauce (1 meal)

SPICES
poultry seasoning
garlic powder
curry powder
thyme
cumin
rosemary
basil
pressed red pepper

DAIRY/DAIRY CASE
eggs (you'll need 1)
Romano cheese, grated (you'll need 6 teaspoons)
**cheese for grilled cheese sandwiches (1 meal)

DRY GOODS
1 pound lentils
1 pound brown rice
flour

BEEF FAJITAS

Serves 6

2 limes, juiced
¼ cup rice vinegar
5 teaspoons cumin
4 cloves garlic, pressed
2 tablespoons olive oil
1 pound flank steak, cut into thin strips
1 medium onion, sliced
1 small green bell pepper, sliced
1 small red bell pepper, sliced
½ cup cilantro, chopped
6 flour tortillas

Prepare the marinade: lime juice, vinegar, cumin, half the garlic and half the olive oil in a plastic zipper-topped bag. Squish it around to mix and add beef; then squish the beef around. Throw the bag in the fridge and get your veggies ready.

In a skillet or a wok (perfect tool for fajitas), heat the remaining olive oil over medium-high heat. Sauté onion and remaining garlic till translucent but don't let brown. Add bell peppers and cook till crisp-tender; set aside.

Remove meat from fridge and take the beef out of the marinade. Discard marinade. Sauté beef till cooked to your liking. Add onion and bell pepper mixture and warm together for a minute. Add cilantro and toss well to mix.

Warm tortillas and serve.

PER SERVING:
449 Calories; 18g Fat (36.1% calories from fat); 23g Protein; 50g Carbohydrate; 4g Dietary Fiber; 39mg Cholesterol; 407mg Sodium. Exchanges: 3 Grain (Starch); 2 Lean Meat; 1 Vegetable; 0 Fruit; 2½ Fat; 0 Other Carbohydrates.

SERVING SUGGESTION: A big green salad is really adequate for this delicious meal.

CHICKEN BALSAMIC

Serves 6

> *3 tablespoons flour*
> *Salt and pepper to taste*
> *6 boneless, skinless chicken breast halves*
> *1 tablespoon olive oil*
> *1 cup balsamic vinegar*
> *1 cup chicken broth*
> *1 teaspoon rosemary, pressed*

On a dinner plate, blend flour and salt and pepper. Dredge chicken and tap off any excess flour.

In a skillet, heat the oil over medium-high heat. Add chicken and brown quickly on both sides, about 2 minutes per side. Then add the vinegar and bring to a boil. Reduce the heat and let simmer until vinegar is reduced by about two-thirds.

Add the chicken broth and continue to simmer until the chicken is tender and fully cooked, about 10 minutes. Remove the chicken and keep warm. Add the rosemary and keep the sauce boiling until it's reduced some more, about another 10 minutes.

Serve with sauce spooned over the top.

PER SERVING:
307 Calories; 5g Fat (16.6% calories from fat); 56g Protein; 6g Carbohydrate; trace Dietary Fiber; 137mg Cholesterol; 281mg Sodium. Exchanges: 0 Grain (Starch); 7½ Lean Meat; 0 Fruit; ½ Fat.

SERVING SUGGESTIONS: Roasted baby red potatoes, steamed broccoli, and baked winter squash will round this off nicely.

BAKED TOMATO BASIL FISH

Serves 6

1 tablespoon olive oil
1 tablespoon lemon juice
6 fish fillets
1 teaspoon basil
Salt and pepper to taste
3 plum tomatoes, sliced into four slices per tomato
6 teaspoons Romano cheese, grated

Preheat oven to 400 degrees F.

In a 9 × 13–inch baking dish, add the olive oil and lemon juice and mix. Next, add fish and turn to coat thoroughly. Sprinkle fish with basil, and salt and pepper to taste. Top each fillet with two slices of tomato.

Cover with foil (don't let foil touch the tomatoes—there is a reaction between aluminum and tomato), and bake for 10–15 minutes or until fish flakes easily with a fork. Top with a teaspoon of Romano cheese and serve.

PER SERVING:
226 Calories; 5g Fat (18.8% calories from fat); 42g Protein; 2g Carbohydrate; trace Dietary Fiber; 102mg Cholesterol; 156mg Sodium. Exchanges: 0 Grain (Starch); 5½ Lean Meat; ½ Vegetable; 0 Fruit; ½ Fat.

SERVING SUGGESTIONS: Serve with brown rice, steamed kale, and steamed baby carrots.

APPLE TURKEY BURGERS

Serves 6

1½ pounds ground turkey
¼ cup chunky applesauce
1 egg
1 teaspoon poultry seasoning
2 teaspoons garlic powder
Salt and pepper to taste
1 tablespoon vegetable oil
6 whole-wheat hamburger buns

In a large bowl, combine turkey, applesauce, egg, seasoning and garlic powder; add salt and pepper to taste. Mix well till fully combined. Divide evenly into six patties using your hands, making them about ½ inch thick.

In a skillet, heat oil over medium-high heat. Add the patties and cook 5 minutes on each side or until thoroughly cooked. Be careful when you turn them—they're fragile.

Serve on warmed hamburger buns, adding your favorite condiments.

PER SERVING:
378 Calories; 15g Fat (37.0% calories from fat); 28g Protein; 31g Carbohydrate; 3g Dietary Fiber; 121mg Cholesterol; 416mg Sodium. Exchanges: 2 Grain (Starch); 3 Lean Meat; 0 Fruit; 1 Fat.

SERVING SUGGESTIONS: Serve with more applesauce, baby carrots, and a green salad.

CURRIED CHICKEN AND RICE SOUP

Serves 6

1 tablespoon olive oil
1 onion, chopped
3 cans chicken broth
1 can stewed tomatoes, with juice
3 boneless, skinless chicken breast halves, cut into ½-inch pieces
½ cup brown rice, cooked
1½ teaspoons curry powder
1 teaspoon garlic powder
½ teaspoon thyme
Salt and pepper to taste

In a soup pot, heat the oil over medium-high heat. Add the onion and cook till onion is translucent. Add chicken broth and stewed tomatoes, and bring to a boil.

Stir in the remaining ingredients; when chicken is thoroughly cooked, soup is ready.

PER SERVING:
249 Calories; 5g Fat (18.5% calories from fat); 32g Protein; 18g Carbohydrate; 1g Dietary Fiber; 68mg Cholesterol; 471mg Sodium. Exchanges: 1 Grain (Starch); 4 Lean Meat; 1 Vegetable; ½ Fat.

SERVING SUGGESTIONS: Serve with grilled cheese sandwiches on wheat and a big spinach salad.

Serves 6

IN PRAISE OF THE LOWLY LENTIL

If you lived during the lifetime of Hippocrates, the father of medicine, you might have had lentils prescribed for your ailing liver. Although lentils were mostly thought to be a peasant's food, Louis XV's wife Marie made them hip and they were dubbed the "lentils of the queen." And check this out—there are over fifty varieties of lentils grown throughout the world. One cup of lentils is loaded with nutrition: protein, calcium, magnesium, potassium, iron, and a whopping 10 grams of fiber. That's more than a third of your daily requirement.

The versatility of lentils, plus how quickly they cook, makes them the ultimate healthy fast food. From start to finish, you can have lentil soup in less than 30 minutes. You just can't beat that! So even if you hadn't given much thought to lentils in the past, this lovely legume will evoke cravings after you've had some of the recipes in this book.

3 cups chicken broth
1 can Italian tomatoes, undrained
1 can tomato paste
½ cup red wine, optional
1 teaspoon thyme
¾ teaspoon basil
¼ teaspoon pressed red pepper
1 onion, chopped
3 carrots, sliced into rounds
2 stalks celery, chopped
3 cloves garlic, pressed
1 pound lentils, rinsed
Salt and pepper to taste

In a Crock-Pot, add all ingredients, except salt and pepper. Cover and cook on low for 10–12 hours. Salt and pepper to taste before serving.

PER SERVING:
337 Calories; 2g Fat (4.5% calories from fat); 25g Protein; 55g Carbohydrate; 26g Dietary Fiber; 0mg Cholesterol; 601mg Sodium. Exchanges: 3 Grain (Starch); 2 Lean Meat; 2 Vegetable; 0 Fat.

SERVING SUGGESTIONS: Serve with a big salad and some whole-grain rolls.

❉ Week Eight

SHOPPING LIST

MEAT
6 boneless, skinless chicken breast halves
1¼ pounds extra-lean ground beef
6 fish fillets
2 cups turkey breast, boneless, skinless, cooked,
    and shredded
½ pound ground turkey

CONDIMENTS
olive oil
lime juice
ketchup
white wine, optional

PRODUCE
3 pounds onions (keep on hand)
8 cloves garlic
russet potatoes (2 meals; **3 meals, if following
    Serving Suggestions)
1 large tomato
1 bunch celery (you'll need 1 stalk)
**kale (1 meal)
**winter squash (1 meal)
**broccoflower (1 meal)
**broccoli (1 meal)
**cilantro (1 meal)
**spinach (I like baby spinach) (1 meal)

**baby carrots (1 meal)
**sweet potatoes (2 meals)
**2–3 heads lettuce (*not* Iceberg)

CANNED GOODS
1½ 28-ounce cans or jars spaghetti sauce
4 14-ounce cans chicken broth
beef broth (you'll need ½ cup)
1 jar salsa (your favorite)
1 16-ounce can refried beans
1 can diced tomatoes

SPICES
thyme
cumin
nutmeg
rosemary
bay leaves
cayenne pepper
paprika
garlic powder
onion powder

DAIRY/DAIRY CASE
butter
1¼ cups low-fat sour cream
2¾ cups low-fat Cheddar cheese, shredded
6 ounces Provolone cheese
¾ cup low-fat cottage cheese
6 ounces part-skim-milk mozzarella cheese,
    shredded

DRY GOODS
cornstarch
oats (you'll need 1 cup)
1 pound ziti pasta

1 pound dry navy beans
2 10-ounce bags baked tortilla chips

BAKERY
**whole-grain rolls (1 meal)

🍁 Recipe Rave:
GARLIC LIME CHICKEN

Serves 6

"Oh that Garlic Lime Chicken! I think I could serve that a few times a week and my husband and kids would be thrilled!"

—KATE BROWN

1 teaspoon salt
¾ teaspoon pepper
¼ teaspoon cayenne pepper
¼ teaspoon paprika
1 teaspoon garlic powder
½ teaspoon onion powder
½ teaspoon thyme
6 boneless, skinless chicken breast halves
2 tablespoons butter
2 tablespoons olive oil
4 tablespoons lime juice
½ cup chicken broth

On a dinner plate, mix together first seven ingredients. Sprinkle mixture on both sides of chicken breasts.

In a skillet heat butter and olive oil together over medium-high heat. Sauté chicken until golden brown about 5 minutes on each side. Remove chicken and add lime juice and chicken broth to the pan, whisking up the browned bits off the bottom of the pan. Keep cooking until sauce has reduced slightly. Add chicken back to the pan to thoroughly coat and serve.

PER SERVING:
343 Calories; 11g Fat (31.1% calories from fat); 55g Protein; 2g Carbohydrate; trace Dietary Fiber; 147mg Cholesterol; 612mg Sodium. Exchanges: 0 Grain (Starch); 7½ Lean Meat; 0 Fruit; 1½ Fat.

SERVING SUGGESTIONS: Serve with garlic mashed potatoes (make mashed potatoes; add garlic powder to taste), steamed broccoflower, or baked sweet potatoes.

DO AHEAD TIP: Make extra mashed potatoes (you'll need 2½ cups) for tomorrow's Shepherd's Skillet.

SHEPHERD'S SKILLET

Serves 6

2 teaspoons olive oil
1 onion, chopped
1 clove garlic
1 pound extra-lean ground beef
1 cup oats
3 squirts ketchup (3 tablespoons, if you have to measure)
1 teaspoon cumin
¼ teaspoon nutmeg
Salt and pepper to taste
½ cup beef broth
1 tablespoon cornstarch
2½ cups mashed potatoes
½ cup low-fat sour cream
¾ cup low-fat Cheddar cheese, shredded

Preheat the broiler.

In a skillet (ovenproof), heat the oil over medium-high heat. Add onion, garlic, and beef and cook till beef is browned and crumbled. Drain beef and blot with paper towels (with this step the fat grams will be lower than what shows up in nutritional info below). Add oats and stir well to incorporate.

Add ketchup, spices, beef broth, and cornstarch; stir well and allow to simmer on low and to thicken slightly. Heat mashed potatoes and set aside. Add sour cream to beef mixture and mix again. Remove skillet from heat and spoon potatoes as evenly as possible over the entire skillet. Top with Cheddar cheese and place skillet under the broiler until the cheese is melted and bubbly. (Make sure the skillet is oven safe!)

PER SERVING:
405 Calories; 21g Fat (47.5% calories from fat); 24g Protein; 29g Carbohydrate; 4g Dietary Fiber; 66mg Cholesterol; 581mg Sodium. Exchanges: 1½ Grain (Starch); 2½ Lean Meat; ½ Vegetable; 3 Fat; ½ Other Carbohydrates.

SERVING SUGGESTIONS: Some broccoli and baked sweet potatoes.

FISH IN A BAG

Serves 6

3 potatoes, peeled and sliced ¼ inch thick
6 fish fillets
2 tablespoons olive oil
Salt and pepper to taste
1 large tomato, diced
½ cup white wine, optional
3 teaspoons thyme

Preheat oven to 400 degrees F.

On a piece of foil (about 12 × 20 inches) spread potatoes on the bottom, put one piece of fish on top, drizzle with a little olive oil, and salt and pepper to taste. Then sprinkle with tomato, add a little wine, and finish with thyme on the top.

Bring opposite corners together and crimp, then bring the other opposite corners and crimp together. Then crimp the seams of the foil so you have a nice seal on your little foil package. Do this with all your fish fillets.

Place fish packets on a baking sheet and bake until fish is cooked, about 20 minutes or until fish flakes.

ONE POTATO, SWEET POTATO

I often get asked about the difference between sweet potatoes and yams. Interestingly, they're not even remotely related as most people assume. Sweet potatoes are aptly named— they're sweet. Yams are not sweet at all and are more starchy, more like a regular potato than a sweet one. Sweet potatoes are hands down nutritionally superior to a yam, and you can see that in their colors. Yams are light yellow, and sweet potatoes are a bright orange to a deep red, depending on the variety you choose. And lastly, sweet potatoes are readily available, and yams are more of a specialty produce item, although there are produce departments in grocery stores mislabeling sweet potatoes all the time as yams—go figure. In this book, I yam, what I yam (to quote Popeye) and it's sweet potatoes all the way!

❧ If there is one thing that
every kitchen should not be
without, it's a peppermill. Pepper, the freshly ground variety,
will do more for a dish than an
exotic herb. Why grind, you say?
Well for starters, peppercorns
have delicate oils in them that
are released immediately upon
grinding. That's bad news for the
preground variety of pepper because by the time it makes it
from the can to your shaker and
into the dish you're preparing,
it's flat, bland, and doesn't offer
the punch that's available from
the do-it-yourself sort.

With just a flick of the wrist,
your soups, salads, entrées, and
anything else you're cooking will
take on a new dimension—it's
truly amazing what freshly
ground pepper will do.

That's why annoying waiters
all over America can be seen
wielding huge peppermills on
steroids anytime you order a
salad. Fresh pepper makes a big
difference—no matter what the
size of the peppermill.

Be careful opening packet so that you don't get burned by the steam.
Carefully slide fish onto plates, and don't forget the elegant sauce you
just made, too.

PER SERVING:
293 Calories; 6g Fat (20.4% calories from fat); 42g Protein; 12g Carbohydrate; 1g Dietary
Fiber; 99mg Cholesterol; 130mg Sodium. Exchanges: 1 Grain (Starch); 5½ Lean Meat; 1 Fat.

SERVING SUGGESTIONS: Serve with steamed kale and baked winter
squash.

LAYERED TURKEY NACHOS

Serves 6

3 tablespoons lime juice
2 tablespoons olive oil
1 teaspoon ground cumin
1 teaspoon garlic powder
2 cups turkey breast, boneless, skinless, cooked, and shredded
Salt and freshly ground pepper to taste
2 10-ounce bags baked tortilla chips
1 16-ounce can refried beans
2 cups low-fat Cheddar cheese, shredded
1 16-ounce jar salsa (your favorite)
Low-fat sour cream optional
Chopped cilantro, optional

Heat oven to 425 degrees F.

Whisk together lime juice, olive oil, cumin, and garlic powder; toss
with turkey in a small bowl and season with salt and pepper.

Make a layer of tortilla chips to cover the bottom of a 9 × 13–inch
baking dish. Evenly spoon refried beans over chips (use the entire can
of beans). Top with turkey and sprinkle with 1 cup shredded cheese.

Make another layer of tortilla chips. Spoon half the salsa evenly
over chips. Top with remaining cup of cheese.

Bake nachos until heated through and cheese melts and begins to
bubble, 15–20 minutes. Serve hot with remaining salsa, sour cream, and
cilantro, if desired.

PER SERVING:

674 Calories; 26g Fat (34.8% calories from fat); 37g Protein; 73g Carbohydrate; 8g Dietary Fiber; 69mg Cholesterol; 1336mg Sodium. Exchanges: 4½ Grain (Starch); 3 Lean Meat; 1 Vegetable; 0 Fruit; 3½ Fat.

SERVING SUGGESTIONS: A big spinach salad and some baby carrots to share around the table.

BAKED ZITI

Serves 6

1 pound ziti pasta
1½ tablespoons olive oil
1 onion, chopped
4 cloves garlic, pressed
1 teaspoon rosemary
¾ cup low-fat sour cream
¾ cup low-fat cottage cheese
½ pound ground turkey
¼ pound extra-lean ground beef
1½ jars spaghetti sauce
6 ounces Provolone cheese
6 ounces mozzarella cheese, part-skim-milk, shredded

Preheat oven to 350 degrees F.

Prepare pasta according to package directions. In a skillet, heat olive oil and sauté onion till translucent. Add garlic and rosemary, remove from pan, and set aside. Meanwhile, in a small bowl, mix the sour cream and cottage cheese together and set aside.

In that same skillet, cook the turkey and beef together till crumbly and brown. Drain off grease and blot with paper towels (with this step the fat grams will be lower than what shows up in nutritional info below).

Return the onion mixture back to the skillet. Add the spaghetti sauce and put on low heat to simmer.

In the 9 × 13–inch pan, start layering. First spread sauce on the bottom, then a layer of ziti then sour cream mixture, then a layer of Provolone, then sauce, ziti, sour cream mixture, etc. Keep going till it's all gone. Then top with mozzarella.

Bake in a preheated oven uncovered for 20 minutes or until heated through.

PER SERVING:
544 Calories; 21g Fat (35.2% calories from fat); 31g Protein; 56g Carbohydrate; 3g Dietary Fiber; 64mg Cholesterol; 682mg Sodium. Exchanges: 3 Grain (Starch); 3 Lean Meat; 1½ Vegetable; 2½ Fat; 0 Other Carbohydrates.

SERVING SUGGESTION: A big green salad is entirely adequate for this rich pasta dish.

DO AHEAD TIP: Soak your beans overnight for Crock Navy Bean Soup tomorrow.

CROCK NAVY BEAN SOUP

Serves 6

1 pound dried navy beans, rinsed and drained
6 cups chicken broth
1 onion, chopped
1 stalk celery, chopped
2 cloves garlic, pressed
½ bay leaf
1 can diced tomatoes, undrained
Salt and pepper to taste

In a Crock-Pot, combine the first six ingredients. Cook on high for 1 hour, turn it down to low and cook for 8–10 hours.

When beans are tender, add tomatoes and salt and pepper to taste.

PER SERVING:
231 Calories; 2g Fat (7.1% calories from fat); 17g Protein; 38g Carbohydrate; 14g Dietary Fiber; 0mg Cholesterol; 587mg Sodium. Exchanges: 2½ Grain (Starch); 1 Lean Meat; ½ Vegetable.

SERVING SUGGESTIONS: A big green salad and some whole-grain rolls are adequate.

WINTER

The chill is on as winter forges ahead. Food truly takes on new meaning as the warmth factor of comfort foods takes off winter's icy edge. Warm soups, delicious stews, and home-baked casseroles keep the tummy warmed and the soul satisfied. This next batch of menus will definitely soften winter's bite.

Week One

DAY ONE: Skillet Chicken with Spinach

DAY TWO: Tuna Fusilli

DAY THREE: Cube Steak Stroganoff

DAY FOUR: Sweet Bean Burritos

DAY FIVE: Herb-Crusted Chicken Piccata

DAY SIX: Crock-Pot Corn Chowder

SHOPPING LIST

MEAT

12 boneless, skinless chicken breast halves

6 cube steaks

CONDIMENTS

vegetable oil

extra-virgin olive oil

Dijon mustard

white wine, optional

PRODUCE

1 lemon (3 tablespoons juice)

1 bunch cilantro

5 russet potatoes

1 pound red potatoes

3 pounds onions (keep on hand)

1 head garlic

1 pound mushrooms

1 bunch celery (you'll need 2 stalks)

1 bag spinach (**additional bag spinach if using Serving
    Suggestions)

2 medium sweet potatoes (**additional potatoes for 1 meal
    if using Serving Suggestions)
**1 bunch kale (1 meal)
**baby carrots (2 meals)
**broccoli (2 meals)
**butternut squash
**1–2 heads lettuce (*not* Iceberg)

CANNED GOODS
4 14½-ounce cans chicken broth
1 12-ounce can solid white tuna in water
1 small jar roasted peppers
2 15-ounce cans black beans
2 15¼-ounce cans corn

SPICES
thyme
basil
tarragon
cumin
garlic powder

DAIRY/DAIRY CASE
low-fat Cheddar cheese (you'll need about 1 cup, shredded)
milk (2 cups)
low-fat sour cream (you'll need ½ cup)
butter (you'll need 5 tablespoons)

DRY GOODS
12 ounces fusilli
flour (you'll need 2 teaspoons)
Italian bread crumbs (you'll need 4 tablespoons)
**1 pound brown rice
**pasta (your choice)

FROZEN FOODS
green beans

SKILLET CHICKEN WITH SPINACH

Serves 6

1 tablespoon olive oil

6 boneless, skinless chicken breast halves

2 onions, chopped

1 pound red potatoes, cut in ½-inch cubes

1 cup chicken broth

⅓ cup white wine

1 teaspoon thyme

Salt and pepper to taste

3 cups spinach

In a skillet, heat oil over medium heat. Add chicken and cook till browned on both sides. Add onions, potatoes, chicken broth, wine, thyme, and salt and pepper. Lower heat; cover and simmer for 10 minutes or until chicken is cooked. Serve on ½ cup raw spinach and let the heat of the chicken perfectly wilt the spinach. Keep the spinach together as much as you can so it wilts correctly. Serve.

PER SERVING:
372 Calories; 6g Fat (14.3% calories from fat); 58g Protein; 18g Carbohydrate; 2g Dietary Fiber; 137mg Cholesterol; 299mg Sodium. Exchanges: 1 Grain (Starch); 7½ Lean Meat; ½ Vegetable; ½ Fat.

SERVING SUGGESTION: Serve with baked butternut squash.

✳ I get e-mails all the time from intrepid cooks wondering what the heck to do with the marvelous butternut squash I suggested for the week's Menu-Mailer. It can be intimidating until you've learned the secret of unlocking the winter squash.

The cookbooks I've read all tell you the same thing when preparing winter squash: "Use a sharp knife and cut the squash in half." Well, if you're buying quality squash (look for firm squash—no soft spots allowed), that thing is harder to break into than a childproof top on a bottle of aspirin. Give me a break! Here's the way I do squash:

First off, wash it and stab it a few times. (No Norman Bates imitations. Go easy.) Next, put your stabbed darling into a preheated (350 degree F oven) for about 10–15 minutes, depending on the size. Throw it right on the rack—no pan necessary.

When the time is up, pull the squash from the oven and set it aside. Now futz with your salad or whatever else you need to do to get dinner ready. When the squash is cool enough to handle, proceed with the peeling, deseeding, and cubing of your gourd. Place in a baking dish and bake till tender. You can add a little orange juice, water, broth—anything to give it a little moisture. Top with a little bit of herbs, too. If you used orange juice, try some cinnamon or nutmeg. If you added water, go with just about anything. If you used broth, a little sage or thyme works well. When the squash is tender, it's done. Use a fork to smush it into a puree, add a little honey or maple syrup if you cooked it with cinnamon and nutmeg, and enjoy—you've earned that delicious squash!

TUNA FUSILLI

Serves 6

12 ounces fusilli
2 tablespoons butter, divided
1 onion, chopped
1 clove garlic, pressed
1 12-ounce can tuna in water, drained
1 teaspoon basil
1 jar roasted peppers, diced
1 package frozen green beans (thawed)
2 teaspoons flour
1 cup milk
½ cup low-fat Cheddar cheese, shredded
Salt and pepper to taste

Cook pasta according to package directions, drain, and set aside.

In a skillet over medium heat, melt 1 tablespoon butter. Add onion and garlic and sauté till translucent. Add drained tuna and basil, mixing well. Add diced peppers and green beans; mix well and remove from skillet.

In the same skillet over medium heat, add remaining butter and add flour gradually, whisking well to form a roux. Add milk and keep whisking till mixture is fully incorporated. Keep whisking and add cheese. Allow sauce to thicken, careful to not let it boil.

Add tuna mixture and pasta back to the cheese sauce, add salt and pepper to taste, and serve.

PER SERVING:
346 Calories; 7g Fat (17.5% calories from fat); 24g Protein; 47g Carbohydrate; 2g Dietary Fiber; 33mg Cholesterol; 255mg Sodium. Exchanges: 3 Grain (Starch); 2 Lean Meat; ½ Vegetable; 0 Non-Fat Milk; 1 Fat.

SERVING SUGGESTIONS: Serve with steamed broccoli, a bowl of baby carrots, and a salad.

CUBE STEAK STROGANOFF

Serves 6

3 teaspoons vegetable oil
6 cube steaks
Salt and pepper to taste
1 onion, chopped
1 pound mushrooms, sliced
¾ cup chicken broth
½ cup low-fat sour cream, room temperature
1 teaspoon Dijon mustard
1 teaspoon tarragon

In a skillet over medium-high heat, heat 1 teaspoon oil and brown cube steaks on both sides, salting and peppering both sides as they cook. When cooked to your liking, remove from skillet and keep warm.

In the same skillet, heat remaining oil and add onions and mushrooms, cooking until wilted and all liquid is evaporated. Add chicken broth and stir, scraping up any browned bits on the bottom of the pan. Bring to a boil, reduce heat, and cook for about a minute until reduced slightly. Remove pan from heat (important—your sauce will break otherwise). Add sour cream, mustard, and tarragon. Salt and pepper to taste, add the beef (juice and all), and heat through. Serve.

PER SERVING:
282 Calories; 17g Fat (55.1% calories from fat); 24g Protein; 8g Carbohydrate; 1g Dietary Fiber; 67mg Cholesterol; 187mg Sodium. Exchanges: 0 Grain (Starch); 3 Lean Meat; 1 Vegetable; 1½ Fat; 0 Other Carbohydrates.

SERVING SUGGESTIONS: Serve with pasta, baked sweet potatoes, and steamed kale.

DO AHEAD TIP: Bake 2 extra sweet potatoes for tomorrow's Sweet Bean Burritos.

SWEET BEAN BURRITOS

Serves 6

2 tablespoons olive oil
1 onion, chopped
3 cloves garlic, pressed
2 cans black beans, drained
2 medium sweet potatoes, cooked and mashed
1 teaspoon cumin
6 flour tortillas
6 tablespoons cilantro, chopped
6 tablespoons low-fat Cheddar cheese

In a skillet, heat oil over medium-high heat and cook onion and garlic until soft. Add beans, stir in the mashed sweet potatoes, add the cumin, and mix well.

Heat tortillas and plop bean mixture inside, add the cilantro and Cheddar cheese and roll up burrito-style. Serve.

PER SERVING:
567 Calories; 11g Fat (17.8% calories from fat); 23g Protein; 94g Carbohydrate; 14g Dietary Fiber; 1mg Cholesterol; 401mg Sodium. Exchanges: 6 Grain (Starch); 1 Lean Meat; ½ Vegetable; 2 Fat.

SERVING SUGGESTION: Add a spinach salad, and you're set.

HERB-CRUSTED CHICKEN PICCATA

Serves 6

4 tablespoons Italian bread crumbs
1 teaspoon garlic powder
Black pepper to taste
6 boneless, skinless chicken breast halves
1 tablespoon butter, divided
⅓ cup chicken broth
3 tablespoons lemon juice

On a dinner plate or pie plate, combine first three ingredients and set aside.

In a large zipper-topped plastic bag, add three chicken breast halves, close bag (but leave open a little so it won't pop) and roll them out with a rolling pin to flatten. Do this again with the other three. It will just take a second and make them cook faster. Dredge chicken in bread-crumb mixture and set aside.

In a skillet, melt half the butter over medium-high heat. Add the chicken and cook about 4 minutes on each side or until done. Remove chicken from skillet when cooked and keep warm. Add broth, lemon juice, and remaining butter using a wire whisk to get everything up off the bottom. Cook 1 minute and spoon sauce over chicken.

PER SERVING:
171 Calories; 4g Fat (19.7% calories from fat); 28g Protein; 5g Carbohydrate; trace Dietary Fiber; 74mg Cholesterol; 271mg Sodium. Exchanges: ½ Grain (Starch); 4 Lean Meat; 0 Fruit; ½ Fat.

SERVING SUGGESTIONS: Serve with brown rice, steamed broccoli, and steamed baby carrots.

CROCK-POT CORN CHOWDER

Serves 6

5 *russet potatoes, peeled and cubed*
2 *onions, chopped*
2 *stalks celery, chopped*
2 *cans corn, undrained*
2 *tablespoons butter*
1 *can chicken broth*
1 *cup milk*

In a Crock-Pot, add everything but the milk and cook on low for 8–9 hours.

Add the milk and cook another 30 minutes, then serve it up.

PER SERVING:
157 Calories; 6g Fat (32.5% calories from fat); 5g Protein; 23g Carbohydrate; 3g Dietary Fiber; 16mg Cholesterol; 207mg Sodium. Exchanges: 1 Grain (Starch); 0 Lean Meat; ½ Vegetable; 0 Non-Fat Milk; 1 Fat.

SERVING SUGGESTIONS: A big salad and some whole-grain rolls will work great.

Week Two

DAY ONE: Ginger Beef
DAY TWO: Romano Turkey Burgers
DAY THREE: Butternut Ravioli Stew
DAY FOUR: Fish Nicoise
DAY FIVE: Dijon Maple Chicken
DAY SIX: Crock Bean Soup with Kale

SHOPPING LIST

MEAT

6 boneless, skinless chicken breast halves
1 pound beef round steak
1½ pounds ground turkey
6 fish fillets

CONDIMENTS

extra-virgin olive oil
Dijon mustard (3 tablespoons)
white wine (you need ½ cup)
peanut butter (6 tablespoons)
Tabasco sauce
soy sauce, low sodium
maple syrup (or pancake syrup)
**mayonnaise for coleslaw

PRODUCE

1 piece gingerroot
1 bunch green onions
3 pounds onions (keep on hand)
1 head garlic
1 butternut squash (about 3 pounds)
1 pint cherry tomatoes
1 bunch carrots
1 bunch kale
**sweet potatoes (1 meal)

**red potatoes (1 meal)
**potatoes (for oven fries) (1 meal)
**cauliflower (1 meal)
**broccoli (1 meal)
**spinach (1 meal)
**baby carrots (1 meal)
**coleslaw (1 meal)
**2–3 heads lettuce (*not* Iceberg)

CANNED GOODS
7 14½-ounce cans chicken broth
Kalamata olives (you'll need ½ cup)
1 small can tomato sauce (you'll need ¼ cup)

SPICES
red pepper flakes
garlic powder
nutmeg
cinnamon
ginger

DAIRY/DAIRY CASE
butter (you'll need 5 tablespoons)
Romano cheese, grated (you'll need ¾ cup)
Neufchatel cheese (¾ cup)
half and half (you'll need 1¼ cups)

DRY GOODS
egg noodles, yolk-free (you'll need 3 cups)
1 pound cannellini beans (or use white beans, if
    unavailable)
**1 pound brown rice

FROZEN FOODS
1 package Asian-style vegetables
1 pound ravioli, cheese-filled

GINGER BEEF

Serves 6

1 tablespoon olive oil
1 pound beef round steak, sliced in 1-inch strips
3 teaspoons gingerroot
Salt and pepper to taste
1 package frozen Asian-style vegetables
3 cups egg noodles, yolk-free
6 tablespoons peanut butter
6 tablespoons green onions, chopped
½ teaspoon red pepper flakes
6 teaspoons soy sauce, low sodium

In a wok or a skillet, heat oil and sauté beef with the ginger till the middle of the beef is pink. Salt and pepper to taste.

Remove meat with a slotted spoon and keep warm. Add veggies to the skillet, right into the remaining liquid, and sauté till crisp-tender, about 3–4 minutes.

Meanwhile, cook noodles according to package directions, drain, and return to pot.

Add the peanut butter, green onions, red pepper flakes, and soy sauce to the hot noodles. Add beef and vegetables, toss well, and serve.

PER SERVING:
456 Calories; 19g Fat (36.9% calories from fat); 29g Protein; 45g Carbohydrate; 9g Dietary Fiber; 46mg Cholesterol; 404mg Sodium. Exchanges: 1½ Grain (Starch); 2½ Lean Meat; 5 Vegetable; 2 Fat.

SERVING SUGGESTION: Serve with a big salad.

ROMANO TURKEY BURGERS

Serves 6

1½ pounds ground turkey
¾ cup Romano cheese, grated
½ cup onion, minced
1 teaspoon garlic powder
Salt and pepper to taste
6 whole-wheat hamburger buns

Turn on broiler. In a bowl, mix all ingredients (except hamburger buns) together well and shape into six patties.

Place patties on a broiler pan and broil for 10 minutes, turning once. Patties are done when they are no longer pink in the middle. Serve on warmed hamburger buns.

PER SERVING:
400 Calories; 16g Fat (36.8% calories from fat); 31g Protein; 31g Carbohydrate; 3g Dietary Fiber; 104mg Cholesterol; 575mg Sodium. Exchanges: 2 Grain (Starch); 3½ Lean Meat; 0 Vegetable; 1 Fat.

SERVING SUGGESTIONS: Serve with coleslaw (see recipe on page 259), baked oven fries (see recipe on page 258), and some baby carrots for the table.

DO AHEAD TIP: Prepare butternut squash per instructions for tomorrow's Butternut Ravioli Stew.

BUTTERNUT RAVIOLI STEW

Serves 6

2 tablespoons butter
2 onions, chopped
3 pounds butternut squash (stab, microwave to soften, peel, deseed, and cube)
½ cup white wine
3 cans chicken broth
1 pinch nutmeg
1 pinch cinnamon

1 pinch ginger
1 pound frozen ravioli, cheese-filled
¾ cup Neufchatel cheese
¾ cup half and half
Salt and pepper to taste

In a soup pot, heat butter over medium-high heat. When hot and melted, add onions and sauté till translucent. Add the squash, wine, and chicken broth. Add the spices. Reduce heat and simmer for 10 minutes.

Meanwhile, cook ravioli according to package directions. Drain and set aside.

In a blender, blend half the stew and all the Neufchatel cheese to a smooth consistency, add back to the stew. Now add ravioli and carefully incorporate. Add half and half, heat till almost a simmer, salt and pepper to taste, if necessary, and serve.

PER SERVING:
431 Calories; 17g Fat (34.3% calories from fat); 14g Protein; 58g Carbohydrate, 6g Dietary Fiber; 132mg Cholesterol; 710mg Sodium. Exchanges: 3½ Grain (Starch); 1 Lean Meat; ½ Vegetable; 0 Non-Fat Milk; 2½ Fat.

SERVING SUGGESTIONS: A big spinach salad and some whole-grain rolls would round this off nicely.

FISH NICOISE

Serves 6

3 teaspoons Tabasco sauce
3 tablespoons soy sauce, low sodium
6 fish fillets
1 tablespoon butter
1 pint cherry tomatoes, halved
½ cup Kalamata olives
1 teaspoon garlic powder
Salt and pepper to taste

In a small shallow bowl, combine Tabasco and soy sauce. Dip the fish fillets on both sides and set aside.

Meanwhile, in a skillet, heat butter over medium-high heat. Add fish and cook 3–4 minutes on each side. Remove the fish, set aside, and keep warm.

Add the tomatoes and olives to the pan and sauté for 1 minute. Add garlic powder and salt and pepper to taste. Top the fish with tomato/olive mixture and serve.

PER SERVING:
276 Calories; 9g Fat (29.7% calories from fat); 42g Protein; 5g Carbohydrate; 1g Dietary Fiber; 105mg Cholesterol; 774mg Sodium. Exchanges: 0 Grain (Starch); 5½ Lean Meat; ½ Vegetable; 0 Fruit; 1½ Fat.

SERVING SUGGESTIONS: Baked red potatoes, steamed broccoli, and cauliflower.

DIJON MAPLE CHICKEN

Serves 6

6 boneless, skinless chicken breast halves
Salt and pepper to taste
2 tablespoons butter, divided
½ cup onion, chopped
1 cup chicken broth
½ cup half and half
3 tablespoons Dijon mustard
1½ tablespoons maple syrup (you can use pancake syrup)

Season chicken with salt and pepper. In a skillet, melt half the butter over medium-high heat and cook chicken till browned on both sides. Remove chicken from skillet and keep warm.

In the same skillet, add the rest of the butter and cook onion till translucent. Stir in broth with a whisk, making sure to whisk the browned bits up off the bottom of the pan. Add half and half, mustard, and maple syrup. Bring to a low simmer and cook till thickened slightly, about 5 minutes. Pour sauce over chicken and serve.

350 Calories; 10g Fat (25.8% calories from fat); 56g Protein; 6g Carbohydrate; trace Dietary Fiber; 155mg Cholesterol; 423mg Sodium. Exchanges: 7½ Lean Meat; 0 Vegetable; 0 Non-Fat Milk; 1½ Fat; ½ Other Carbohydrates.

SERVING SUGGESTIONS: Serve with brown rice, baked sweet potatoes, and a big green salad.

DO AHEAD TIP: Presoak beans.

CROCK BEAN SOUP WITH KALE

Serves 6

3 tablespoons olive oil
3 onions, chopped
1 carrot, chopped
3 cloves garlic, pressed
1 bunch kale, trimmed and sliced
1 pound cannellini beans, soaked overnight
¼ teaspoon red pepper flakes
3 cans chicken broth
¼ cup tomato sauce
Salt and pepper to taste

In a skillet, heat olive oil over medium-high heat. Add onions, carrot, and garlic. Cook until onions are translucent. Add kale and cook till wilted, about 3 minutes.

In a Crock-Pot, place the soaked beans, red pepper flakes, and the contents of the skillet; and cover with broth. Cook on high 8 hours or until beans are tender. Once beans are tender, add the tomato sauce and salt and pepper to taste.

PER SERVING:
349 Calories; 8g Fat (19.0% calories from fat); 19g Protein; 54g Carbohydrate; 13g Dietary Fiber; 0mg Cholesterol; 85mg Sodium. Exchanges: 3 Grain (Starch); 1 Lean Meat; 1½ Vegetable; 1½ Fat.

SERVING SUGGESTIONS: A big green salad and some whole-grain rolls are all you need.

Week Three

DAY ONE: Spicy Honey-Glazed Chicken
DAY TWO: Cube Steak Skillet Stew
DAY THREE: Basic Black Bean Soup
DAY FOUR: Garlic Lime Salmon
DAY FIVE: Spinach Pasta Casserole
DAY SIX: Crock-Pot Chicken Jambalaya

SHOPPING LIST

MEAT
12 boneless, skinless chicken breast halves
6 cube steaks
6 salmon fillets
½ pound kielbasa

CONDIMENTS
extra-virgin olive oil
honey (you need ½ cup)
Worcestershire sauce

PRODUCE
1–2 limes (you'll need 2 tablespoons juice)
1 bunch green onions
3 pounds onions (keep on hand)
1 head garlic
1 small red bell pepper
1 small green bell pepper
1 bunch celery (you'll need 1 stalk)
1 bunch cilantro
**broccoli (1 meal)
**butternut squash (1 meal)
**kale (1 meal)
**sweet potatoes (1 meal)
**potatoes (for mashed potatoes) (1 meal)
**spinach (2 meals)
**baby carrots (2 meals)
**1–2 heads lettuce (*not* Iceberg)

CANNED GOODS

3 14½-ounce cans chicken broth

1 14½-ounce can beef broth

2 15-ounce cans black beans

1 39-ounce jar spaghetti sauce (your favorite)

1 14-ounce can tomatoes

SPICES

red pepper flakes

thyme

oregano

cumin

Cajun seasoning

cayenne pepper

DAIRY/DAIRY CASE

butter (you'll need 2 tablespoons, more if you like it in potatoes)

1 wedge Romano cheese, grated (you'll need 4 ounces)

6 ounces part-skim-milk mozzarella cheese, shredded

1 egg (keep 1 dozen on hand)

DRY GOODS

flour (you'll need 3 tablespoons)

10 ounces fusilli

Italian bread crumbs (you'll need ½ cup)

**corn muffin mix, or ingredients to make from scratch

**2–3 pounds brown rice (3 meals)

FROZEN FOODS

Orange juice concentrate (you'll need 2 tablespoons)

1 10-ounce bag peas (petite peas are best; you'll need
   2 cups)

1 10-ounce bag chopped spinach

BAKERY

**corn muffins (if you buy instead of make)

Serves 6

¼ cup honey

2 tablespoons frozen orange juice concentrate

2 cloves garlic, pressed

⅛ teaspoon red pepper flakes

1 tablespoon butter

½ teaspoon olive oil

6 boneless, skinless chicken breast halves

Salt and pepper to taste

cilantro, chopped

green onions, chopped

In a small bowl, combine honey, orange juice, garlic, and red pepper flakes.

In a skillet, heat butter and olive oil over medium heat, add chicken, salt and pepper to taste, and brown, about 4 minutes on each side.

Add honey mixture to the skillet and cook, turning to thoroughly coat the chicken. Cook 2 more minutes or until sauce begins to thicken.

To serve, place chicken on plate, spoon sauce over the top and sprinkle with cilantro and green onions.

PER SERVING:
204 Calories; 4g Fat (16.9% calories from fat); 28g Protein; 14g Carbohydrate; trace Dietary Fiber; 74mg Cholesterol; 97mg Sodium. Exchanges: 0 Grain (Starch); 4 Lean Meat; 0 Vegetable; 0 Fruit; ½ Fat; 1 Other Carbohydrates.

SERVING SUGGESTIONS: Serve with brown rice, steamed broccoli, and baked butternut squash.

CUBE STEAK SKILLET STEW

Serves 6

3 tablespoons flour
Salt and pepper to taste
6 cube steaks
1 tablespoon butter, divided
1 tablespoon olive oil
1 onion, chopped
2 cloves garlic, pressed
1 can beef broth
½ teaspoon thyme
1 teaspoon Worcestershire sauce
2 cups frozen peas (petite peas are best)

On a dinner plate, combine flour and salt and pepper to taste. Mix well. Dredge meat in flour on both sides.

In a skillet, heat half the butter and half the olive oil together over medium-high heat. Add onion and garlic and sauté till translucent but not brown. Turn down heat if necessary. Add remaining oil and butter, then add meat, cooking on both sides till browned.

Stir in broth, using a spatula to scrape up the browned bits from the bottom of the pan. Turn the heat down to a simmer, add thyme and Worcestershire sauce and allow to cook for 15 minutes more, stirring occasionally. Add peas, salt and pepper to taste, and serve.

PER SERVING:
276 Calories; 18g Fat (58.3% calories from fat); 23g Protein; 6g Carbohydrate; 1g Dietary Fiber; 69mg Cholesterol; 296mg Sodium. Exchanges: 0 Grain (Starch); 3 Lean Meat; ½ Vegetable; 1½ Fat; 0 Other Carbohydrates.

SERVING SUGGESTIONS: Mashed potatoes, steamed baby carrots, and a spinach salad.

BASIC BLACK BEAN SOUP

Serves 6

1 tablespoon olive oil
1 onion, chopped
4 cloves garlic, pressed
1 small red bell pepper, chopped
½ teaspoon oregano
½ teaspoon thyme
1 teaspoon cumin
Pinch red pepper flakes
2 cans chicken broth
2 cans black beans, drained
Salt and pepper to taste

In a soup pot, heat oil over medium-high heat and add onion, garlic, and bell pepper. Cook till peppers are wilted and onion is translucent. Do not let garlic brown. Add spices and chicken broth; bring to a boil.

Add beans, bring back to a boil, salt and pepper to taste.

In a blender, puree half the soup (in batches! Don't do it all at once or you'll have bean soup on your ceiling till the next millennium). Add puree back to soup, reheat, and serve.

PER SERVING:
270 Calories; 4g Fat (12.3% calories from fat); 16g Protein; 44g Carbohydrate; 11g Dietary Fiber; 0mg Cholesterol; 260mg Sodium. Exchanges: 2½ Grain (Starch); 1 Lean Meat; ½ Vegetable; ½ Fat.

SERVING SUGGESTIONS: Serve with a big spinach salad and some corn muffins (homemade, from a mix, or store bought).

GARLIC LIME SALMON

Serves 6

¼ cup olive oil
1 onion, chopped
2 tablespoons lime juice
2 cloves garlic, pressed
6 salmon fillets

In a plastic zipper-topped bag, add the first 4 ingredients. Squish around to mix. Add the salmon, turning several times to get evenly coated. Let sit in the fridge for an hour if you have the luxury of time; if not, go ahead and start the broiling.

Turn on the broiler. Place salmon on a broiler pan and broil 5 minutes or more depending on how the salmon is cooking. (All broilers are different.) Then turn over and cook on the other side. Fish is done when it flakes easily with a fork.

PER SERVING:
287 Calories; 15g Fat (47.8% calories from fat); 34g Protein; 2g Carbohydrate; trace Dietary Fiber; 88mg Cholesterol; 115mg Sodium. Exchanges: 5 Lean Meat; ½ Vegetable; 0 Fruit; 2 Fat.

SERVING SUGGESTIONS: Brown rice, steamed kale, and baked sweet potatoes.

MAKING MEASUREMENTS MEANINGFUL

❋ I get e-mails by the bagful—if they could be measured that way. Occasionally, I get someone complaining about a cookie, muffin, fill-in-the-blank type of recipe that was too dry. After a lot of thought and some time in the test kitchen (that would be the one I live with), I know why I get these e-mails: incorrect measuring.

There are two types of measuring cups: dry and liquid measurements. The glass one is for liquid. Those cute little nesting measuring cups are for dry ingredients. Use the proper measuring cups for each ingredient—it makes a difference.

When you measure in glass, make sure you put your eyeball right there by the measurement line. If you are standing up, looking down on the cup, your measurement will be way off.

When measuring dry ingredients, don't forget the old spoon-it-in-and-level-it-off routine. If you stick your dry measuring cup into a bag of flour, you will come out with more flour than you intended. The flour will pack down into the cup, making your measurement considerably more. So remember to spoon the flour (or other dry ingredient) into the dry measuring cup and use the back of a knife to level it off. The only dry ingredient that should be packed is brown sugar.

Your measurement will then be correct and you can now effectively say good-bye to dry.

SPINACH PASTA CASSEROLE

10 ounces fusilli

1 egg

⅛ cup olive oil

10 ounces frozen chopped spinach, thawed and drained

½ cup Italian bread crumbs

39 ounces spaghetti sauce

6 ounces mozzarella cheese, part-skim-milk, shredded

4 ounces Romano cheese, grated

Preheat oven to 350 degrees F.

Cook fusilli according to package directions, drain, and place in a large bowl.

In a smaller bowl, mix together the egg and oil. Add to the pasta and toss. Add the spinach and bread crumbs and toss again.

On the bottom of a 11 × 7–inch baking pan, pour half of the spaghetti sauce. Add half the pasta mixture. Sprinkle half the cheeses. Now finish it by adding the rest of the sauce, the rest of the pasta, the rest of the cheeses.

Bake for 45 minutes till bubbly and slightly browned on top.

PER SERVING:
627 Calories; 25g Fat (35.6% calories from fat); 27g Protein; 75g Carbohydrate; 9g Dietary Fiber; 66mg Cholesterol; 1603mg Sodium. Exchanges: 3 Grain (Starch); 2 Lean Meat; 6 Vegetable; 4 Fat.

SERVING SUGGESTIONS: This is rich! Just a salad and little bowl of baby carrots are sufficient.

CROCK-POT CHICKEN JAMBALAYA

Serves 6

6 boneless, skinless chicken breast halves, cut into 1-inch cubes
½ pound kielbasa, sliced
1 can tomatoes, undrained
½ bell pepper, chopped
½ cup chicken broth
1 teaspoon oregano
1 teaspoon Cajun seasoning
¼ teaspoon cayenne pepper
1 onion, chopped
1 stalk celery, chopped

Put everything in a Crock-Pot and turn on low for 7 hours.

PER SERVING:
270 Calories; 12g Fat (41.0% calories from fat); 34g Protein; 5g Carbohydrate; 1g Dietary Fiber; 94mg Cholesterol; 693mg Sodium. Exchanges: 0 Grain (Starch); 4½ Lean Meat; ½ Vegetable; 1½ Fat; 0 Other Carbohydrates.

SERVING SUGGESTIONS: Serve with brown rice and a big salad.

Week Four

DAY ONE: Oven-Fried Mustard Chicken
DAY TWO: Easy Creamy Tomato Pasta
DAY THREE: Apricot Fish
DAY FOUR: Layered Enchilada Casserole
DAY FIVE: Turkey with Apples and Cheddar
DAY SIX: Crock-Pot Italian Chicken

SHOPPING LIST

MEAT
12 boneless, skinless chicken breast halves
¼ pound Italian sausage
6 fish fillets
¾ pound extra-lean ground beef
6 turkey breast cutlets

CONDIMENTS
Dijon mustard (you'll need ½ cup)
apricot preserves (you'll need ½ cup)
white vinegar
chili sauce (1 cup)
Italian salad dressing

PRODUCE
3 pounds onions (keep on hand)
1 small red bell pepper
1 lime
2 apples
6 potatoes (**additional potatoes for 2 more meals, if using Serving Suggestions)
1–2 bags baby carrots (**you need 12; additional carrots for 1 meal if using Serving Suggestions)
**2 bags spinach (2 meals)
**sweet potatoes (2 meals)
**kale (1 meal)

**broccoli (3 meals)
**winter squash (your choice) (1 meal)
**1–2 heads lettuce (*not* Iceberg)

CANNED GOODS

1 16-ounce jar spaghetti sauce
1 16-ounce can tomato sauce
1 small can black olives (you need 1 cup)
1 7-ounce can diced green chilies

SPICES

tarragon
garlic powder
Italian seasoning

DAIRY/DAIRY CASE

Parmesan cheese, grated (you'll need ½ cup)
low-fat Cheddar cheese (you'll need 1½ cups, shredded)
part-skim-milk Ricotta cheese, (you'll need 1 cup)
Romano cheese, grated (you'll need ½ cup)
low-fat sour cream (you'll need 2 cups)
butter (you'll need 2 tablespoons)

DRY GOODS

1 pound penne pasta
oats (you'll need 1 cup)
brown sugar (you'll need 1 tablespoon)
1 bag baked tortilla chips
1 canister Italian bread crumbs (you'll need 1¼ cups)
**1 pound brown rice
**pasta (your choice)

FROZEN FOODS

corn (you'll need 1 cup)

OVEN-FRIED MUSTARD CHICKEN

Serves 6

1¼ cups Italian bread crumbs
½ cup Parmesan cheese, grated
½ cup Dijon mustard
6 boneless, skinless chicken breast halves

Preheat oven to 350 degrees F. In a shallow bowl, combine bread crumbs and cheese. In another bowl, place the mustard.

Dip the chicken first into the mustard, then the bread crumbs, then place on a baking sheet, lightly sprayed with oil (I use a pump sprayer and avoid the aerosol can types). Bake for 20 minutes or until chicken is done.

PER SERVING:
267 Calories; 5g Fat (17.3% calories from fat); 34g Protein; 19g Carbohydrate; 2g Dietary Fiber; 74mg Cholesterol; 114mg Sodium. Exchanges: 1 Grain (Starch); 4½ Lean Meat; ½ Fat; 0 Other Carbohydrates.

SERVING SUGGESTIONS: Mashed potatoes, sweet potatoes, and steamed broccoli.

EASY CREAMY TOMATO PASTA

Serves 6

2 tablespoons butter
1 onion, chopped
1 small red bell pepper, chopped
1 pound penne pasta
¼ pound Italian sausage, removed from casings
1 pound spaghetti sauce
1 cup low-fat sour cream

In a skillet over medium heat, melt butter and sauté onion and pepper. Meanwhile, be heating the water to cook your pasta according to package directions. Add Italian sausage to onion mixture and continue to cook till sausage is crumbled and well cooked; drain fat and blot well with paper towels.

In the same pot in which you cooked the pasta, add the spaghetti sauce and heat through. Then add the pasta, sausage mixture, and the sour cream. Cook until heated through, about 5 minutes.

PER SERVING:
512 Calories; 15g Fat (27.4% calories from fat); 16g Protein; 75g Carbohydrate; 6g Dietary Fiber; 33mg Cholesterol; 599mg Sodium. Exchanges: 3½ Grain (Starch); ½ Lean Meat; 3 Vegetable; 3 Fat; ½ Other Carbohydrates.

SERVING SUGGESTIONS: Serve pasta with a spinach salad and some baby carrots.

APRICOT FISH

Serves 6

½ cup apricot preserves
2 tablespoons white vinegar
½ teaspoon tarragon
6 fish fillets

Preheat broiler. In a small bowl, mix preserves, vinegar, and tarragon. Place fish on broiler pan and broil, about 4 minutes on each side. One minute before fish is ready, brush preserves mixture on the top of fish, allowing it to cook into fish during the last minute.

PER SERVING:
255 Calories; 2g Fat (5.8% calories from fat); 41g Protein; 18g Carbohydrate; trace Dietary Fiber; 99mg Cholesterol; 136mg Sodium. Exchanges: 0 Grain (Starch); 5½ Lean Meat; 1 Other Carbohydrates.

SERVING SUGGESTIONS: Serve with baked potatoes, steamed broccoli, and baked winter squash (your choice).

LAYERED ENCHILADA CASSEROLE

Serves 6

¾ *pound extra-lean ground beef*
1 *cup oats*
1 *teaspoon garlic powder*
1 *cup black olives, chopped*
1 *can tomato sauce*
1 *cup low-fat sour cream*
1 *cup Ricotta cheese, part-skim-milk*
1 *can diced green chilies*
1 *bag baked tortilla chips*
1 *cup low-fat Cheddar cheese*

Preheat oven to 350 degrees F. In a skillet, brown the beef and drain well. Blot with paper towels to remove some more of the grease (with this step fat grams will be lower than what shows up in nutritional info below). Add oats and stir well to incorporate. Add garlic powder, olives, and tomato sauce.

In a bowl, mix together sour cream, Ricotta cheese, and green chilies.

Crush tortilla chips and place half of them on the bottom of a 2-quart casserole dish. Add half the meat mixture and then half the sour cream mixture, and finally the cheese. Repeat the layers. Bake uncovered for 30–40 minutes.

PER SERVING:
392 Calories; 20g Fat (45.3% calories from fat); 26g Protein; 27g Carbohydrate; 4g Dietary Fiber; 64mg Cholesterol; 937mg Sodium. Exchanges: 1 Grain (Starch); 3 Lean Meat; 1 Vegetable; 0 Fruit; 2½ Fat; ½ Other Carbohydrates.

SERVING SUGGESTIONS: Add a big salad and some steamed broccoli to this meal.

TURKEY WITH APPLES
AND CHEDDAR

Serves 6

1 lime, juiced
6 turkey breast cutlets
Salt and pepper to taste
1 tablespoon brown sugar
1 cup chili sauce
2 apples, chopped
1 cup frozen corn
½ cup low-fat Cheddar cheese, shredded

In a bowl, toss together lime juice and turkey cutlets; salt and pepper to taste. Set aside while you prepare the rest. Preheat broiler.

In a saucepan, toss together the remaining ingredients except the cheese. Simmer on low heat for 10 minutes.

Place turkey on a broiler pan and broil turkey on both sides, 3 minutes or less, depending on thickness. Serve hot apple/corn sauce over turkey and top with a little shredded Cheddar cheese.

PER SERVING:
165 Calories; 2g Fat (11.0% calories from fat); 21g Protein; 18g Carbohydrate; 3g Dietary Fiber; 47mg Cholesterol; 229mg Sodium. Exchanges: ½ Grain (Starch); 2½ Lean Meat; ½ Fruit; 0 Other Carbohydrates.

SERVING SUGGESTIONS: Serve with brown rice, sweet potatoes, and steamed kale.

CROCK-POT ITALIAN CHICKEN

Serves 6

6 potatoes, cut in wedges
12 baby carrots
6 boneless, skinless chicken breast halves
½ cup Italian salad dressing
2 teaspoons Italian seasoning
½ cup Romano cheese, grated

In a Crock-Pot, place potatoes and baby carrots on the bottom. Place chicken on top and add remaining ingredients, including cheese. Cook on low for about 6–8 hours or until chicken and vegetables are tender.

PER SERVING:
362 Calories; 14g Fat (34.2% calories from fat); 33g Protein; 26g Carbohydrate; 2g Dietary Fiber; 78mg Cholesterol; 357mg Sodium. Exchanges: 1½ Grain (Starch); 4 Lean Meat; ½ Vegetable; 0 Fruit; 2 Fat.

SERVING SUGGESTIONS: Serve with steamed spinach and a green salad.

Week Five

DAY ONE: Spiced Chicken Breast Halves
DAY TWO: Upside-Down Meat Loaf
DAY THREE: Cracker-Crusted Dijon Fish
DAY FOUR: White Turkey Chili
DAY FIVE: Winter Vegetable Chowder
DAY SIX: Crock-Pot Chicken Stew

SHOPPING LIST

MEAT
12 boneless, skinless chicken breast halves
1¼ pounds extra-lean ground beef
¾ pound ground turkey
6 fish fillets
turkey bacon (you'll need 4 slices)

CONDIMENTS
extra-virgin olive oil
Dijon mustard (you'll need ¼ cup)
ketchup
currant jelly
apple cider (you'll need 2 cups)

PRODUCE
3 pounds onions (keep on hand)
1 head garlic
3 leeks
1 medium butternut squash
1 16-ounce bag baby carrots (**additional bag if using
    Serving Suggestions)
2 large russet potatoes
**potatoes (for mashed potatoes) (1 meal)
**sweet potatoes (1 meal)
**winter squash (your choice) (1 meal)
**broccoli (1 meal)

**kale (1 meal)
**2 bags spinach (2 meals)
**1 head lettuce (*not* Iceberg)

CANNED GOODS

4 14½-ounce cans chicken broth
1 16-ounce can cannellini beans (or substitute white beans if
    unavailable)
1 11-ounce can corn with red and green peppers
1 15-ounce can tomatoes with garlic and onion
1 16-ounce jar salsa (your favorite)

SPICES

thyme
nutmeg
cinnamon
cumin
ginger
rosemary

DAIRY/DAIRY CASE

butter (you'll need 2 tablespoons)
3 eggs
buttermilk (you'll need ¾ cup)
half and half (you'll need 1 cup)
**low-fat Cheddar cheese, shredded (1 meal)

DRY GOODS

brown sugar (you'll need ½ cup)
oats (you'll need 1¾ cups)
crackers (you'll need ¾ cup, pressed)
flour (you'll need 1 tablespoon)
**2 pounds brown rice (3 meals)

FROZEN FOODS

**peas (1 meal)

SPICED CHICKEN BREAST HALVES

Serves 6

1 teaspoon salt
1 teaspoon thyme
½ teaspoon cinnamon
½ teaspoon black pepper
⅛ teaspoon nutmeg
⅛ teaspoon cumin
6 boneless, skinless chicken breast halves
1 tablespoon olive oil
¼ cup currant jelly
⅔ cup chicken broth

In a medium bowl, combine the spices well. Add chicken; toss to coat. Set aside.

In a skillet, heat oil over medium-high heat until hot. Add chicken and cook about 5 minutes on each side or until cooked through.

Remove chicken from the skillet and keep warm. Add currant jelly and chicken broth to pan drippings and scrape up browned bits off the bottom of the skillet, stirring well to make a sauce. Bring to a quick boil, lower temperature, and spoon sauce over the top of the chicken.

PER SERVING:
190 Calories; 4g Fat (19.1% calories from fat); 28g Protein; 10g Carbohydrate; trace Dietary Fiber; 68mg Cholesterol; 522mg Sodium. Exchanges: 0 Grain (Starch); 4 Lean Meat; ½ Fat; ½ Other Carbohydrates.

SERVING SUGGESTIONS: Brown rice, steamed broccoli, and baked winter squash.

UPSIDE-DOWN MEAT LOAF

Serves 6

½ cup brown sugar
½ cup ketchup
1¼ pounds extra-lean ground beef
1¾ cups oats
¾ cup buttermilk
2 eggs
1 teaspoon salt
1 onion, chopped
¼ teaspoon ginger

Preheat oven to 350 degrees F. Lightly grease a 5 × 9–inch loaf pan.

On the bottom of the pan, press brown sugar, then spread the ketchup over the sugar.

Meanwhile, in a large mixing bowl, combine remaining ingredients. Make a loaf out of mixture and place it carefully on top of the sugar/ketchup mixture in the loaf pan.

Bake for 45 minutes to an hour or until juice runs clear.

PER SERVING:
420 Calories; 19g Fat (41.7% calories from fat); 25g Protein; 36g Carbohydrate; 3g Dietary Fiber; 129mg Cholesterol; 712mg Sodium. Exchanges: 1 Grain (Starch); 3 Lean Meat; ½ Vegetable; 0 Non-Fat Milk; 2 Fat; 1 Other Carbohydrates.

SERVING SUGGESTIONS: Serve with mashed potatoes, peas, and steamed baby carrots.

CRACKER-CRUSTED DIJON FISH

Serves 6

1 egg, slightly beaten
¼ cup Dijon mustard
1 teaspoon thyme
¾ cup crackers, pressed
6 fish fillets
2 tablespoons butter, melted

Preheat oven to 475 degrees F. In a small bowl, mix egg, mustard, and thyme. On a dinner plate, evenly spread cracker crumbs. Dip fish into mustard mixture first, then dredge in cracker crumbs and place on an ungreased cookie sheet. Drizzle butter evenly over the top and cook for 10–15 minutes or until golden brown, turning fish once.

PER SERVING:
371 Calories; 10g Fat (25.1% calories from fat); 45g Protein; 22g Carbohydrate; 1g Dietary Fiber; 141mg Cholesterol; 683mg Sodium. Exchanges: 1½ Grain (Starch); 5½ Lean Meat; 1½ Fat; 0 Other Carbohydrates.

SERVING SUGGESTIONS: Serve with steamed spinach, brown rice, and baked sweet potatoes.

WHITE TURKEY CHILI

Serves 6

1 tablespoon olive oil
1 onion, chopped
2 cloves garlic, pressed
¾ pound ground turkey
Salt and pepper to taste
1 can cannellini beans, drained
1 can corn with red and green peppers, drained
1 16-ounce jar salsa
1 15-ounce can tomatoes with garlic and onion

In a skillet, heat olive oil over medium-high heat. Add onion and garlic and cook till translucent, add turkey and brown, salting and peppering to taste. Drain, then blot meat with paper towels to absorb excess grease.

Add the rest of the ingredients and heat till bubbly and completely heated through.

PER SERVING:
411 Calories; 8g Fat (16.9% calories from fat); 30g Protein; 58g Carbohydrate; 13g Dietary Fiber; 45mg Cholesterol; 458mg Sodium. Exchanges: 3½ Grain (Starch); 2½ Lean Meat; 1 Vegetable; ½ Fat.

SERVING SUGGESTIONS: A huge green salad and some whole-grain rolls would round this off nicely. You could top this delicious chili with some low-fat Cheddar cheese, if desired.

WINTER VEGETABLE CHOWDER

Serves 6

1 tablespoon olive oil
3 leeks, washed and sliced
4 slices turkey bacon, cut into 1-inch pieces
2 large russet potatoes, cut into 1-inch cubes
1 medium butternut squash, cut into 1-inch cubes
2 cans chicken broth
½ teaspoon thyme
Salt and pepper to taste
1 cup half and half

In a soup pot, heat olive oil over medium-high heat. Add leeks and cook to soften; add bacon pieces and continue cooking till leeks are completely cooked and bacon is browned. Add potatoes and squash; cook another 3 minutes. Add chicken broth, thyme, and salt and pepper to taste; simmer covered till veggies are soft, about 20–30 minutes.

With a potato masher, mash half the veggies, leaving some intact to give the chowder a nice thick consistency and texture. Add half and half and heat thoroughly, but don't let it boil or the half and half will break. Correct the seasoning if necessary, and serve immediately.

PER SERVING:
283 Calories; 10g Fat (28.4% calories from fat); 8g Protein; 46g Carbohydrate; 6g Dietary Fiber; 23mg Cholesterol; 415mg Sodium. Exchanges: 2½ Grain (Starch); ½ Lean Meat; 1 Vegetable; 0 Non-Fat Milk; 1½ Fat.

SERVING SUGGESTIONS: Serve with a big spinach salad and whole-grain rolls.

CROCK-POT CHICKEN STEW

Serves 6

1 16-ounce bag baby carrots
2 onions, thinly sliced
6 boneless, skinless chicken breast halves
Salt and pepper to taste
½ teaspoon rosemary, pressed
2 cups apple cider
1 can chicken broth
1 tablespoon flour
¼ cup cold water

In a Crock-Pot, place carrots on the bottom, then onions. Layer chicken on top, salt and pepper to taste and crush the rosemary over the top as well. Add cider and broth. Turn Crock-Pot on low and cook for 8 hours.

When carrots are tender and all is cooked, drain cooking liquid into a saucepan and simmer over medium heat till reduced. In a cup, add 1 tablespoon flour and ¼ cup cold water and blend to make a paste, using a fork. Make sure there are no lumps, then add to simmering cooking juices, blending the entire time with the fork to incorporate flour mixture with the cooking juices. When sauce has thickened, serve over chicken.

PER SERVING:
190 Calories; 2g Fat (9.1% calories from fat); 29g Protein; 13g Carbohydrate; 1g Dietary Fiber; 68mg Cholesterol; 208mg Sodium. Exchanges: 0 Grain (Starch); 4 Lean Meat; ½ Vegetable; ½ Fruit; 0 Fat.

SERVING SUGGESTIONS: Serve with rice and steamed kale.

Week Six

DAY ONE: Honey Mustard Glazed Chicken
DAY TWO: My Big Fat Greek Stuffed Peppers
DAY THREE: Spiced Fish with cilantro and Lime
DAY FOUR: Skillet Turkey Jambalaya
DAY FIVE: Cream of Broccoli Cheddar Soup
DAY SIX: Crock-Pot Tuscan Chicken and Beans

SHOPPING LIST

MEAT

12 boneless, skinless chicken breast halves
½ pound extra-lean ground beef
6 fish fillets
¾ pound kielbasa
turkey breast cutlets (you'll need 4 cups)

CONDIMENTS

extra-virgin olive oil
honey (you'll need ¼ cup)
Dijon mustard (you'll need ⅓ cup)

PRODUCE

1 bunch green onions
3 pounds onions (keep on hand)
2 cloves garlic
2 large tomatoes
1 lime
1 lemon
1 bunch cilantro
1 pound mushrooms (pre-sliced, if available)
1 bunch carrots
1 bunch celery (you'll need 1 stalk)
6 bell peppers
5 pounds potatoes (enough for garlic mashed potatoes with
    1½ cups left over)
**butternut squash (1 meal)

**kale (1 meal)
**sweet potatoes (2 meals)
**spinach (2 meals)
**baby carrots (1 meal)
**cauliflower (1 meal)
**1–2 heads lettuce (*not* Iceberg)

CANNED GOODS

1 14½-ounce can chicken broth
1 2¼-ounce can black olives, sliced
1 small jar roasted peppers
1 small jar marinated artichoke hearts
1 15-ounce can diced tomatoes
1 jar spaghetti sauce (you'll need 1½ cups)
1 15-ounce can cannellini beans (or use white beans if
   unavailable)

SPICES

paprika
curry powder
oregano
basil
thyme
garlic powder
crushed red pepper
Italian seasoning

DAIRY/DAIRY CASE

Feta cheese (you'll need 1 cup)
milk
1 bag low-fat Cheddar cheese, shredded
**1 wedge Romano cheese

DRY GOODS

1 pound brown rice
12 ounces spaghetti

HONEY MUSTARD GLAZED CHICKEN

Serves 6

1 tablespoon olive oil
½ onion, chopped
6 boneless, skinless chicken breast halves
1 teaspoon paprika
Salt and pepper to taste
1 tablespoon lemon juice
⅓ cup Dijon mustard
¼ cup honey
½ teaspoon curry powder

In a skillet, heat olive oil over medium-high heat and add onion. Sauté till translucent. Sprinkle chicken with paprika and salt and pepper to taste, then add to the skillet. Cook chicken till nicely browned on both sides, about 5 minutes per side. Set aside and keep warm.

Meanwhile, in a small bowl, mix together lemon juice, mustard, honey, and curry powder. Add to skillet, mix well, and scrape up the browned bits off the bottom of the pan. Return the chicken to the skillet and simmer a minute in the sauce. Serve, spooning the sauce over the top of the chicken.

PER SERVING:
208 Calories; 4g Fat (19.1% calories from fat); 28g Protein; 14g Carbohydrate; 1g Dietary Fiber; 68mg Cholesterol; 245mg Sodium. Exchanges: 0 Grain (Starch); 4 Lean Meat; 0 Vegetable; 0 Fruit; ½ Fat; 1 Other Carbohydrates.

SERVING SUGGESTIONS: Serve with brown rice, steamed cauliflower, and sweet potatoes.

DO AHEAD TIP: Prepare rice for tomorrow's My Big Fat Greek Stuffed Peppers.

MY BIG FAT GREEK STUFFED PEPPERS

Serves 6

6 bell peppers, halved and seeded
2 tablespoons olive oil
1 onion, chopped
½ pound extra-lean ground beef
Salt and pepper to taste
1 teaspoon oregano
½ teaspoon basil
2 large tomatoes, diced
3 cups brown rice, cooked
1 cup Feta cheese, crumbled

Preheat oven to 400 degrees F. Lightly grease a baking sheet and put peppers, cut side down, on the surface. Roast in the oven for 20–30 minutes or until they're tender and skin begins to brown.

While peppers are roasting, heat the olive oil over medium-high heat and add onion. Cook onion till translucent, then add beef, crumbling well; add salt and pepper to taste. Drain well and blot with paper towels (with this step the fat grams will be lower than what shows up in the nutritional info below).

Add seasonings to beef mixture; then add the tomatoes and rice. Mix well. Add the Feta cheese and mix well again.

In a baking dish, place peppers cut side up this time and fill with meat and cheese mixture. Cook for an additional 5–10 minutes or until heated through.

PER SERVING:
352 Calories; 15g Fat (23% calories from fat); 15g Protein; 35g Carbohydrate; 5g Dietary Fiber; 48mg Cholesterol; 312mg Sodium. Exchanges: 1½ Grain (Starch); 1½ Lean Meat; 2 Vegetable; 2½ Fat.

SERVING SUGGESTIONS: Serve with baked sweet potatoes and a spinach salad.

SPICED FISH WITH CILANTRO AND LIME

Serves 6

¾ teaspoon thyme
⅛ teaspoon salt
½ teaspoon garlic powder
⅛ teaspoon curry powder
⅛ teaspoon pressed red pepper
6 fish fillets
1 lime, cut in 6 wedges
Cilantro, chopped

Set oven to broil. In a small bowl, mix seasonings together and generously sprinkle on both sides of the fish. Place seasoned fish on broiler pan and broil, about 5 minutes each side, or until fish flakes easily with a fork. Serve with lime wedges and cilantro sprinkled over the top.

PER SERVING:
194 Calories; 2g Fat (7.7% calories from fat); 41g Protein; 1g Carbohydrate; trace Dietary Fiber; 99mg Cholesterol; 170mg Sodium. Exchanges: 0 Grain (Starch); 5½ Lean Meat; 0 Fruit; 0 Fat.

SERVING SUGGESTIONS: Mashed garlic potatoes, baked butternut squash, and steamed kale.

DO AHEAD TIP: Make an extra 1½ cups mashed potatoes for the Cream of Broccoli Cheddar Soup. Precook turkey and rice for Skillet Turkey Jambalaya.

SKILLET TURKEY JAMBALAYA

Serves 6

1 tablespoon olive oil
¾ pound kielbasa, sliced in ½-inch pieces
1 onion, chopped
1 pound mushrooms, sliced
4 cups turkey breast cutlets, cooked and cubed
1 2¼-ounce can sliced black olives
1 jar marinated artichoke hearts, drained and chopped
1 can diced tomatoes, undrained
3 cups brown rice, cooked
Salt and pepper to taste
½ cup green onions, chopped

In a skillet, heat olive oil and sauté kielbasa and onion together till sausage is browned and onion is translucent. Add mushrooms and cook till liquid from mushrooms has evaporated.

Add turkey, olives, artichoke hearts, and tomatoes. Cook over low heat for 2 minutes. Add rice and simmer another 2 minutes; salt and pepper to taste. Sprinkle green onions over the top and serve.

PER SERVING:
524 Calories; 23g Fat (40.0% calories from fat); 46g Protein; 33g Carbohydrate; 4g Dietary Fiber; 127mg Cholesterol; 1124mg Sodium. Exchanges: 1½ Grain (Starch); 6 Lean Meat; 1½ Vegetable; 0 Fruit; 3 Fat.

SERVING SUGGESTIONS: A green salad and some baby carrots to pass at the table are really all you need.

CREAM OF BROCCOLI CHEDDAR SOUP

Serves 6

1 tablespoon olive oil
1 onion, chopped
1 bag frozen chopped broccoli
2 cups chicken broth
1½ cups mashed potatoes (leftovers)
2 cups milk
1½ cups low-fat Cheddar cheese, shredded
Salt and pepper to taste

In a soup pot, heat olive oil over medium-high heat and cook onion. When onion is translucent, add broccoli and chicken broth. Cook till broccoli is tender, about 3 minutes or so.

Add mashed potatoes, mixing well till incorporated. Heat for 5 minutes, then add milk and heat a little while longer. Add Cheddar cheese and stir; salt and pepper to taste. Serve.

PER SERVING:
180 Calories; 9g Fat (43.1% calories from fat); 12g Protein; 13g Carbohydrate; 1g Dietary Fiber; 18mg Cholesterol; 591mg Sodium. Exchanges: ½ Grain (Starch); 1 Lean Meat; ½ Vegetable; ½ Non-Fat Milk; 1 Fat.

SERVING SUGGESTIONS: Serve with a big salad and some whole-grain rolls.

CROCK-POT TUSCAN CHICKEN AND BEANS

Serves 6

1 onion, chopped
2 cloves garlic, pressed
2 carrots, chopped
1 stalk celery, chopped
6 boneless, skinless chicken breast halves, cut into 1-inch cubes
1 jar roasted peppers, diced
1 can cannellini beans, drained
1 teaspoon Italian seasoning
Salt and pepper to taste
1½ cups spaghetti sauce
1 cup water
12 ounces spaghetti

In a Crock-Pot, layer onion, garlic, carrots, and celery on the bottom. Add the chicken next then the roasted peppers, beans, Italian seasoning, and salt and pepper to taste. Add spaghetti sauce and water. Cover and cook on low for 4–5 hours or until chicken is tender and cooked.

During the last 15 minutes of cooking, prepare pasta according to package directions, drain, and serve chicken on top.

PER SERVING:
473 Calories; 6g Fat (10.8% calories from fat); 39g Protein; 65g Carbohydrate; 8g Dietary Fiber; 68mg Cholesterol; 408mg Sodium. Exchanges: 3½ Grain (Starch); 4 Lean Meat; 3 Vegetable; ½ Fat.

SERVING SUGGESTIONS: Serve with a big spinach salad and a little grated Romano cheese over the top of the pasta and chicken, if you like.

Week Seven

DAY ONE: Green Chile Chicken Casserole
DAY TWO: Pasta with Garlicky Greens and Beans
DAY THREE: Double Potato Soup
DAY FOUR: Thai Roll-ups
DAY FIVE: Salmon Burgers
DAY SIX: Crock-Pot Beef Stew

SHOPPING LIST

MEAT

6 boneless, skinless chicken breast halves
¾ pound turkey breast
1 pound round steak

CONDIMENTS

olive oil
soy sauce (low sodium if available)
vegetable oil
Dijon mustard
Worcestershire sauce
peanut butter (you'll need 3 tablespoons)
balsamic vinegar
**mustard
**mayonnaise
**ketchup

PRODUCE

1 small red bell pepper
1 small green bell pepper
1 head garlic
3 pounds onions (keep on hand)
1 bunch kale (**one more bunch, if using Serving Suggestions)
2 sweet potatoes
10–12 russet potatoes (you'll need 6, plus enough for 4 cups
    mashed potatoes)

1 piece gingerroot

1 lime

1 bunch cilantro

1 bunch green onions

1 bag baby carrots (**one more bag, if using Serving
  Suggestions)

1 bunch celery (you'll need 1 stalk)

**2 heads lettuce (*not* Iceberg)

**sweet potatoes (1 meal)

**1 bag spinach (baby is best)

**tomatoes

**butternut squash

** kale

SPICES

garlic powder

cumin

thyme

cayenne pepper

dill

CANNED GOODS

1 28-ounce can green enchilada sauce

2 15-ounce cans cannellini beans (or substitute white
  beans)

3 14½-ounce cans chicken broth

1 14½-ounce can beef broth

1 16-ounce can salmon

DAIRY/DAIRY CASE

1 (16-ounce) bag shredded low-fat Cheddar cheese

1 8-ounce container low-fat sour cream

1 wedge Romano cheese (you need ½ cup grated)

1 16-ounce container half and half

1 3-ounce package Neufchatel cheese

1 dozen eggs (you'll need 1)

GREEN CHILE CHICKEN CASSEROLE

Serves 6

6 boneless, skinless chicken breast halves
1 teaspoon cumin
1 teaspoon garlic powder
12 corn tortillas, cut into fourths
16 ounces low-fat Cheddar cheese, shredded
1 cup low-fat sour cream
1 can green enchilada sauce

Preheat oven to 350 degrees F. In a baking dish, arrange chicken and sprinkle with cumin and garlic powder. Bake until chicken is cooked, 30 minutes or more depending on the thickness of your chicken. When cooled, shred chicken for casserole.

Line the bottom of a medium-sized baking dish with half of the tortillas. Top with half the chicken, a third of the cheese, half of the sour cream, and a third of the enchilada sauce (you will end with cheese and enchilada sauce). Repeat layers, top with remaining sauce and cheese.

Tent with aluminum foil (not touching or the cheese will bake onto the foil). Bake for 45 minutes or until hot and bubbly—don't let cheese brown. Let stand 5 minutes before digging in.

PER SERVING:
451 Calories; 12g Fat (23.9% calories from fat); 52g Protein; 33g Carbohydrate; 3g Dietary Fiber; 98mg Cholesterol; 725mg Sodium. Exchanges; 1½ Grain (Starch); 6½ Lean Meat; ½ Vegetable; 1 Fat; ½ Other Carbohydrates.

SERVING SUGGESTIONS: What more do you need than just a nice big salad and maybe a little bowl of baby carrots?

PASTA WITH GARLICKY GREENS AND BEANS

Serves 6

1 tablespoon olive oil
6 cloves garlic, pressed
1 small red bell pepper, diced
1 bunch kale, washed and chopped, with stems removed
¼ cup chicken broth
2 tablespoons balsamic vinegar
1 pound ziti pasta
2 cans cannellini beans, drained
½ cup Romano cheese, grated
Freshly ground black pepper

In a skillet, heat olive oil over medium-high heat. Add garlic and red bell pepper and sauté for about 2 minutes. Don't let the garlic brown. Add greens and cook another minute. Now add broth and vinegar and cover pan and cook until greens are wilted, about 5 minutes. In the meantime, get your water started for the pasta and cook according to package directions, drain, and set aside.

After greens have cooked, add the drained beans and incorporate. Now add the pasta and toss gently to mix. Serve with grated Romano and some freshly ground black pepper on top.

PER SERVING:
579 Calories; 7g Fat (10.4% calories from fat); 29g Protein; 101g Carbohydrate; 13g Dietary Fiber; 10mg Cholesterol; 166mg Sodium. Exchanges: 6½ Grain (Starch); 1½ Lean Meat; ½ Vegetable; 0 Fruit; ½ Fat.

SERVING SUGGESTION: Serve with baked sweet potatoes.

DOUBLE POTATO SOUP

1 tablespoon olive oil
2 onions, chopped
2 sweet potatoes, peeled and cubed
2 russet potatoes, peeled and cubed
3 cloves garlic, pressed
2 cans chicken broth
1 teaspoon thyme
⅛ teaspoon cayenne pepper
Salt and pepper to taste
2 cups half and half

In a soup pot, heat olive oil over medium-high heat. Add onions and cook till translucent. Add sweet potatoes, potatoes and garlic and cook another two minutes. Add the chicken broth, thyme, and cayenne pepper and bring to a boil. Reduce heat and simmer covered until the potatoes are tender, about 10–15 minutes.

Use a potato masher and squish the lumps in the soup as best you can. This soup is better not processed in a blender as it is heartier this way; however, if you prefer it smoother, go ahead and blend away. Just remember to process it in batches or it'll get all over the ceiling.

Heat soup to a simmer, and salt and pepper to taste, add half and half and warm till hot, but don't boil or it will break.

PER SERVING:
220 Calories; 12g Fat (49.2% calories from fat); 6g Protein; 23g Carbohydrate; 2g Dietary Fiber; 30mg Cholesterol; 296mg Sodium. Exchanges: 1 Grain (Starch); 0 Lean Meat; ½ Vegetable; ½ Non-Fat Milk; 2½ Fat.

SERVING SUGGESTIONS: Spinach salad and some whole-grain rolls.

DO AHEAD TIP: While you're peeling potatoes, peel a few extra and make 4 cups mashed potatoes for the Salmon Burgers scheduled for the day after tomorrow.

THAI ROLL-UPS

Serves 6

1 lime, juiced

3 tablespoons soy sauce, low sodium

3 tablespoons peanut butter

1 tablespoon brown sugar

2 teaspoons gingerroot, grated

2 cloves garlic, pressed

¾ pound cooked turkey breast, cut into strips

6 whole-wheat tortillas

6 tablespoons Neufchatel cheese

3 tablespoons cilantro, chopped

3 tablespoons green onions, minced

In a medium bowl, combine lime juice, soy sauce, peanut butter, brown sugar, ginger, and garlic. Add turkey and mix into the sauce well. Refrigerate for about an hour for the best flavor. If you can't wait, that's okay. Proceed to the next step.

On each whole-wheat tortilla, evenly spread 1 tablespoon of the Neufchatel cheese. Drain turkey of marinade if necessary and line up along the middle of the tortilla, vertically. Sprinkle cilantro and green onions over the top then roll up burrito-style and serve.

PER SERVING:
380 Calories; 11g Fat (26.7% calories from fat); 23g Protein; 46g Carbohydrate; 3g Dietary Fiber; 43mg Cholesterol; 737mg Sodium. Exchanges: 3 Grain (Starch); 2 Lean Meat; ½ Vegetable; 0 Fruit; 2 Fat; 0 Other Carbohydrates.

SERVING SUGGESTIONS: Serve with some leftover soup if you have it and a great big green salad.

SALMON BURGERS

Serves 6

3 tablespoons vegetable oil

2 small onions, chopped

1 small green bell pepper, chopped

1 pound canned salmon, drained and flaked

1 egg, beaten

4 cups mashed potatoes

1 teaspoon Dijon mustard

1 teaspoon Worcestershire sauce

1 teaspoon dill

Salt and pepper to taste

6 whole-wheat hamburger buns

In a skillet, add half the oil and sauté onions and bell pepper together till soft.

Meanwhile, mix salmon, egg, potatoes, and seasonings together in a bowl. When onion mixture has cooled a bit, add to the salmon mixture. Make into 6 salmon patties. Heat remaining oil in skillet over medium heat and cook patties 5 minutes each side or until completely cooked. Serve on warmed hamburger buns.

PER SERVING:
478 Calories; 18g Fat (34.4% calories from fat); 26g Protein; 52g Carbohydrate; 7g Dietary Fiber; 76mg Cholesterol; 1076mg Sodium. Exchanges: 3 Grain (Starch); 2 Lean Meat; 1 Vegetable; 2½ Fat; 0 Other Carbohydrates.

SERVING SUGGESTIONS: Serve with the usual fixings for hamburgers—lettuce, tomato, onion, mustard, mayonnaise, ketchup. A green salad will round this off nicely.

CROCK-POT BEEF STEW

Serves 6

2 tablespoons olive oil

2 onions, chopped

2 cloves garlic, pressed

¼ cup flour

1 pound round steak, cubed

4 potatoes, peeled and cubed

12 baby carrots

1 stalk celery, finely chopped

½ cup water

1 can beef broth

1 teaspoon thyme

Salt and pepper to taste

In a skillet, heat the oil over medium-high heat and sauté onions and garlic till translucent. In the meantime, dump the flour in a plastic bag and toss beef cubes in there to coat. Add beef to onion mixture and continue to cook till meat is browned.

In a Crock-Pot, place potatoes, carrots, and celery on the bottom. Top with beef mixture. Now take the skillet and begin heating, adding ½ cup of water to the browned skillet. Use a wire whisk to get these browned bits up and pour the browned water over the top of the meat in the Crock-Pot. Add beef broth, thyme, and salt and pepper; cover and cook on low for 8 hours or until meat is tender.

PER SERVING:
302 Calories; 14g Fat (41.6% calories from fat); 19g Protein; 25g Carbohydrate; 3g Dietary Fiber; 45mg Cholesterol; 271mg Sodium. Exchanges: 1 Grain (Starch); 2½ Lean Meat; 1 Vegetable; 1½ Fat.

SERVING SUGGESTIONS: Serve with baked butternut squash and steamed kale.

A CASE FOR OIL

❋ Pretend with me, for a minute, that I am a nutritional attorney defending a bottle of olive oil in a non-fat Court of Food. I am giving closing arguments to Judge JuJu Bee. Shhh . . . come on into the Food Court, and take a listen:

"Judge, let me just summarize the defendant's right to be included in a healthy diet by giving the court these facts:

"*Fact One:* A developing child (before and after birth and throughout childhood) must have fat for normal brain development.

"*Fact Two:* Olive oil is a monounsaturated fat that reduces the bad cholesterol (LDL) while not affecting the good cholesterol (HDL).

"*Fact Three:* It satiates and helps with that 'full' feeling—helping people to not overeat.

"*Fact Four:* It helps keep skin and hair healthier looking.

"*Fact Five:* It helps food taste better," I said, motioning dramatically to my client, the olive oil.

The judge was unmoved and eyed me like a piece of lettuce lodged in her tooth.

"Everything you say may be true, Ms. Healthy-Foods, but isn't it true that oils are unstable?" she said, arching her eyebrows and drawing out the last word for emphasis.

"That is true, Judge. But this is easily overcome by purchasing the right oil. For example, a cold pressed or expeller pressed oil most often found in health food stores is always a good oil and is labeled as such. Never mind the instability problem—if the oils are stored correctly in the refrigerator after opening, their fatty acids are preserved and no more rancid oils!" I said triumphantly, taking my seat. But I could see the judge wasn't willing to back down. She asked the question I had been dreading.

"Well, margarine is made from oil, and yet you told me earlier that it was hydrogenated and a bad choice! So you have the audacity to tell the food court to eat *butter*!" she bellowed, startling the poor olive oil.

I sighed and shifted nervously in my chair. Here we go again, I thought. Slowly rising to my weary feet, I pitch one more time.

"Honorable Judge, while it is true that butter is a saturated fat, it is still real food and is digestible by the body. *If* it is eaten in mass quantities, it will be problematic both for your thighs and your heart. Margarine, on the other hand, is hydrogenated oil with fake colors and flavorings. This is a product filled with *trans*-fatty acids, which will actually *raise* LDL levels and reduce the HDL levels. Not only that, but the *trans*-fatty acids will age you faster than sitting in a tanning booth with your face slathered in baby oil," I said, slamming the well-oiled table with my open hand.

Judge JuJu Bee removed her glasses, rubbed her eyes, and sat for a moment. The tension could be cut with a butter knife.

"Thank you, Counselor," said the judge finally. "Obviously, we can all use all the help we can get with our health, and as far as I'm concerned, with regard to the *Non-Fat People vs. Olive Oil,* case dismissed!" She slammed her gavel down and smiled for the first time.

A cheer went up in the audience. The safflower oil and peanut oil embraced as the butter melted in its chair. It was emotional for every oil and almost every fat . . . however, the Crisco and margarine left in a huff.

Week Eight

DAY ONE: Rosemary Chicken Breast Halves
DAY TWO: Country Fried Steaks
DAY THREE: Orange Honey Mustard Fish
DAY FOUR: Turkey with Spiced Squash and Apples
DAY FIVE: Tuscan Bean and Sausage Soup
DAY SIX: Crock-Pot Taco Chicken

SHOPPING LIST

MEAT
6 boneless, skinless chicken breast halves
6 boneless, skinless chicken thighs
6 cube steaks
6 fish fillets
6 turkey breast cutlets
¾ pound Italian sausage links

CONDIMENTS
olive oil
vegetable oil
Dijon honey mustard (you'll need ⅓ cup)
orange marmalade (you'll need 3 tablespoons)
maple syrup (you'll need 3 tablespoons)
red wine (you'll need ⅓ cup)
**salsa (your favorite)

PRODUCE
1–2 lemons (you'll need 3 tablespoons lemon juice)
1 head garlic
3 pounds onions (keep on hand)
mushrooms (you'll need 2 cups, sliced)
3 red apples
1 acorn squash (about a pound)
1 yellow squash
1 bag spinach (you'll need 2 cups, shredded)
**1 bunch broccoli (1 meal)

**1 bag baby carrots (1 meal)
**sweet potatoes (1 meal)
**1 bunch kale (1 meal)
**winter squash (your choice, 1 meal)
**brussels sprouts (1 meal)
**broccoflower (cauliflower if unavailable, 1 meal)
**2 heads lettuce (*not* Iceberg—two meals)

SPICES
rosemary
garlic powder
white pepper
ginger
Italian seasoning
cinnamon
nutmeg
1 package taco seasoning mix

CANNED GOODS
2 14½-ounce cans beef broth
2 14½-ounce cans chicken broth
apple juice (you'll need ¼ cup)
2 15-ounce cans white beans
1 14-ounce can Italian tomatoes
2 14-ounce cans tomatoes with green chilies

DAIRY/DAIRY CASE
skim milk (1¼ cups)
1 dozen eggs (you'll need 1 egg white)
1 wedge Romano cheese (you'll need 3 tablespoons)
**shredded low-fat Cheddar cheese

DRY GOODS
flour (you'll need 1 cup)
**1 pound brown rice

ROSEMARY CHICKEN BREAST HALVES

Serves 6

5 tablespoons olive oil
3 tablespoons lemon juice
6 cloves garlic, pressed
1½ teaspoons dried rosemary
6 boneless, skinless chicken breast halves
Salt and pepper to taste
1 lemon, cut into 6 wedges

In a big zipper-topped plastic bag, combine 4 tablespoons olive oil, lemon juice, garlic, and rosemary. Place chicken in the bag and refrigerate. Do this in the morning to have it perfect by dinnertime. If you can, turn the bag during the day a few times.

In a skillet over medium-high heat, heat remaining olive oil and cook chicken for approximately 5 minutes on each side, depending on the thickness of the chicken. Salt and pepper to taste and serve with lemon wedges.

PER SERVING:
237 Calories; 13g Fat (49.5% calories from fat); 27g Protein; 2g Carbohydrate; trace Dietary Fiber; 68mg Cholesterol; 77mg Sodium. Exchanges: 0 Grain (Starch); 4 Lean Meat; 0 Vegetable; 0 Fruit; 2½ Fat.

SERVING SUGGESTIONS: Steamed broccoli, baby carrots, and brown rice.

Serves 6

1¼ cups skim milk
1 egg white
1 cup flour, reserve 3 tablespoons
1 teaspoon garlic powder
¼ teaspoon white pepper
Salt and pepper to taste
2 tablespoons vegetable oil
6 cube steaks
1 onion, chopped
2 cups mushrooms, sliced
2 cups beef broth

In a shallow bowl, combine milk and egg white. In another shallow bowl, combine flour with spices. Take turns dipping cube steaks first in the egg white mixture, then in the flour mixture.

In a skillet, heat 1 tablespoon vegetable oil over medium-high heat. Add steaks and cook 3 minutes on each side. Remove from pan and keep warm.

To that same skillet, add another tablespoon vegetable oil and heat over medium heat. Add onion and mushrooms, sautéing onion till translucent and mushrooms are soft with all liquid evaporated.

In a jar, combine reserved flour and beef broth, shaking vigorously to combine. Make sure you don't have lumps. Add broth mixture to pan and bring to a boil, cooking about a minute, stirring constantly and whisking up the browned bits off the bottom of the pan. Serve steaks immediately with mushroom gravy over the top.

PER SERVING:
395 Calories; 18g Fat (42.3% calories from fat); 32g Protein; 24g Carbohydrate; 1g Dietary Fiber; 64mg Cholesterol; 871mg Sodium. Exchanges: 1 Grain (Starch); 4 Lean Meat; ½ Vegetable; 0 Non-Fat Milk; 1½ Fat.

SERVING SUGGESTIONS: Mashed potatoes, sweet potatoes, and steamed kale.

ORANGE HONEY MUSTARD FISH

Serves 6

6 *fish fillets*
⅓ *cup Dijon honey mustard*
3 *tablespoons orange marmalade*
1 *teaspoon ginger*

Preheat broiler. Place fish fillets on broiler pan.

In a bowl, combine mustard, orange marmalade, and ginger.

Broil fish 3 minutes on each side or just until done. At the last cooking minute, pull fish and brush mustard mixture generously on each fish piece and cook one minute longer.

PER SERVING:
215 Calories; 2g Fat (6.9% calories from fat); 41g Protein; 7g Carbohydrate; trace Dietary Fiber; 99mg Cholesterol; 129mg Sodium. Exchanges: 0 Grain (Starch); 5½ Lean Meat; 0 Fat; ½ Other Carbohydrates.

SERVING SUGGESTIONS: Winter squash, steamed brussels sprouts, and brown rice.

TURKEY WITH SPICED SQUASH AND APPLES

Serves 6

1 *pound acorn squash, seeded and cut into 6 wedges*
3 *red apples, peeled and quartered*
3 *tablespoons maple syrup*
¼ *cup apple juice*
½ *teaspoon cinnamon*
¼ *teaspoon nutmeg*
6 *turkey breast cutlets*

Preheat oven to 350 degrees F. In a baking dish, arrange squash wedges and apple quarters together in the pan. In a small bowl, mix together syrup, apple juice, cinnamon, and nutmeg. Pour half the syrup mixture over the top of the squash and apples. Bake for 30 minutes or until nearly fully cooked. Add turkey cutlets and remaining syrup mixture, spooning sauce over the cutlets. Return to the oven and bake for an additional 20 minutes or until turkey and squash are both completely cooked.

PER SERVING:
175 Calories; 1g Fat (6.8% calories from fat); 18g Protein; 25g Carbohydrate; 3g Dietary Fiber; 45mg Cholesterol; 163mg Sodium. Exchanges: ½ Grain (Starch); 2½ Lean Meat; 1 Fruit; 0 Fat; ½ Other Carbohydrates.

SERVING SUGGESTIONS: Steamed broccoflower and brown rice.

TUSCAN BEAN AND SAUSAGE SOUP

Serves 6

¾ pound Italian sausage links, removed from casing and cut into
    ½-inch pieces
1 onion, chopped
2 cloves garlic, pressed
1 yellow squash, sliced
2 cans white beans, rinsed and drained
1 can Italian tomatoes, undrained
2 cans chicken broth
⅓ cup red wine
2 cups spinach, shredded
1 teaspoon Italian seasoning
3 tablespoons Romano cheese, grated

In a soup pot over medium-high heat, brown sausage and fully cook. Drain grease. Add onion and garlic and cook till translucent. Add squash and sauté about 1 minute.

Add remaining ingredients except cheese, and simmer till heated through, about 10 minutes. Serve with cheese on top.

PER SERVING:
474 Calories; 20g Fat (38.1% calories from fat); 27g Protein; 45g Carbohydrate; 11g Dietary Fiber; 47mg Cholesterol; 741mg Sodium. Exchanges: 2½ Grain (Starch); 2½ Lean Meat; ½ Vegetable; 3 Fat.

SERVING SUGGESTIONS: A big green salad and whole-grain rolls.

CROCK-POT TACO CHICKEN

Serves 6

6 boneless, skinless chicken thighs
2 cans tomatoes with green chilies
1 package taco seasoning mix

In a Crock-Pot, add all ingredients and cook on low 7–9 hours or until chicken is tender and easily shreddable.

PER SERVING:
111 Calories; 3g Fat (23.0% calories from fat); 15g Protein; 6g Carbohydrate; 1g Dietary Fiber; 57mg Cholesterol; 770mg Sodium. Exchanges: 2 Lean Meat; ½ Vegetable; 0 Other Carbohydrates.

SERVING SUGGESTIONS: Serve with warmed corn tortillas, shredded cheese, salsa, and whatever else you like with your tacos. Add a big salad, and you're set.

SPRING

*Spring offers the promise that the cold is over, the
barrenness of winter is gone, and everything is new.
Nowhere is that more prevalent than at a roadside produce
stand. The colors from the vegetables themselves almost
seem to call your name. Green has never looked more
beautiful and fresh. Tender lettuces and young peas are at
their very best. Asparagus and green beans, gorgeous
young spinach and kale all vie for your attention.*

*Cooking this time of year can take on new meaning
and enjoyment. Like puppies at the pound, the produce
begs to be taken home and enjoyed by your family. And
when you're turned on to cooking by season, you're ready
to deliver! These next few weeks of menus will help you to
produce delicious spring meals. Enjoy!*

Week One

DAY ONE: Chicken Pasta with Artichokes
DAY TWO: Asian Burritos with Ginger Salsa
DAY THREE: Succotash Soup
DAY FOUR: Mediterranean Fish
DAY FIVE: Turkey Wraps
DAY SIX: Orange Thyme Crock-Pot Chicken

SHOPPING LIST

MEAT
9 boneless, skinless chicken breast halves
¾ pound extra-lean ground beef
6 pieces of white fish (cod, halibut, or whatever is available, fresh or frozen)
1 package white turkey meat (you'll need 1½ cups, cooked and chopped)

CONDIMENTS
cornstarch
hoisin sauce
soy sauce
plum sauce, optional
vegetable oil
olive oil
Dijon mustard
dry white wine or apple juice (you'll need ½ cup)

PRODUCE
1 lemon (you'll need 2 tablespoons juice)
1 pound mushrooms (you'll need two cups, sliced)
1 head cabbage (red or green)
1 head napa cabbage
1 bunch carrots

garlic (you'll need one clove)

1 large tomato

1 bunch cilantro

1 piece gingerroot (you'll need 1 teaspoon)

3 pounds onions (keep on hand)

1 red bell pepper

1 bunch celery (you'll need ½ cup, chopped)

1 bunch green onions

**spinach (2 meals)

**sweet potatoes (1 meal)

**green beans (1 meal)

**baby carrots (2 meals)

**broccoli (1 meal)

**1–2 heads lettuce (*not* Iceberg)

SPICES

cayenne pepper

thyme

nutmeg

garlic powder

CANNED GOODS

3 14½-ounce cans chicken broth (you'll have some left over and can freeze it in a freezer bag)

1 14½-ounce can whole tomatoes

1 11-ounce can whole kernel corn

1 14½-ounce can diced tomatoes with roasted garlic, onion, and oregano

1 4½-ounce can sliced olives

1 6-ounce jar marinated artichoke hearts

1 7-ounce jar roasted red peppers

DAIRY/DAIRY CASE

1 bag low-fat shredded Cheddar cheese (you'll need 6 tablespoons)

1 package low-fat cream cheese

DRY GOODS

cornstarch

1 12–16-ounce package fusilli pasta (or other medium-size pasta)

oats (you'll need 1 cup)

**1 pound brown rice (3 meals)

FROZEN FOODS

1 6-ounce can frozen concentrated orange juice

1 10-ounce bag frozen lima beans

BAKERY

12 flour tortillas (whole wheat, if available)

**whole-grain rolls (1 meal)

CHICKEN PASTA WITH ARTICHOKES

Serves 6

3 cups uncooked fusilli pasta (or other medium-size pasta)

1 6-ounce jar marinated artichoke hearts, undrained

3 boneless, skinless chicken breast halves, cut into ½-inch slices

2 cups sliced mushrooms

1 clove garlic, pressed

1 7-ounce jar roasted red peppers, sliced

¾ cup chicken broth

½ cup dry white wine, optional (substitute apple juice if not using wine)

1 tablespoon cornstarch

Salt and pepper to taste

Cook and drain pasta as directed on package. Drain liquid from artichokes into 10-inch skillet; heat over medium-high heat. Cook chicken in liquid for 3 minutes, stirring occasionally. Stir in mushrooms and garlic. Cook about 4 minutes or so, stirring occasionally, until chicken is light brown and no longer pink. Stir in artichokes and peppers.

In a medium bowl, mix broth, wine, and cornstarch together till well blended. Gradually stir the broth mixture into the chicken mixture. Heat to boiling, stirring constantly. Boil and stir 1 minute, till thickened. Toss with pasta, salt and pepper to taste, and serve.

PER SERVING:
341 Calories; 4g Fat (10% calories from fat); 27g Protein; 46g Carbohydrate; 2g Fiber; 44mg Cholesterol; 514mg Sodium. Exchanges: 2½ Grain (Starch); 2½ Lean Meat; 1 Vegetable; 0 Fruit; ½ Fat; 0 Other Carbohydrates.

SERVING SUGGESTION: A nice big spinach salad would complement this meal wonderfully!

ASIAN BURRITOS WITH GINGER SALSA

Serves 6

¾ pound extra-lean ground beef
1 cup oats
¼ cup hoisin sauce
3 tablespoons water
2 tablespoons soy sauce
⅛ teaspoon cayenne pepper
6 whole-wheat tortillas
2 cups shredded cabbage
1 medium carrot, shredded
plum sauce, optional

Ginger Salsa

Mix together the following:

1 large tomato (1 cup), finely chopped
1 tablespoon chopped fresh cilantro
1 teaspoon finely chopped gingerroot

Prepare Ginger Salsa. Then, in a skillet, cook ground beef till browned. Drain and blot up any remaining grease with paper towels. Stir in oats till well incorporated, then add hoisin sauce, water, soy sauce, and cayenne pepper. Let simmer a few minutes till well blended.

Warm tortillas and fill each tortilla with beef mixture. Top with cabbage and carrot. Serve with plum sauce and serve, burrito-style.

PER SERVING:
195 Calories (kcal); 11g Fat (48% calories from fat); 11g Protein; 15g Carbohydrate; 3g Fiber; 28mg Cholesterol; 389mg Sodium. Exchanges: ½ Grain (Starch); 1½ Lean Meat; ½ Vegetable; 0 Fruit; 1½ Fat; 0 Other Carbohydrates

SERVING SUGGESTIONS: A big green salad and some baked sweet potatoes would round this out beautifully!

SUCCOTASH SOUP

Serves 10 (good recipe to freeze, or save to have with Turkey Wraps)

1 bag frozen lima beans
1 cup water
2 14½-ounce cans chicken broth
1 tablespoon vegetable oil
1 cup chopped onion
¾ cup chopped red bell pepper
½ cup chopped celery
¾ cup chopped green onions
2½ teaspoons dried whole thyme
Salt and pepper to taste
Dash cayenne pepper
1 14½-ounce can whole tomatoes, drained and chopped
1 11-ounce can whole kernel corn

Place beans in a large Dutch oven. Cover with water to 2 inches above beans, bring to a boil, and cook 2 minutes. Remove from heat, cover, and let stand 1 hour.

Drain beans; add 1 cup water and broth. Bring to a boil; cover, reduce heat, and simmer 40 minutes or until beans are tender.

Heat vegetable oil in a large skillet over medium-high heat. Add onion; sauté 2 minutes. Add bell pepper and celery; sauté 2 minutes.

Add green onions; sauté 1 minute. Add onion mixture, thyme, and remaining ingredients to bean mixture; bring to a boil. Cover, reduce heat, and simmer 20 minutes.

PER SERVING:
172 Calories (kcal); 3g Fat (12% calories from fat); 12g Protein; 31g Carbohydrate; 12g Fiber; 0mg Cholesterol; 136mg Sodium. Exchanges: 1½ Grain (Starch); ½ Lean Meat; 1 Vegetable; 0 Fruit; ½ Fat; 0 Other Carbohydrates.

SERVING SUGGESTIONS: A big green salad, some whole-grain rolls, and you're good to go!

MEDITERRANEAN FISH

Serves 6

> 1 tablespoon olive oil
> 1 large onion, chopped
> 1 14½-ounce can diced tomatoes with roasted garlic, onion, and oregano
> 1 4½-ounce can sliced olives, drained
> Salt and pepper to taste
> 6 pieces of white fish (cod, halibut, or whatever is available, fresh or frozen)
> 2 tablespoons lemon juice

Heat oil in a skillet over medium-high heat and sauté onion, stirring occasionally, until crisp-tender. Add the tomatoes, olives, and salt and pepper; heat to boiling. Arrange fish fillets in single layer in tomato mixture. Sprinkle with a little lemon juice; reduce heat to medium high. Cover and cook 8–10 minutes or until fish flakes easily with fork.

PER SERVING:
201 Calories (kcal); 8g Fat (33% calories from fat); 22g Protein; 11g Carbohydrate; 2g Fiber; 49mg Cholesterol; 831mg Sodium. Exchanges: 0 Grain (Starch); 2½ Lean Meat; 1½ Vegetable; 0 Fruit; 1½ Fat; 0 Other Carbohydrates.

SERVING SUGGESTIONS: Steamed broccoli, steamed baby carrots, and brown rice will work well with this dinner. Salad is always a good thing!

DO AHEAD TIP: Cook turkey for tomorrow's Turkey Wraps.

TURKEY WRAPS

Serves 6

6 tablespoons low-fat Cheddar cheese, shredded
1 tablespoon thinly sliced green onions
2 teaspoons Dijon mustard
1 package low-fat cream cheese
6 flour tortillas
1½ cups cooked turkey breast, diced
1½ cups shredded napa cabbage

Combine first 4 ingredients in a bowl; stir well. Spread 3 tablespoons cheese mixture over each tortilla. Top each with ¼ cup turkey, ¼ cup cabbage. Roll up and serve.

PER SERVING:
332 Calories (kcal); 8g Fat; (20% calories from fat); 22g Protein; 43g Carbohydrate; 4g Fiber; 27mg Cholesterol; 1270mg Sodium. Exchanges: 2½ Grain (Starch); 2 Lean Meat; ½ Vegetable; 0 Fruit; 1 Fat; 0 Other Carbohydrates.

SERVING SUGGESTIONS: Serve with leftover Succotash Soup and a bowl of baby carrots on the table.

ORANGE THYME CROCK-POT CHICKEN

Serves 6

6-ounce can frozen orange juice concentrate, thawed
½ teaspoon thyme
Dash ground nutmeg
Dash garlic powder
6 boneless, skinless chicken breast halves
¼ cup water
2 tablespoons cornstarch

Combine thawed orange juice concentrate (not regular orange juice) in bowl along with the thyme, nutmeg, and garlic powder. Dip each piece of chicken into the orange juice to coat completely. Place in Crock-Pot. Pour the remaining orange juice mixture over the chicken.

Cover and cook on low for 6–7 hours or on high for about 4 hours.

When chicken is done, remove and keep warm. Pour the sauce that remains in your Crock-Pot into a saucepan. Mix the cornstarch and ¼ cup water well (no lumps!) and stir into the juice in pan. Cook over medium heat, stirring constantly, until thick and bubbly. Serve the sauce over the chicken.

PER SERVING:
305 Calories (kcal); 13g Fat (40% calories from fat); 31g Protein; 13g Carbohydrate; 1g Fiber; 93mg Cholesterol; 93mg Sodium. Exchanges: 0 Grain (Starch); 4½ Lean Meat; 0 Vegetable; ½ Fruit; 0 Fat; 0 Other Carbohydrates.

SERVING SUGGESTIONS: Serve with brown rice, steamed green beans, and a big spinach salad.

Week Two

DAY ONE: Pan-Roasted Chicken and Potatoes
DAY TWO: Pasta Beef Satay
DAY THREE: Black and White Checkered Chili
DAY FOUR: Blackened Salmon
DAY FIVE: Mexican Torta
DAY SIX: Crock Italian Veggie Stew

SHOPPING LIST

MEAT

6 boneless, skinless chicken breast halves
1½ pounds boneless top sirloin
½ pound lean boneless round steak
6 salmon fillets, ½ to ¾ inch thick
½ pound ground turkey

CONDIMENTS

olive oil
mayonnaise
Dijon mustard
teriyaki sauce
vegetable oil
creamy peanut butter (you'll need 2 tablespoons)

PRODUCE

1 pound small red potatoes
3 pounds onions (keep on hand)
1 head garlic
2 carrots
1 large zucchini
1 bag spinach (baby, if available) (**plus enough for
   2 meals, if you follow Serving Suggestions)
1 bunch cilantro
**baby carrots (2 meals)
**sweet potatoes (2 meals)

**1 bunch asparagus (1 meal)
**2–3 heads of lettuce (*not* Iceberg)

CANNED GOODS
2 4-ounce cans chopped green chilies
3 14¼-ounce cans chicken broth
1 14¼-ounce can beef broth
2 14½-ounce cans diced tomatoes
1 15-ounce can black beans
1 15–16-ounce can cannellini beans (or white beans, if
    unavailable)
1 16-ounce can fat-free refried beans
1 7-ounce jar roasted red bell peppers
1 jar salsa (your favorite)

SPICES
garlic powder
ground ginger
cayenne pepper
chili powder
paprika
white pepper
onion powder
dried thyme
dried oregano
cumin
sage
nutmeg
1 envelope taco seasoning (low sodium, if available)

DAIRY/DAIRY CASE
1 pound butter (keep on hand in the freezer for when needed)
16 ounces shredded reduced-fat Monterey Jack cheese
1 wedge Romano cheese
8 ounces low-fat sour cream

DRY GOODS
12 ounces thin spaghetti
½ cup elbow macaroni, or other small pasta
1 cup dried white beans
1 package pearl barley
**1 pound brown rice (1 meal)

BAKERY
16 corn tortillas
**corn muffins (or homemade, if preferred)
**whole-grain rolls

PAN-ROASTED CHICKEN AND POTATOES

Serves 6

⅓ cup mayonnaise
3 tablespoons Dijon mustard
6 boneless, skinless chicken breast halves, cut in half
1 pound small red potatoes, cut in quarters
2 cloves garlic, pressed
Salt and pepper to taste

Preheat oven to 350 degrees F. Lightly grease a 13 × 9–inch pan. In a large mixing bowl, whisk mayonnaise and Dijon mustard together well. Place chicken and potatoes in bowl, turning to coat completely. Place everything plus the garlic in the 13 × 9–inch pan; salt and pepper well.

Bake uncovered 30–35 minutes or until potatoes are tender and juice of chicken is no longer pink when center of thickest piece is cut.

PER SERVING:
285 Calories (kcal); 12g Fat (38% calories from fat); 29g Protein; 15g Carbohydrate; 1g Fiber; 73mg Cholesterol; 245mg Sodium. Exchanges: 1 Grain (Starch); 4 Lean Meat; 0 Vegetable; 0 Fruit; 1 Fat; 0 Other Carbohydrates.

SERVING SUGGESTIONS: Steamed baby carrots, steamed spinach, and a salad.

PASTA BEEF SATAY

Serves 6

1½ pounds boneless top sirloin, cut into 1-inch strips
5 tablespoons teriyaki sauce, divided
12 ounces thin spaghetti
2 tablespoons creamy peanut butter
1 tablespoon water
½ teaspoon ground ginger
¼ teaspoon cayenne pepper
2 tablespoons vegetable oil

Put a pot of water on high heat to boil for pasta (boils faster with a lid on). In the meantime, in a medium bowl, combine beef and 2 tablespoons of the teriyaki sauce and toss to coat and set aside. When water comes to a boil, add pasta.

In smaller bowl, combine remaining teriyaki sauce, peanut butter, 1 tablespoon water, ginger, and cayenne pepper. In the meantime, your pasta should be nearly ready. Drain pasta when cooked and toss with peanut butter mixture to coat; keep warm.

Meanwhile, in a skillet or wok, heat oil over medium-high heat until hot. Add beef (half at a time) and stir-fry 1–2 minutes or until outside surface is no longer pink. (Do *not* overcook.) Add to pasta; toss lightly. Serve immediately.

PER SERVING:
394 Calories; 12g Fat (28% calories from fat); 29g Protein; 41g Carbohydrate; 1g Fiber; 66mg Cholesterol; 663mg Sodium. Exchanges: 2½ Grain (Starch); 3½ Lean Meat; ½ Vegetable; 0 Fruit; 1½ Fat; 0 Other Carbohydrates.

SERVING SUGGESTIONS: Baked sweet potatoes and a big green salad would be perfect.

BLACK AND WHITE CHECKERED CHILI

Serves 6

1 tablespoon vegetable oil
1 medium onion, chopped
1 clove garlic, pressed
1 can chopped green chilies
3 cups chicken broth
1 tablespoon chili powder
1 can diced tomatoes, drained
1 15-ounce can black beans, drained
1 15-ounce can cannellini beans, rinsed and drained
½ cup cilantro, chopped

Heat oil in 3-quart saucepan over medium-high heat. Sauté onion and garlic till translucent.

Stir in remaining ingredients, except cilantro. Heat to boiling; reduce heat. Cover and simmer for 30 minutes, stirring occasionally. Sprinkle with chopped cilantro and serve.

PER SERVING:
159 Calories (kcal); 2g Fat (10% calories from fat); 10g Protein; 25g Carbohydrate; 14g Fiber; 1mg Cholesterol; 769mg Sodium. Exchanges: 1½ Grain (Starch); ½ Lean Meat; 1 Vegetable; 0 Fruit; 0 Fat; 0 Other Carbohydrates.

SERVING SUGGESTIONS: Some corn muffins (homemade or store bought) and a big spinach salad will round this off nicely.

BLACKENED SALMON

1 tablespoon paprika

½ teaspoon cayenne pepper

1 teaspoon salt

½ teaspoon black pepper

½ teaspoon white pepper

1 teaspoon onion powder

1 teaspoon garlic powder

½ teaspoon dried thyme

½ teaspoon dried oregano

1 dash cumin

¼ cup butter

6 salmon fillets, (½ to ¾ inch thick)

Mix dry ingredients on large plate.

In a skillet, melt butter over medium-high heat. Pour off all but 3 tablespoons into an 8-inch square pan.

Turn on hood vent and turn heat to high. Dip each fillet in the melted butter (very lightly) and then dip in the dry ingredients, patting the fillets by hand.

In the same skillet, cook fish on each side for 2–3 minutes, being careful when turning over. The fish will look charred—"blackened"—and there may be some smoke, but not enough so that you need to call the fire department.

PER SERVING:
274 Calories; 14g Fat (46% calories from fat); 34g Protein; 2g Carbohydrate; 1g Fiber; 109mg Cholesterol; 548mg Sodium. Exchanges: 0 Grain (Starch); 5 Lean Meat; 0 Vegetable; 0 Fruit; 1½ Fat; 0 Other Carbohydrates.

SERVING SUGGESTIONS: Serve with brown rice, steamed asparagus, and steamed baby carrots.

MEXICAN TORTA

Serves 6

1 tablespoon olive oil
2 medium onions, chopped
2 cloves garlic, pressed
½ pound ground turkey
1 envelope taco seasoning (low sodium, if available)
1 4-ounce can chopped green chilies, drained
16 corn tortillas, cut into wedges
2 cups shredded reduced-fat Monterey Jack cheese
1 16-ounce can refried beans (use fat-free)
1 7-ounce jar roasted red bell peppers, drained
Salsa, optional
Low-fat sour cream, optional

In a skillet, heat olive oil over medium-high heat and cook onions till translucent. Add garlic and cook another minute. Then add turkey, and cook until browned, breaking into small pieces, as you go. Add the taco seasoning according to package directions, mixing well and allowing to simmer for a couple of minutes until slightly thickened. Stir in the chilies and set aside.

Heat oven to 400 degrees F. Lightly grease a 10-inch pie plate. Place one-fourth of the tortilla pieces on the bottom of the pie plate (till covered). Spread with half of the turkey mixture; sprinkle with 1 cup of the Jack cheese. Place another one-fourth of the tortillas on cheese; spread with beans. Place yet another one-fourth of the tortillas on beans; top with roasted peppers. And finally, place the remaining tortillas on the roasted peppers and spread with remaining turkey mixture. Top with remaining 1 cup cheese. Cover and bake 30–40 minutes or until cheese is melted and center is hot. Let sit 10 minutes before cutting into your masterpiece.

Can be served with salsa and sour cream, if desired.

PER SERVING:

339 Calories (kcal); 9g Fat (25% calories from fat); 20g Protein; 42g Carbohydrate; 4g Fiber; 34mg Cholesterol; 942mg Sodium. Exchanges: 2½ Grain (Starch); 2 Lean Meat; 1 Vegetable; 0 Fruit; 1 Fat; 0 Other Carbohydrates.

SERVING SUGGESTIONS: A big spinach salad and baked sweet potatoes.

DO AHEAD TIPS: Soak white beans overnight for Crock Italian Veggie Stew. You can also cook pasta ahead and refrigerate, if desired.

CROCK ITALIAN VEGGIE STEW

Serves 6–8

4 cups water

2 cups chopped onion

1½ cups quartered small red potatoes

1 cup dried white beans

2 carrots, peeled and sliced

½ cup uncooked pearl barley

½ pound lean boneless round steak, cut into ½-inch pieces

1 14½-ounce can diced tomatoes, undrained

1 14¼-ounce can beef broth

3 cloves garlic, pressed

1 large zucchini, sliced

1 cup torn spinach (don't chop with a knife; use your hands)

1 teaspoon thyme

1 teaspoon sage

¼ teaspoon nutmeg

½ cup elbow macaroni, or other small pasta (cooked)

½ cup grated Romano cheese

Combine first 10 ingredients in a Crock-Pot. Cover with the lid, and cook on high for 6 hours, or until beef is tender.

Add zucchini and next 4 ingredients (zucchini through nutmeg); cover and cook on high an additional 30 minutes or until beans are tender. Now add the pasta and stir for 2 minutes till pasta is heated through. Top with cheese before serving.

PER SERVING:
295 Calories (kcal); 6g Fat (17% calories from fat); 20g Protein; 44g Carbohydrate; 15g Fiber; 21mg Cholesterol; 501mg Sodium. Exchanges: 2½ Grain (Starch); 1½ Lean Meat; 1½ Vegetable; 0 Fruit; ½ Fat; 0 Other Carbohydrates.

SERVING SUGGESTIONS: Serve in big bowls with whole-grain rolls and a big stomping salad.

Week Three

DAY ONE: Low Country Beef and Rice
DAY TWO: Spiced Baked Halibut
DAY THREE: Recipe Rave: Caramelized Garlic Chicken
DAY FOUR: Mexican Stuffed Pitas
DAY FIVE: Pepper Steak
DAY SIX: Moroccan Chicken

SHOPPING LIST

MEAT

3 boneless, skinless chicken thighs

6 boneless, skinless chicken breast halves

¾ pound extra-lean ground beef

1 pound flank steak

6 halibut or lean whitefish fillets, about 1 inch thick

6 ounces cooked turkey (or buy turkey breast fillets and cook yourself—your choice)

CONDIMENTS

olive oil

Cajun/Creole seasoning

balsamic vinegar

Worcestershire sauce

PRODUCE

1 bunch celery (you'll need 1 stalk)

4 medium tomatoes

1 bunch green onions (you'll use 1 tablespoon, chopped)

3 pounds onions (keep on hand)

1 head lettuce (your choice—*not* Iceberg; you'll use 2 cups, shredded)

1–2 heads garlic (you'll use 11 cloves)

green bell peppers (you'll use 1 small plus enough to have 2 cups strips)

1 small red bell pepper

1 small red onion

1 avocado
2 jalapeño chilies, optional
1 bunch cilantro, optional
**russet potatoes (1 meal)
**sweet potatoes (2 meals)
**baby red potatoes (1 meal)
**broccoli (1 meal)
**kale (1 meal)
**fresh green beans (1 meal)
**baby carrots (4 meals)
**2 heads lettuce (*not* Iceberg; use color as your guide, the
    darker the green, the better)

CANNED GOODS
1 28-ounce jar spaghetti sauce
2 14-ounce cans broth (one chicken and one beef; you'll use ¼
    cup chicken broth and ¼ cup beef broth)
1 jar salsa (your favorite; you'll need 1 tablespoon)
1 small can tomato paste (you'll need 2 tablespoons)
1 12-ounce can diced tomatoes
1 16-ounce can whole tomatoes
2 11½-ounce cans V-8 juice
2 16-ounce cans garbanzo beans
1 jar peanut butter (you'll need 2 tablespoons)

SPICES
cumin
ground coriander

DAIRY/DAIRY CASE
3 ounces Monterey Jack cheese (you'll need ¾ cup shredded)
low-fat sour cream (you'll need 3 tablespoons)

DRY GOODS
golden raisins (you'll need ½ cup)
oats (you'll need 1 cup)
brown sugar (you'll need 6 teaspoons)

1 pound brown rice (you'll need 3 cups, cooked)
**pasta (1 meal)
**whole-wheat or regular couscous (1 meal)

BAKERY
6 whole-wheat pitas

LOW COUNTRY BEEF AND RICE

Serves 6

¾ pound extra-lean ground beef
1 stalk celery, chopped fine
1 large onion, chopped
1 small green bell pepper, chopped
1 teaspoon Cajun or Creole seasoning (Paul Prudhomme makes a
  good one)
1 cup oats
3 cups brown rice, cooked
3 medium tomatoes, chopped (1½ cups)
2 11½-ounce cans V-8 juice

In a skillet, over medium-high heat, cook beef, celery, onion, bell pepper, and Cajun seasoning in skillet about 4 minutes, stirring frequently, until beef is brown and vegetables are tender. With paper towels, blot any excess grease. Stir in oats well. Then add remaining ingredients. Reduce heat to medium low. Keep uncovered and simmer about 5 minutes.

PER SERVING:
417 Calories (kcal); 8g Fat (18% calories from fat); 19g Protein; 67g Carbohydrate; 7g Fiber; 35mg Cholesterol; 749mg Sodium. Exchanges: 3 Grain (Starch); 1½ Lean Meat; 3 Vegetable; 0 Fruit; ½ Fat; 0 Other Carbohydrates.

SERVING SUGGESTIONS: Sweet potatoes and a big green salad would be my choice.

SPICED BAKED HALIBUT

Serves 6

1 tablespoon olive oil
1 large onion, sliced
2 cloves garlic, pressed
2 jalapeño chilies, seeded, deribbed, and chopped, optional
1 16-ounce can whole tomatoes, drained and chopped
2 tablespoons balsamic vinegar
2 teaspoons ground cumin
¾ teaspoon ground coriander
6 halibut or other lean white fish, about 1 inch thick
Chopped fresh cilantro, if desired

Heat oven to 350 degrees F. In a skillet, add olive oil and sauté onion, garlic, and chilies over medium heat, stirring frequently, until onion is translucent and tender. Then reduce heat. Stir in remaining ingredients except fish and cilantro. Simmer uncovered over low heat 5 minutes, stirring occasionally.

Arrange fish in an ungreased 11 × 7–inch pan. Spoon tomato mixture over fish. Bake uncovered 25 to 30 minutes or until fish flakes easily with fork. Sprinkle with cilantro, if desired.

PER SERVING:
228 Calories (kcal); 8g Fat (34% calories from fat); 37g Protein; 9g Carbohydrate; 2g Fiber; 54mg Cholesterol; 262mg Sodium. Exchanges: 0 Grain (Starch); 5 Lean Meat; 1½ Vegetable; 0 Fruit; 0 Fat; 0 Other Carbohydrates.

SERVING SUGGESTIONS: Roasted baby red potatoes (cut them in half, add a little olive oil and garlic, and roast them in the oven while you make the fish). Steamed broccoli and baby carrots will round it off.

❦ Recipe Rave:
CARAMELIZED GARLIC CHICKEN

Serves 6

"The Carmelized Garlic Chicken was just about the best chicken I've ever eaten, and my man, the one who had all but refused to eat any more chicken, loved it also."

—BEV

3 teaspoons olive oil, plus additional for greasing foiled pan
6 cloves garlic, pressed
6 teaspoons brown sugar
6 boneless, skinless chicken breast halves

Heat oven to 500 degrees F. Line shallow roasting pan with foil, lightly grease the foil with a little oil.

Heat oil in small skillet over medium-low heat until hot. Add garlic and cook 1–2 minutes or until garlic begins to soften. (*Don't* let garlic get brown!) Remove from heat and stir in brown sugar until well mixed. Set aside.

Place chicken breasts on greased foil-lined pan, spreading the garlic mixture evenly over chicken.

Bake for 10–15 minutes or until chicken is fork-tender and juices run clear.

PER SERVING:
295 Calories (kcal); 5g Fat (16% calories from fat); 55g Protein; 4g Carbohydrate; 137mg Cholesterol; 155mg Sodium. Exchanges: 0 Grain (Starch); 7½ Lean Meat; 0 Vegetable; 0 Fruit; ½ Fat; 0 Other Carbohydrates.

SERVING SUGGESTIONS: Baked potatoes with all the fixin's (if you like, butter and sour cream), baked sweet potatoes, steamed broccoli.

DO AHEAD TIP: If you opted to buy uncooked turkey, cook it now for tomorrow's Mexican Stuffed Pitas.

MEXICAN STUFFED PITAS

Serves 6

1 avocado, sliced into sixths
6 whole-wheat pitas
6 ounces cooked turkey, diced
2 cups lettuce, shredded
1 medium tomato, chopped
¾ cup Monterey Jack cheese (3 ounces), shredded

Sour Cream Salsa

Mix together the following:

3 tablespoons low-fat sour cream
1 tablespoon salsa

Place slice of avocado in pita bread. Then top with turkey, lettuce, tomato, and cheese. Finish your masterpiece with Sour Cream Salsa and garnish with green onions.

PER SERVING:
314 Calories (kcal); 10g Fat (28% calories from fat); 18g Protein; 38g Carbohydrate; 3g Fiber; 36mg Cholesterol; 466mg Sodium. Exchanges: 2 Grain (Starch); 1½ Lean Meat; ½ Vegetable; 0 Fruit; 1½ Fat; 0 Other Carbohydrates.

SERVING SUGGESTIONS: A big salad and a bowl of baby carrots will do the trick.

PEPPER STEAK

Serves 6

1 tablespoon olive oil, divided
1 pound flank steak, cut in ¼-inch strips
2 cups green pepper strips
1 medium onion, thinly sliced
1 27–28-ounce jar spaghetti sauce (your favorite)
¾ cup beef broth
2 tablespoons Worcestershire sauce

In a large saucepan over medium-high heat, heat 1 teaspoon of olive oil and cook meat, stirring frequently until done to your liking. Remove meat and pan juices and set aside.

In that same saucepan, add remaining oil and stir in peppers and onion, cooking 5 minutes or until tender, stirring frequently.

Stir in pasta sauce, broth, Worcestershire sauce, and meat (plus all those wonderful pan juices) and heat to boiling. Reduce heat and let simmer about 10 minutes or till the sauce reduces slightly.

PER SERVING:
379 Calories; 11g Fat (26.1% calories from fat); 25g Protein; 45g Carbohydrate; 5g Dietary Fiber; 39mg Cholesterol; 521mg Sodium. Exchanges: 2½ Grain (Starch); 2 Lean Meat; 1 Vegetable; 1 Fat; 0 Other Carbohydrates.

SERVING SUGGESTIONS: Serve with pasta, steamed kale, and steamed baby carrots.

MOROCCAN CHICKEN

Serves 6

2 16-ounce cans garbanzo beans, drained
1 12-ounce can diced tomatoes
1 small red bell pepper, seeded, cut into 1-inch squares
1 small red onion, chopped
½ cup golden raisins
2 tablespoons tomato paste
¼ cup chicken broth

3 cloves garlic, minced

1½ teaspoons ground cumin

3 boneless, skinless chicken thighs, cut into 1-inch cubes

2 tablespoons peanut butter

Place garbanzo beans, tomatoes, bell pepper, onion, raisins, tomato paste, broth, garlic, and cumin in a Crock-Pot. Mix until well combined.

Place chicken on top of bean mixture. Cover. Cook on low heat setting 6–7 hours, or until chicken is tender. Stir in peanut butter.

PER SERVING:
507 Calories (kcal); 15g Fat (26% calories from fat); 41g Protein; 53g Carbohydrate; 93mg Fiber; 9g Cholesterol; 599mg Sodium. Exchanges: 2½ Grain (Starch); 4½ Lean Meat; 1 Vegetable; ½ Fruit; 1 Fat; 0 Other Carbohydrates.

SERVING SUGGESTIONS: Serve with whole-wheat couscous (or regular couscous), steamed green beans, and baby carrots.

THE STOCK MARKET: BROTH IN A CAN

The secret to any decent soup is stock. In an ideal world, we would have the time to make a good homemade stock. But the reality of a busy life being what it is means that most often, the stock will come from a can—at least at my house it will.

Here are a couple of hints for purchasing a good canned stock or broth:

- Go with a low-salt variety. The less salt, the more the flavor there is, generally.

- Skip any broth containing MSG.

- Don't be duped into believing that brand has anything to do with good stock. Just make sure the above criteria are followed.

- Forget about bouillon cubes unless you're looking for too much salt and too little flavor.

Week Four

DAY ONE: Blackberry Balsamic Chicken
DAY TWO: Polenta Pie
DAY THREE: Thai Beef
DAY FOUR: Honey Barbecued Salmon
DAY FIVE: Creamy Ziti
DAY SIX: Sweet Lentil Stew

SHOPPING LIST

MEAT
6 boneless, skinless chicken breast halves
6 salmon fillets
turkey bacon (you'll need 3 slices)
12 ounces lean turkey ham
1 pound flank steak

CONDIMENTS
olive oil
vegetable oil
cooking spray
balsamic vinegar (you'll need 2 tablespoons)
barbecue sauce (you'll need ¼ cup)
Dijon mustard (you'll need ¼ cup)
hot sauce or Tabasco sauce (you'll need ¾ teaspoon)
teriyaki sauce (you'll need ½ cup)
rice vinegar (you'll need 2 tablespoons)
honey (you'll need ⅛ cup)

PRODUCE
1 red onion
3 pounds onions (keep on hand)
2 lemons
2 red bell peppers
1 bunch parsley (you'll need ¼ cup, chopped)
dill (you'll need 2 tablespoons, minced)
1 piece fresh gingerroot

1 head garlic
1 large sweet potato
1 large potato
**red rose baby potatoes (1 meal)
**sweet potatoes (1 meal)
**green beans (2 meals)
**spinach (2 meals)
**baby carrots (1 meal)
**broccoli (1 meal)
**baking potatoes (1 meal)
**1–2 heads lettuce (*not* Iceberg)

CANNED GOODS
seedless blackberry preserves (you need ⅓ cup)
1 15-ounce can chili beans
1 28-ounce jar spaghetti sauce

SPICES
dried thyme
garlic powder
red pepper flakes

DAIRY/DAIRY CASE
eggs (you'll need 1 egg)
Monterey Jack cheese (you'll need ¾ cup,
    shredded)
non-fat sour cream (you'll need 1 cup)
skim milk (you'll need ¾ cup)

DRY GOODS
cornmeal (you'll need ¼ cup)
baked tortilla chips (you'll need ⅓ cup)
1 pound ziti, penne, or other medium-size pasta
lentils (you'll need 1 cup)
**brown rice (1 meal)

BLACKBERRY BALSAMIC CHICKEN

Serves 6

1 teaspoon vegetable oil
Cooking spray
½ cup chopped red onion
Salt and pepper to taste
½ teaspoon dried thyme
6 boneless, skinless chicken breast halves
⅓ cup seedless blackberry preserves
2 tablespoons balsamic vinegar

Heat oil in a large nonstick skillet coated with cooking spray over medium-high heat until hot. Add onion and sauté till translucent.

Sprinkle salt, pepper, and thyme over the top of the chicken. Add chicken to skillet and sauté 6 minutes on each side or until done. Remove chicken from skillet and keep warm. Reduce heat to medium low. Add preserves, vinegar, and salt and pepper, stirring constantly until the preserves melt. Spoon the sauce over chicken to serve.

PER SERVING:
213 Calories; 3g Fat (11% calories from fat); 27g Protein; 20g Carbohydrate; 1g Fiber; 66mg Cholesterol; 350mg Sodium. Exchanges: 0 Grain (Starch); 3½ Lean Meat; ½ Vegetable; 0 Fruit; 0 Fat; 1 Other Carbohydrates.

SERVING SUGGESTIONS: Roasted baby red rose potatoes (cut potatoes in half, toss with a little olive oil, salt and pepper, and roast at 450 degrees F till done), steamed green beans, and baked sweet potatoes.

POLENTA PIE

Serves 6

½ cup cornmeal

2 cups water

¼ teaspoon salt

1 egg, slightly beaten

1 15-ounce can chili beans, drained

¾ cup shredded Monterey Jack cheese

⅓ cup tortilla chips, crushed

Heat oven to 375 degrees F and lightly grease a 9-inch pie pan. Mix cornmeal, water, and salt in 2-quart saucepan. Heat to boiling, stirring constantly; reduce heat to medium. Cook about 6 minutes, stirring frequently, until mixture is very thick; remove from heat. Quickly stir in egg. Let stand 5 minutes.

Spread cornmeal mixture in pie plate. Bake uncovered 15 minutes. Spread beans over cornmeal mixture. Sprinkle with cheese and corn chips. Bake uncovered about 20 minutes or until center is set. Let stand 5 minutes before cutting.

PER SERVING:
168 Calories (kcal); 7g Fat (34% calories from fat); 9g Protein; 20g Carbohydrate; 4g Fiber; 46mg Cholesterol; 880mg Sodium. Exchanges: 1 Grain (Starch); 1 Lean Meat; 0 Vegetable; 0 Fruit; ½ Fat; 0 Other Carbohydrates.

SERVING SUGGESTION: A big spinach salad ought to cover all bases.

THAI BEEF

Serves 6

½ cup teriyaki sauce
4 tablespoons vegetable oil, divided
3 tablespoons fresh gingerroot, finely chopped
6 cloves garlic, minced
1 teaspoon red pepper flakes
2 tablespoons rice vinegar
1 pound flank steak

In a large zipper-topped plastic bag, prepare marinade by mixing teriyaki sauce, half the vegetable oil, ginger, garlic, red pepper flakes, and rice vinegar. Add beef and let sit for 30 minutes in the fridge.

In the meantime, prepare your side dishes (either follow the ones I have suggested below or whatever you have chosen).

In a skillet, over medium-high heat, add remaining oil, heat, and sauté steak till cooked to your liking.

PER SERVING:
241 Calories; 17g Fat (63.6% calories from fat); 16g Protein; 6g Carbohydrate; trace Dietary Fiber; 39mg Cholesterol; 974mg Sodium. Exchanges: 0 Grain (Starch); 2 Lean Meat; 1 Vegetable; 2½ Fat; 0 Other Carbohydrates.

SERVING SUGGESTIONS: Serve atop a bed of brown rice and steamed broccoli and baby carrots.

HONEY BARBECUED SALMON

Serves 6

6 *salmon fillets*
½ *teaspoon salt*
½ *teaspoon pepper*
½ *teaspoon garlic powder*
3 *strips turkey bacon*
1 *medium onion, sliced*
1 *lemon, sliced*
¼ *cup barbecue sauce*
⅛ *cup honey*

Preheat oven to 400 degrees F.

In a 9 × 13–inch baking pan, place fillets and sprinkle first with salt, pepper, and garlic powder. Then top with ½ strip of turkey bacon, a slice of onion, and a slice of lemon.

In a bowl, mix together barbecue sauce and honey. Pour sauce evenly over the top of each fillet. Place a sheet of foil securely over the top and bake for 20 minutes or until fish flakes easily.

PER SERVING:
352 Calories; 6g Fat (27% calories from fat); 34g Protein; 1g Carbohydrate; 1g Dietary Fiber; 88mg Cholesterol; 114mg Sodium. Exchanges: 0 Grain (Starch); 5 Lean Meat; 0 Vegetable; 0 Fruit; 0 Fat; 0 Other Carbohydrates.

SERVING SUGGESTIONS: Serve with baked potatoes, steamed green beans, and a spinach salad.

✓

Serves 6

garnish w/ toasted pine nuts

1 pound ziti, penne, or other medium-size pasta
½ teaspoon olive oil
12 ounces lean turkey ham, cut into bite-size pieces
1 red bell pepper (about 1 cup), diced
1 cup non-fat sour cream
1 10-ounce package frozen spinach, thawed and drained well
¾ cup skim milk
¼ cup Dijon mustard
¼ cup chopped fresh parsley
| ~~3~~ tablespoons minced fresh dill
1 tablespoon lemon juice
~~¾ teaspoon hot sauce~~
Salt and pepper to taste
2 T olive oil

Prepare pasta according to package directions. While waiting for the water to boil or while pasta is cooking, warm the oil over medium heat in a large skillet. Add the ham and red pepper and cook until browned. Meanwhile, puree the sour cream, spinach, milk, mustard, parsley, dill, lemon juice, and hot sauce in a food processor or blender until very smooth. Add the puree to the ham mixture and heat to a simmer.

When pasta is done, drain it well. Toss pasta with sauce, season with salt and pepper, and serve.

PER SERVING:
419 Calories; 5g Fat (11.1% calories from fat); 26g Protein; 67g Carbohydrate; 4g Dietary Fiber; 37mg Cholesterol; 792mg Sodium. Exchanges: 4 Grain (Starch); 2 Lean Meat; ½ Vegetable; 0 Fruit; 0 Non-Fat Milk; 0 Fat; ½ Other Carbohydrates.

SERVING SUGGESTION: A great big salad is all you really need.

SWEET LENTIL STEW

1¾ cups dried lentils, washed
1 large sweet potato, peeled and cut in 1-inch chunks
1 jar spaghetti sauce
1 small red bell pepper, diced
1 large potato, diced
1 medium onion, chopped
2 cloves garlic, pressed
3 cups water
1 tablespoon olive oil

In a Crock-Pot, mix all ingredients except olive oil.

Cover and cook on low 8–10 hours or until the vegetables and lentils are tender. Stir in the olive oil just before serving.

PER SERVING:
423 Calories; 3g Fat (5% calories from fat); 21g Protein; 81g Carbohydrate; 26g Dietary Fiber; 0mg Cholesterol; 227mg Sodium. Exchanges: 4½ Grain (Starch); 1½ Lean Meat; 2½ Vegetable; 1 Fat.

SERVING SUGGESTIONS: Some whole-grain rolls and a big salad is all you need.

Week Five

DAY ONE: Chicken Parmesan
DAY TWO: Mexican Lasagna
DAY THREE: Beef and Spinach Pitas
DAY FOUR: Chicken Broccoli Soup
DAY FIVE: Halibut Piccata
DAY SIX: Greens and Beans

SHOPPING LIST

MEAT
8–9 boneless, skinless chicken breast halves
½ pound ground turkey
1 pound extra-lean ground beef
6 pieces white fish (your choice)

CONDIMENTS
olive oil
capers
balsamic vinegar

PRODUCE
1 lemon (you'll need 3 tablespoons)
1 head garlic
8 ounces mushrooms
1 bag spinach
1 tomato
1 bunch broccoli (**extra, for 2 meals, if following
    Serving Suggestions)
1 bunch parsley
greens (kale, collards, mustard greens—your choice; enough
    for 4 cups)
3 pounds onions (keep on hand)
**baby carrots (2 meals)
**baby spinach (1 meal)
**sweet potatoes (2 meals)

**russet potatoes (1 meal)
**2–3 heads lettuce (*not* Iceberg)

SPICES
1 package taco seasoning mix
thyme

CANNED GOODS
1 14½-ounce can chicken broth
1 28-ounce jar spaghetti sauce
1 28-ounce can enchilada sauce
1 15-ounce can diced tomatoes
1 8-ounce jar salsa
1 15-ounce can black beans
3 15-ounce cans white beans

DAIRY/DAIRY CASE
1 dozen eggs
1 wedge Parmesan cheese
16 ounces low-fat cottage cheese
shredded low-fat Cheddar cheese (4½ cups total)
8 ounces low-fat sour cream
part-skim-milk mozzarella cheese, shredded (you'll need ¾ cup)
1 pint half and half

DRY GOODS
6 ounces wide egg noodles
9 ounces lasagna noodles
6 whole-wheat pitas
1 container Italian seasoned bread crumbs
flour (you'll need 2 tablespoons)
**1 pound brown rice (1 meal)

BAKERY
6 whole-wheat pitas
**whole-grain rolls (1 meal)

CHICKEN PARMESAN

Serves 6

HERE A CHICK, THERE A CHICK

❦ Nearly every week, the shopping lists will contain boneless, skinless chicken breast halves. These are the kind you can buy frozen, individually flash frozen, and in large 3-pound bags. I suggest you use the frozen ones (as opposed to the fresh) for several reasons. One, they're usually less expensive this way. Very often markets will have them on sale—buy one/get one free. And if you're like me, you hate paying retail, so it's a win/win situation. Two, the frozen factor is helpful for recipes that need the chicken cut in strips, cubes, etc. Semifrozen chicken is much easier to cut than fresh, wiggly chicken. So keep that in mind when you're going to the market with your grocery list.

6 boneless, skinless chicken breast halves, pounded flat
2 eggs, lightly beaten
¾ cup Italian seasoned bread crumbs
1 tablespoon olive oil
1 jar spaghetti sauce
¾ cup part-skim mozzarella cheese, shredded
3 tablespoons grated Parmesan cheese
3¾ cups (6 ounces) wide egg noodles, uncooked

Heat oven to 350 degrees F.

In a large zipper-topped plastic bag, place 2 chicken breast halves at a time and use a rolling pin to flatten. Take turns with the chicken till it's all flattened.

In a bowl, place your lightly beaten eggs; in another bowl, place the bread crumbs. Dip chicken in egg first, then in bread crumbs to coat thoroughly. In a large skillet, heat oil; add chicken. Cook on both sides until lightly browned; drain well on paper towels.

Pour ½ cup spaghetti sauce into an 8-inch-square baking dish. Layer chicken in the dish and pour about ¾ cup sauce evenly over the chicken. Sprinkle with the cheeses and bake 25 minutes or until bubbly.

Meanwhile, cook noodles according to package directions and drain. Heat remaining sauce. To serve, place noodles on the bottom, spoon sauce over noodles, and arrange chicken pieces on top.

PER SERVING:
380 Calories; 10g Fat (24.4% calories from fat); 40g Protein; 30g Carbohydrate; 2g Dietary Fiber; 163mg Cholesterol; 707mg Sodium. Exchanges: 2 Grain (Starch); 4½ Lean Meat; 1 Fat.

SERVING SUGGESTIONS: Steamed broccoli and a spinach salad. Put a bowl of baby carrots on the table to pass, too.

MEXICAN LASAGNA

Serves 6

½ pound ground turkey
½ envelope taco seasoning mix
1 can enchilada sauce
1 can diced tomatoes
¾ cup salsa
1 can black beans, drained
9 ounces lasagna noodles
2 cups low-fat cottage cheese
3 cups low-fat Cheddar cheese, shredded

In a skillet, brown turkey; drain and blot grease. Add taco seasoning and, using half the recommended water on seasoning packet, simmer for 5 minutes. Set aside.

In the meantime, preheat oven to 375 degrees F. In a medium bowl, combine enchilada sauce, tomatoes (and their juice), and salsa. Mix well and add black beans.

To make lasagna: in the bottom of a 13 × 9–inch pan, spoon a third of the tomato sauce mixture and spread evenly. Top with uncooked lasagna noodles till sauce is covered. Then add all the meat, spreading evenly, add 1 cup of the cottage cheese and 1 cup of the Cheddar. Spoon half the remaining sauce on top.

Add another layer of noodles, remaining cottage cheese and 1 cup of the Cheddar. Add another layer of noodles, remaining tomato sauce, and remaining 1 cup Cheddar cheese. Tent with foil (so the cheese doesn't stick to it) and tightly cover.

Bake for 45 minutes or until noodles are tender. Let stand 5 minutes before digging in.

PER SERVING:
547 Calories; 13g Fat (22.2% calories from fat); 44g Protein; 62g Carbohydrate; 7g Dietary Fiber; 57mg Cholesterol; 1072mg Sodium. Exchanges: 3½ Grain (Starch); 4½ Lean Meat; 1 Vegetable; 1 Fat; 0 Other Carbohydrates.

SERVING SUGGESTION: A big green salad is really all you need.

BEEF AND SPINACH PITAS

Serves 6

1 pound extra-lean ground beef
1 large onion, chopped
2 cloves garlic, pressed
8 ounces mushrooms, sliced
1 bag spinach
½ teaspoon thyme
Salt and pepper to taste
6 whole-wheat pitas
1 tomato, chopped
½ cup low-fat sour cream

In a skillet, cook beef and onion over medium-high heat till browned. Drain and blot beef with paper towels to absorb excess grease.

Add garlic, mushrooms, spinach, and thyme and cook for about 3 minutes till spinach wilts.

Salt and pepper to taste.

Spoon beef mixture into pitas and top with tomato and sour cream.

PER SERVING:
394 Calories; 16g Fat (35.2% calories from fat); 23g Protein; 42g Carbohydrate; 6g Dietary Fiber; 56mg Cholesterol; 421mg Sodium. Exchanges: 2½ Grain (Starch); 2 Lean Meat; 1 Vegetable; 2 Fat; 0 Other Carbohydrates.

SERVING SUGGESTIONS: A green salad and a bowl of baby carrots work.

CHICKEN BROCCOLI SOUP

Serves 6

1 tablespoon olive oil
2 onions, chopped
2 tablespoons flour
2 cans chicken broth
5 cups broccoli, chopped
1½ cups low-fat Cheddar cheese
1½ cups cooked chicken, chopped
1 cup half and half

In a large saucepan, heat oil over medium-high heat and add onions. Cook till translucent, about 3 minutes.

Stir in flour and cook about 1 minute. Add broth and heat till boiling, stirring until thickened. Add broccoli and cook till tender, 5 minutes.

Stir in cheese, chicken, and half and half. Reduce heat (Important! or the soup will break) and cook another minute or until cheese is melted and incorporated in the soup.

PER SERVING:
235 Calories; 11g Fat (42.7% calories from fat); 23g Protein; 11g Carbohydrate; 3g Dietary Fiber; 51mg Cholesterol; 488mg Sodium. Exchanges: 0 Grain (Starch); 2½ Lean Meat; 1 Vegetable; 0 Non-Fat Milk; 1½ Fat.

SERVING SUGGESTIONS: A nice big salad and some whole-grain rolls.

HALIBUT PICCATA

Serves 6

¾ teaspoon black pepper
6 pieces halibut (or other firm white fish)
1½ tablespoons parsley, finely chopped
3 tablespoons lemon juice
3 tablespoons capers

GARNISH : *lemon rounds*

Preheat broiler. Pepper fish and place in a broiling pan. Broil fish for 2½ minutes on each side or until flesh turns opaque. Remove fish from broiling pan and keep warm. Sprinkle with parsley, lemon juice, and capers. Garnish with lemon rounds.

PER SERVING:
106 Calories; 3g Fat (30.1% calories from fat); 17g Protein; 1g Carbohydrate; trace Dietary Fiber; 33mg Cholesterol; 90mg Sodium. Exchanges: 0 Grain (Starch); 2½ Lean Meat; 0 Vegetable; 0 Fruit; 0 Fat; 0 Other Carbohydrates.

SERVING SUGGESTIONS: Baked potatoes, steamed broccoli, and sweet potatoes.

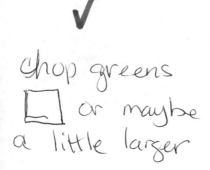

chop greens
☐ or maybe
a little larger

Serves 6

1 tablespoon olive oil
2 medium onions, chopped
4 cloves garlic, pressed
4 cups greens, chopped
3 cans white beans, drained
1 tablespoon balsamic vinegar
Salt and pepper to taste

In a large skillet, over medium heat, heat the oil and sauté the onions till wilted. Add garlic and continue to cook another 2 minutes, making sure not to brown the garlic. Add the greens and sauté till wilted and bright green, but not cooked. It will be a little dry when you sauté, but that's okay. You're just trying to wilt the greens, not cook them.

In a Crock-Pot, add the beans and the greens from the skillet, mixing well. Cover and cook on low for 3–4 hours or until the greens are tender (cooking time will vary depending on which greens you choose).

When you're ready to serve, add vinegar and salt and pepper to taste.

PER SERVING:
383 Calories; 3g Fat (7.4% calories from fat); 25g Protein; 67g Carbohydrate; 17g Dietary Fiber; 0mg Cholesterol; 27mg Sodium. Exchanges: 4 Grain (Starch); 1½ Lean Meat; 1 Vegetable; 0 Fruit; ½ Fat.

SERVING SUGGESTIONS: Some brown rice, baked sweet potatoes, and a salad make this a wonderful dinner.

Week Six

DAY ONE: Mashed Potato Pie
DAY TWO: Baked Citrus Fish
DAY THREE: Chicken Fajita Orzo
DAY FOUR: Quick Tri-Bean Soup
DAY FIVE: Skillet Pizza
DAY SIX: Crock Stroganoff

SHOPPING LIST

MEAT
1½ pounds ground turkey
6 fish fillets
4 boneless, skinless chicken breast halves
1 pound extra-lean ground beef
1½ pounds round steak

CONDIMENTS
Worcestershire sauce
olive oil

PRODUCE
1 bunch carrots
3 pounds onions (keep on hand)
1 large red onion
1 lemon
1 bunch cilantro (you'll need 3 tablespoons, chopped)
2 large red bell peppers
1 small red bell pepper (you'll need half of it; you can put
   the rest in your salad)
4 medium tomatoes
1 bunch green onions
1 jalapeño pepper
1 head garlic
4–6 limes (for ¾ cup juice plus 1 lime)
1–2 oranges (for ⅓ cup juice)
1½ cups mushrooms

**broccoli (2 meals)
**sweet potatoes (1 meal)
**kale (1 meal)
**spinach (1 meal)
**baby carrots (1 meal)
**1–3 heads lettuce (*not* Iceberg)

CANNED GOODS
1 15-ounce can white beans
1 15-ounce can kidney beans
1 15-ounce can black beans
1 14½-ounce can chicken broth
1 14½-ounce can beef broth
1 15-ounce can diced tomatoes
1 14-ounce jar spaghetti sauce

SPICES
garlic powder
basil

DAIRY/DAIRY CASE
eggs (you'll need 2)
butter (you'll need 3 tablespoons)
low-fat Cheddar cheese, shredded (you'll need ¾ cup)
part-skim-milk mozzarella cheese (you'll need 1 cup,
    shredded)
1 wedge Romano cheese (you'll need 6 tablespoons)
16 ounces low-fat sour cream (you'll need 1¼ cups)
skim milk (you'll need ½ cup)

DRY GOODS
1 pound orzo, ditalini, or other small-size pasta
oats (you'll need 1 cup)
flour (you'll need about ⅔ cup)
1 package egg noodles, yolk-free
1 container Italian bread crumbs
**1 pound brown rice (1 meal)

MASHED POTATO PIE

Serves 6

1½ *pounds ground turkey*
2 *carrots, grated*
1 *onion, chopped fine*
¾ *cup Italian bread crumbs*
1 *egg*
½ *tablespoon Worcestershire sauce*
1 *teaspoon garlic powder*
Salt and pepper to taste
1 *pound hash browns, frozen*
1 *tablespoon butter, melted*
¾ *cup low-fat Cheddar cheese, shredded*

Preheat oven to 350 degrees F.

In a large bowl, combine first 8 ingredients, mixing well. In a 10-inch pie plate, press turkey mixture evenly into the bottom and up the sides of the pie plate to fashion a shell. Top with hash browns and drizzle with the melted butter.

Bake 40 minutes or until meat is thoroughly cooked. Top with cheese and bake 5 minutes longer, or until cheese is melted.

PER SERVING:
358 Calories; 14g Fat (35.4% calories from fat); 28g Protein; 29g Carbohydrate; 3g Dietary Fiber; 129mg Cholesterol; 657mg Sodium. Exchanges: 1½ Grain (Starch); 3½ Lean Meat; 1 Vegetable; ½ Fat; 0 Other Carbohydrates.

SERVING SUGGESTIONS: Serve with steamed broccoli and a big green salad.

BAKED CITRUS FISH

Serves 6

2 tablespoons butter
⅓ cup orange juice
1 lime, juiced
½ lemon, juiced
6 fish fillets
Salt and pepper to taste
1 tablespoon cilantro, chopped

In a small saucepan, melt butter and add citrus juices. Heat until well blended, but don't burn the butter.

Heat oven to 400 degrees F. In a 13 × 9–inch baking dish, arrange fish fillets. Salt and pepper the fish to your taste. Pour the sauce over the fish and bake uncovered until the fish flakes easily with a fork, about 8–12 minutes, depending on the thickness of your fish. Serve with lemon wedges made from the other half of your lemon. Sprinkle with chopped cilantro.

PER SERVING:
232 Calories; 5g Fat (21.7% calories from fat); 41g Protein; 3g Carbohydrate; trace Dietary Fiber; 110mg Cholesterol; 164mg Sodium. Exchanges: 5½ Lean Meat; 0 Fruit; 1 Fat.

SERVING SUGGESTIONS: Serve with baked sweet potatoes, brown rice, and steamed kale.

CHICKEN FAJITA ORZO

Serves 6

1 pound orzo, ditalini, or other small-size pasta, uncooked
1 teaspoon olive oil
4 boneless, skinless chicken breast halves, cut in strips
2 large red bell peppers, diced fine
1 large red onion, sliced thin
4 medium tomatoes, finely chopped
1 bunch green onions, finely chopped
1 jalapeño pepper, seeded and minced
¾ cup lime juice

½ teaspoon salt
¼ cup low-fat sour cream

Prepare pasta according to package directions; drain and set aside.

Meanwhile, in a skillet, heat the oil till hot over medium-high heat. Add chicken and stir frequently to avoid burning. Next add the red bell peppers and onions, and continue cooking till both the chicken and vegetables are cooked, about 5 minutes.

In a medium bowl, make the salsa by mixing the tomatoes, green onions, jalapeño, lime juice, and salt.

Toss together the cooked pasta, salsa, and chicken mixture till well incorporated.

Top each serving with a dollop of sour cream.

PER SERVING:
468 Calories; 15g Fat (28.3% calories from fat); 13g Protein; 74g Carbohydrate; 6g Dietary Fiber; 0mg Cholesterol; 648mg Sodium. Exchanges: 4 Grain (Starch); 1½ Vegetable; 0 Fruit; 3 Fat; ½ Other Carbohydrates.

SERVING SUGGESTION: Serve with a big salad.

QUICK TRI-BEAN SOUP

Serves 6

1 onion, chopped
2 cloves garlic, pressed
1 tablespoon olive oil
1 can white beans, drained
1 can kidney beans, drained
1 can black beans, drained
1 can chicken broth
1 teaspoon basil
1 can diced tomatoes
6 tablespoons Romano cheese
Salt and pepper to taste

In a saucepan, over medium-high heat, cook the onion and garlic in olive oil until translucent.

Add the rest of the ingredients except the Romano cheese and stir well. Salt and pepper to taste, and heat till nice and hot.

Top each bowlful with a tablespoon of Romano cheese and serve.

PER SERVING:
179 Calories; 5g Fat (23.4% calories from fat); 11g Protein; 24g Carbohydrate; 6g Dietary Fiber; 7mg Cholesterol; 220mg Sodium. Exchanges: 1½ Grain (Starch); 1 Lean Meat; ½ Vegetable; ½ Fat.

SERVING SUGGESTIONS: Serve with a big salad and some whole-grain rolls.

SKILLET PIZZA

Serves 6

1 pound extra-lean ground beef
1 onion, chopped
1 cup oats
½ small red bell pepper, chopped
1 jar spaghetti sauce
½ cup flour
½ cup skim milk
1 egg
1 cup part-skim-milk mozzarella cheese, shredded

Preheat oven to 350 degrees F.

In an ovenproof skillet, cook beef and onions over medium-high heat, till beef is browned and crumbled. Drain grease and blot beef with paper towels (with this step the fat grams will be lower than what shows up in the nutritional info below). Add oats, mixing well; cover while you prepare bell pepper. Add chopped pepper and spaghetti sauce and simmer on low for about 4 minutes.

In a bowl, whisk together flour, milk, and egg until well blended. Add ½ cup of the cheese to the mixture. Sprinkle remaining cheese evenly over the top of the meat mixture in the skillet, then top that evenly with the batter.

Place the skillet in the oven and bake 20 minutes or until golden. Let rest 2 minutes and cut into wedges to serve.

PER SERVING:
392 Calories; 20g Fat (45.9% calories from fat); 25g Protein; 27g Carbohydrate; 4g Dietary
Fiber; 94mg Cholesterol; 376mg Sodium. Exchanges: 1 Grain (Starch); 3 Lean Meat; 1½ Vegetable; 0 Non-Fat Milk; 2 Fat.

SERVING SUGGESTIONS: A big spinach salad and a little bowl of baby
carrots to pass would round this hearty meal off nicely.

DO AHEAD TIP: You can cook the noodles for tomorrow's Crock
Stroganoff, if you want.

CROCK STROGANOFF

Serves 6

1½ pounds round steak, cut in strips
2 tablespoons flour
Salt and pepper to taste
1 onion, sliced
1½ cups mushrooms, sliced
1 can beef broth
½ teaspoon Worcestershire sauce
1 cup low-fat sour cream
3 cups egg noodles, yolk-free, cooked

Dredge the strips of beef in flour and place on the bottom of the
Crock-Pot. Salt and pepper to your particular taste. Add the onion,
mushrooms, beef broth, and Worcestershire sauce. Cover and cook on
low for 8–10 hours (or on high for 4–5 hours).

Just before serving, stir the sour cream into the stroganoff. Serve on
a bed of noodles.

PER SERVING:
381 Calories; 16g Fat (39.1% calories from fat); 30g Protein; 27g Carbohydrate; 1g Dietary
Fiber; 75mg Cholesterol; 327mg Sodium. Exchanges: 1½ Grain (Starch); 3½ Lean Meat; ½ Vegetable; 1½ Fat; ½ Other Carbohydrates.

SERVING SUGGESTIONS: Some steamed broccoli and a big salad ought to
do it.

DAY ONE: Cashew Chicken
DAY TWO: Baked Fish with Tomatoes and Olives
DAY THREE: Chili with Corn Bread Dumplings
DAY FOUR: Creamy Spaghetti Carbonara
DAY FIVE: Turkey and Rice Strata
DAY SIX: Crocked Barbecued Beef

SHOPPING LIST

MEAT

4 boneless, skinless chicken breast halves
6 fish fillets (your choice, use what's available and affordable)
¾ pound extra-lean ground beef
9 ounces turkey bacon
small package white meat turkey (you'll need 1½ cups, cooked
    and cubed)
2 pounds chuck roast

CONDIMENTS

honey (about ⅔ cup)
soy sauce (you'll need ¼ cup)
vegetable oil
extra-virgin olive oil
ketchup (at least 1½ cups)
balsamic vinegar
Dijon mustard
barbecue sauce
Worcestershire sauce
dry white wine (you'll need 1 cup)

PRODUCE

1 lime (you'll need 1 tablespoon juice)
2 oranges (you'll need ¼ cup juice)
1 bunch green onions
1 bunch carrots
1 bunch celery (you'll need 1 stalk)

4 tomatoes
1 head garlic
1 red onion
3 pounds onions (keep on hand)
1 green bell pepper
1 bunch parsley
1 bunch fresh basil
**sweet potatoes (1 meal)
**potatoes for baking (1 meal)
**potatoes for Oven Fries (1 meal)
**spinach (2 meals)
**baby carrots (1 meal)
**broccoli (1 meal)
**green beans (1 meal)
**asparagus (1 meal)
**cabbage or bagged coleslaw (1 meal)
**butternut squash (1 meal)
**1–2 heads lettuce (*not* Iceberg)

CANNED GOODS
1 15-ounce can pinto beans
1 28-ounce jar spaghetti sauce
1 small jar green olives (you'll need ½ cup, chopped)

SPICES
ground ginger
garlic powder
thyme
dried hot red pepper flakes
chili powder
cumin
oregano
cayenne pepper

DAIRY/DAIRY CASE
eggs (you'll need 4)
low-fat Cheddar cheese (you'll need 1¾ cups, shredded)

part-skim-milk mozzarella cheese, shredded
    (you'll need ¾ cup)
1 wedge Parmesan cheese, grated (you'll need ½ cup)
milk (you'll need ½ cup)
half and half (1 cup)

DRY GOODS
cashews (you'll need 1 cup)
oats (you'll need 1 cup)
8½-ounce package corn muffin mix
1½ pounds spaghetti
2 pounds brown rice (**1 pound is for Serving Suggestions)
flour (you'll need 1 tablespoon)
cornstarch (1 tablespoon)

BAKERY
**whole-grain hamburger buns (1 meal)

CASHEW CHICKEN

Serves 6

¾ *cup orange juice*
⅓ *cup honey*
¼ *cup soy sauce*
1 *tablespoon cornstarch*
1 *teaspoon ground ginger*
1 *teaspoon garlic powder*
½ *teaspoon pepper*
2 *tablespoons vegetable oil, divided*
4 *green onions, chopped*
2 *large carrots, sliced*
1 *celery stalk, sliced*
4 *boneless, skinless chicken breast halves, cut into 1-inch strips*
1 *cup cashews*

In a bowl, combine juice, honey, soy sauce, cornstarch, and seasonings.

In a wok or large skillet, heat 1 tablespoon oil until it begins to smoke. Stir-fry vegetables for several minutes until the onions become fragrant. Set aside and keep warm.

In the same skillet, heat another tablespoon of oil until smoking and stir-fry chicken strips until browned and tender.

Add cooked vegetables, cashews, and sauce mixture. Continue cooking until sauce bubbles and thickens.

PER SERVING:
265 Calories; 15g Fat (48.5% calories from fat); 5g Protein; 31g Carbohydrate; 3g Dietary Fiber; 0mg Cholesterol; 707mg Sodium. Exchanges: ½ Grain (Starch); ½ Lean Meat; 1 Vegetable; 0 Fruit; 3 Fat; 1 Other Carbohydrates.

SERVING SUGGESTIONS: Serve with brown rice and spinach salad.

BAKED FISH WITH TOMATOES AND OLIVES

Serves 6

6 fish fillets (your choice, use what's available and affordable)
Salt and pepper to taste
¼ cup extra-virgin olive oil
1 teaspoon thyme
3 tomatoes, peeled, seeded, and chopped
½ cup coarsely chopped green olives
¼ teaspoon dried hot red pepper flakes
2 garlic cloves, minced
½ cup finely chopped red onion
1 tablespoon fresh lime juice

Preheat oven to 400 degrees F.

Lightly grease a shallow baking dish large enough to hold the fillets in one layer. Arrange fish in the dish, and salt and pepper to taste.

In a bowl, stir together the oil, thyme, tomatoes, olives, red pepper flakes, garlic, onion, and lime juice. Spoon the tomato mixture over the fish and bake the fish, uncovered, in the middle of the oven 15–20 minutes, or until fish flakes easily with a fork.

PER SERVING:
113 Calories; 10g Fat (79.0% calories from fat); 1g Protein; 5g Carbohydrate; 1g Dietary Fiber; 0mg Cholesterol; 105mg Sodium. Exchanges: 0 Grain (Starch); 1 Vegetable; 0 Fruit; 2 Fat.

SERVING SUGGESTIONS: Baked potatoes, steamed green beans, butternut squash.

CHILI WITH CORN BREAD DUMPLINGS

Serves 6

¾ *pound extra-lean ground beef, cooked and drained*
1 *cup oats*
1 *large onion, chopped*
2 *cloves garlic, minced*
1 *15-ounce can pinto beans, drained*
1 *28-ounce jar spaghetti sauce*
2 *tablespoons chili powder*
½ *teaspoon cumin*
½ *teaspoon oregano*
1 *cup low-fat Cheddar cheese, shredded*
1 *8½-ounce package corn muffin mix*

Preheat oven to 400 degrees F.

In a large skillet, thoroughly brown beef; drain fat and blot beef with paper towels (with this step fat grams will be lower than what shows up in nutritional info below). Add oats and incorporate well. Add onion and garlic; sauté lightly. Add beans, sauce, and seasonings; simmer 20 minutes. Spoon into a 13 x 9–inch baking dish. Evenly sprinkle with cheese. Spoon corn muffin batter (prepared according to package directions) like dumplings over the top of the casserole. Bake 20–25 minutes or until corn-bread dumplings test done.

PER SERVING:
704 Calories; 19g Fat (24.0% calories from fat); 35g Protein; 98g Carbohydrate; 24g Dietary Fiber; 43mg Cholesterol; 1155mg Sodium. Exchanges: 4½ Grain (Starch); 3 Lean Meat; ½ Vegetable; 2½ Fat; 2 Other Carbohydrates.

SERVING SUGGESTION: Only a big green salad is necessary for this hearty meal.

CREAMY SPAGHETTI CARBONARA

Serves 6

1½ pounds spaghetti, uncooked
½ cup grated Parmesan cheese
1 tablespoon flour
9 ounces turkey bacon, finely chopped
1½ cloves garlic, minced
1 cup dry white wine
1 cup half and half
½ cup chopped parsley
Salt and freshly ground pepper to taste

Prepare pasta according to package directions. Toss Parmesan cheese with flour and set aside. While pasta is cooking, cook the bacon and garlic in a small sauté pan over medium-low heat until the garlic is aromatic and the bacon is lightly browned, about 3–4 minutes.

Add the wine, increase heat, bring the wine to a boil, and cook until it has reduced by half. Add the half and half and bring back up to a slight simmer (not much—it will break), then whisk in the Parmesan cheese mixture, stirring constantly until thickened. Remove from heat.

When pasta is done, drain it well and add it immediately to the bacon mixture. Add chopped parsley and toss quickly. Season with salt and freshly ground pepper, and serve.

PER SERVING:
587 Calories; 12g Fat (19.6% calories from fat); 24g Protein; 87g Carbohydrate; 3g Dietary Fiber; 43mg Cholesterol; 697mg Sodium. Exchanges: 5½ Grain (Starch); 1½ Lean Meat; 0 Vegetable; 1 Fat.

SERVING SUGGESTIONS: Steamed broccoli and a big spinach salad. Pass a bowl of baby carrots at the table for a little beta-carotene crunch!

DO AHEAD TIPS: Cook turkey and rice for tomorrow's Turkey and Rice Strata.

TURKEY AND RICE STRATA

Serves 6

3 cups brown rice, cooked and cooled to room temperature
1½ cups cooked turkey, cubed
¾ cup finely diced fresh tomatoes
¼ cup sliced green onions
¼ cup finely diced green pepper
1 tablespoon chopped fresh basil
Salt and pepper to taste
⅛ teaspoon cayenne pepper, or to taste
4 eggs, beaten
½ cup milk
¾ cup low-fat Cheddar cheese, shredded
¾ cup mozzarella cheese, shredded

Preheat oven to 350 degrees F.

In a large bowl, combine rice, turkey, tomatoes, onions, green pepper, basil, salt and pepper, cayenne, eggs, and milk and stir well until incorporated. Pour into a greased 9 × 13–inch pan. Top with cheeses and bake for 20–25 minutes or until knife inserted near the center comes out clean.

Cut strata into squares and serve.

PER SERVING:
341 Calories; 15g Fat (40.7% calories from fat); 24g Protein; 27g Carbohydrate; 2g Dietary Fiber; 181mg Cholesterol; 219mg Sodium. Exchanges: 1½ Grain (Starch); 3 Lean Meat; ½ Vegetable; 0 Non-Fat Milk; 1½ Fat.

SERVING SUGGESTIONS: Baked sweet potatoes and steamed asparagus would be wonderful. I would even add a big salad to this meal.

CROCKED BARBECUED BEEF

Serves 6

2 pounds chuck roast, boneless and trimmed of all visible fat
Salt and pepper to taste
1½ cups ketchup
⅛ cup honey
¼ cup balsamic vinegar
2 tablespoons Dijon mustard
¼ cup barbecue sauce
2 tablespoons Worcestershire sauce
1 teaspoon garlic powder

In a Crock-Pot, place chuck roast. Salt and pepper it to your personal taste.

In a large bowl, mix the rest of the ingredients until well blended. Pour on top of the roast, cover, and cook on low for 8–10 hours.

Remove roast from Crock-Pot and shred meat with a fork. Return meat to Crock-Pot, stirring well to coat evenly with the sauce. Cook for another hour and serve.

PER SERVING:
418 Calories; 24g Fat (51.6% calories from fat); 25g Protein; 26g Carbohydrate; 1g Dietary Fiber; 87mg Cholesterol; 984mg Sodium. Exchanges: 0 Grain (Starch); 3½ Lean Meat; 0 Fruit; 2½ Fat; 1½ Other Carbohydrates.

SERVING SUGGESTIONS: Serve on toasted whole-grain hamburger buns with coleslaw, Oven Fries (see page 258), and extra barbecue sauce.

**NUTRITION NOTE: If you trim the fat from the beef before cooking and blot the grease from the sauce, you can substantially lower the fat grams in this recipe and many of the beef recipes in this book. However, the nutrition software won't calculate that, so just know if you do include that step, you're doing yourself a big favor.

Week Eight

DAY ONE: Cajun Chicken

DAY TWO: Make Mine Meat Loaf

DAY THREE: Baked Parmesan Fish

DAY FOUR: Red and Yellow Chowder

DAY FIVE: White Bean and Sausage Pasta

DAY SIX: Crock-Pot Chicken Indonesian

SHOPPING LIST

MEAT

6 boneless, skinless chicken breast halves

1 pound extra-lean ground beef

6 fish fillets (use what is available, fresh or frozen)

1 pound Italian turkey sausage

6 skinless chicken thighs

CONDIMENTS

barbecue sauce (you'll need 1 cup)

salsa

olive oil

balsamic vinegar

soy sauce

sesame oil

peanut butter (you'll need ⅓ cup)

PRODUCE

3 pounds onions (keep on hand)

1 green bell pepper

1 small red bell pepper

2 potatoes

1 head garlic

1 piece gingerroot

**sweet potatoes (2 meals)

**kale (1 meal)

**baby carrots (1 meal)

**broccoli (2 meals)

**asparagus (1 meal)

**potatoes (3 meals)
**spinach (1 meal)
**2–3 heads of lettuce (*not* Iceberg)

CANNED GOODS
1 4-ounce can corn kernels
1 15-ounce can white beans
4 15-ounce cans chicken broth
1 15-ounce can tomatoes

SPICES
paprika
sage
cayenne pepper
garlic powder
chili powder
oregano
red pepper flakes

DAIRY/DAIRY CASE
butter (you'll need 8 tablespoons)
eggs (you'll need 2)
1 wedge Parmesan cheese
half and half (you'll need 1 cup)
1 wedge Romano cheese

DRY GOODS
flour (you'll need 7 tablespoons)
cornmeal (you'll need 5 tablespoons)
rigatoni (you'll need ½ pound)
**brown rice (2 meals)

FROZEN FOODS
1–2 bags corn (you'll need 4 cups)

BAKERY
Soft bread crumbs (you'll need 1 cup)
**whole-grain rolls (1 meal)

CAJUN CHICKEN

Serves 6

1½ tablespoons paprika
1 teaspoon salt
1½ teaspoons sage
¾ teaspoon cayenne pepper
¾ teaspoon black pepper
¾ teaspoon garlic powder
6 boneless, skinless chicken breast halves
3 teaspoons butter

On a large dinner plate, combine seasonings and coat chicken with seasoning mixture on both sides. Heat butter over medium-high heat, but don't let it turn brown. Put chicken in the pan, reduce heat to medium. Cook on both sides until dark brown, a total of 6–8 minutes, or until cooked thoroughly.

PER SERVING:
180 Calories; 9g Fat (46.2% calories from fat); 22g Protein; 2g Carbohydrate; 1g Dietary Fiber; 72mg Cholesterol; 413mg Sodium. Exchanges: 0 Grain (Starch); 3 Lean Meat; ½ Fat.

SERVING SUGGESTIONS: Brown rice, baked sweet potatoes, and steamed kale would be a great dinner.

MAKE MINE MEAT LOAF

Serves 6

1 teaspoon chili powder
Salt and pepper, to taste
1 pound extra-lean ground beef
4 ounces corn kernels, drained and chopped
1 medium onion, chopped
½ cup soft bread crumbs
2 eggs, slightly beaten
¼ cup green bell pepper, chopped
⅓ cup barbecue sauce
Salsa

Preheat oven to 350 degrees F.

Sprinkle chili powder, salt, and pepper over ground beef. Add corn, onion, bread crumbs, eggs, bell pepper, and barbecue sauce, mixing thoroughly. Using your hands, shape beef mixture into blobby loaf and place it on a rack in a shallow roasting pan (so it doesn't swim in grease). Bake for 1½ hours or until cooked through. Cut loaf into slices and spoon salsa over each serving.

PER SERVING:
244 Calories; 15g Fat (55.4% calories from fat); 17g Protein; 10g Carbohydrate; 1g Dietary Fiber; 115mg Cholesterol; 208mg Sodium. Exchanges: ½ Grain (Starch); 2½ Lean Meat; ½ Vegetable; 1½ Fat; 0 Other Carbohydrates.

SERVING SUGGESTIONS: Mashed potatoes, steamed baby carrots, and broccoli.

BAKED PARMESAN FISH

Serves 6

5 tablespoons flour
5 tablespoons cornmeal
½ teaspoon garlic powder
Salt and pepper to taste
3 tablespoons butter
6 fish fillets (use what's available—fresh or frozen)
⅓ cup grated Parmesan cheese

Preheat oven to 400 degrees F.

On a dinner plate, combine flour, cornmeal, and seasonings. Melt butter in shallow baking dish. Dredge fish in flour mixture and place in baking dish. Turn fish to coat with butter; then sprinkle with Parmesan cheese.

Bake for 8–10 minutes or until fish flakes easily with a fork.

PER SERVING:
311 Calories; 9g Fat (26.4% calories from fat); 44g Protein; 11g Carbohydrate; 1g Dietary Fiber; 118mg Cholesterol; 266mg Sodium. Exchanges: ½ Grain (Starch); 6 Lean Meat; 1 Fat.

SERVING SUGGESTIONS: Baked potatoes, steamed asparagus, and a big salad.

RED AND YELLOW CHOWDER

1 tablespoon olive oil
2 tablespoons butter
1 large onion, chopped
1 small red bell pepper, chopped
2 tablespoons flour
3 cans chicken broth
2 potatoes, peeled and chopped
4 cups frozen corn
Salt and pepper to taste
1 cup half and half

In a soup pot, add oil and butter over medium heat. When butter is completely melted, add onion and cook till translucent, 3 minutes. Add bell pepper and cook another 3 minutes. Sprinkle flour over onion and bell pepper and cook, stirring continually, for another 3 minutes.

Add the broth and potatoes and bring to a boil. Cover and cook for about 5 minutes, then uncover and allow potatoes to finish cooking, another 5 minutes.

Add corn, salt, pepper, and half and half, cooking over low heat for about 5 minutes, stirring as necessary. When nice and hot and corn is tender, serve it up!

PER SERVING:
256 Calories; 12g Fat (38.1% calories from fat); 6g Protein; 37g Carbohydrate; 4g Dietary Fiber; 25mg Cholesterol; 62mg Sodium. Exchanges: 2 Grain (Starch); ½ Vegetable; 0 Non-Fat Milk; 2 Fat.

SERVING SUGGESTIONS: A big spinach salad and some whole-grain rolls will round this off nicely.

WHITE BEAN AND SAUSAGE PASTA

Serves 6

½ pound rigatoni
1 pound Italian turkey sausage
2 tablespoons olive oil
1 medium onion, chopped
3 cloves garlic, pressed
1 can white beans
½ teaspoon red pepper flakes
2 teaspoons oregano
1 can chicken broth
1 can tomatoes
2 tablespoons balsamic vinegar
Salt and pepper to taste
¼ cup Romano cheese, grated

Cook pasta; drain and set aside.

In the meantime, in a skillet, sauté sausage meat until browned. Drain grease and blot sausage with paper towels to absorb excess fat. Remove and set aside. Heat oil in skillet over medium-high heat and add onions, cooking till translucent. Add garlic and beans and heat through. Add red pepper flakes, oregano, broth, and tomatoes and simmer gently for 10 minutes. Add balsamic vinegar and continue to simmer until heated through. Season lightly with salt and pepper. Lightly toss bean mixture together with cooked pasta and serve, topped with a sprinkling of Romano cheese.

PER SERVING:
804 Calories; 19g Fat (21.2% calories from fat); 47g Protein; 113g Carbohydrate; 24g Dietary Fiber; 65mg Cholesterol; 520mg Sodium. Exchanges: 7½ Grain (Starch); 3½ Lean Meat; ½ Vegetable; 0 Fruit; 2 Fat.

SERVING SUGGESTION: Serve with a salad.

TO SPRAY OR NOT TO SPRAY?

🌻 I am vehemently opposed to aerosol oil sprays. They are full of propellant—and, if you're a human, propellant isn't generally thought of as food. I very rarely call for an oil spray in any of these recipes, but occasionally I do so simply to keep the fat grams at bay. Still, I don't like those spray cans of oil.

But there is an alternative. You can buy oil sprayers and fill them yourself with your own quality oil. This handy device is composed of a hand pump that puts the air into the container, giving you a decent spritz of oil. These fine contraptions can be purchased inexpensively at huge discount stores, or you can pay more for them at fine department stores. From my experience, it would seem smarter to get several less expensive ones rather than a slick, expensive brand. They all seem to last about the same time, so why not spend less money?

CROCK-POT CHICKEN INDONESIAN

1 tablespoon soy sauce
2 cloves garlic, minced
2 teaspoons grated fresh gingerroot
1½ teaspoons sesame oil
¼ teaspoon cayenne pepper
6 skinless chicken thighs
⅓ cup peanut butter

In a small bowl, combine soy sauce, garlic, ginger, sesame oil, and cayenne pepper. Place chicken in a Crock-Pot. Pour sauce mixture over the top of the chicken. Cover and cook on low heat setting 6½–7 hours or until chicken is tender and fully cooked. Remove chicken from Crock-Pot and stir peanut butter into juices until smooth. Spoon sauce over chicken to serve.

PER SERVING:
139 Calories; 10g Fat (62.4% calories from fat); 10g Protein; 3g Carbohydrate; 1g Dietary Fiber; 16mg Cholesterol; 251mg Sodium. Exchanges: 0 Grain (Starch); 1½ Lean Meat; 0 Vegetable; 1½ Fat.

SERVING SUGGESTIONS: Serve with brown rice, steamed broccoli, and baked sweet potatoes.

SUMMER

Summer means abundance when it comes to vegetables. Tomatoes will never taste better, and the zucchini will never be more prolific. This is a delicious time for eating seasonal foods, even though it is hot outside. The very idea of turning on the oven should cause you to break out into hot sweat, and for that reason, the oven stays off these next eight weeks. All dinners will be prepared either on top of the stove or outside on a fired-up barbecue. Heck, you can do your whole dinner on the barbecue— veggies included!

Week One:

DAY ONE: Skillet Chili Chicken
DAY TWO: Grilled Ginger Fish
DAY THREE: Indian Lentils and Rice
DAY FOUR: Pasta Salad Primavera
DAY FIVE: Hungarian Hamburger Steaks
DAY SIX: Crock-Pot Cabbage Rolls

SHOPPING LIST

MEAT
6 boneless, skinless chicken breast halves
6 fish fillets
1½ pounds extra-lean ground beef
1 pound ground turkey

CONDIMENTS
vegetable oil
soy sauce (I prefer low sodium)
olive oil
cider vinegar
**balsamic vinegar

PRODUCE
3 pounds onions (keep on hand)
1 head garlic (keep on hand)
1 small red onion
1 piece gingerroot (you'll need 1 teaspoon grated)
1 bunch cilantro
1 bunch carrots (keep on hand)
1 bunch broccoli (**additional broccoli for 2 meals if you
    follow Serving Suggestions)

1 red bell pepper
1 head cabbage
**baby carrots (2 meals)
**baby spinach (1 meal)
**yellow squash (1 meal)
**zucchini (1 meal)
**tomatoes (1 meal)
**fresh basil (1 meal)
**potatoes (1 meal)
**cabbage for coleslaw (my preference is a bag of already
    shredded coleslaw mix) (1 meal)
**2–3 heads lettuce (*not* Iceberg)

CANNED GOODS

2 4-ounce cans diced green chilies
2 14-ounce cans chicken broth
1 7-ounce can whole kernel corn
1 8-ounce can tomato sauce

SPICES

chili powder
cayenne pepper
cumin
dry mustard
garlic powder
curry powder
basil
paprika
marjoram

DAIRY/DAIRY CASE

low-fat sour cream (you'll need 1¾ cups) (**additional sour
    cream if you follow Serving Suggestions)
plain yogurt (you'll need ½ cup)
Provolone cheese (6 ounces)
1 egg
**mozzarella cheese (1 meal)

DRY GOODS
flour
brown sugar
lentils (2 cups)
1 box pasta shells
brown rice (**additional brown rice for 2 meals if you follow
    Serving Suggestions)
**couscous (1 meal)
1 box toothpicks

SKILLET CHILI CHICKEN

Serves 6

6 *boneless, skinless chicken breast halves*
3 *teaspoons chili powder*
¼ *teaspoon cayenne pepper*
2 *teaspoons cumin*
Salt and pepper to taste
1 *tablespoon oil*
3 *cloves garlic, pressed*
1 *onion, chopped*
2 *4-ounce cans diced green chilies*
1 *cup chicken broth*
3 *tablespoons flour*
3 *tablespoons water*
¾ *cup low-fat sour cream*

Rub both sides of each chicken breast half with mixture of chili powder, cayenne, cumin, salt, and pepper.

In a skillet, heat oil on medium-high heat and brown chicken on both sides; about 3 minutes each. Add garlic, onion, chilies, and chicken broth. Cover and simmer on low for 15–20 minutes.

Remove chicken pieces to platter, draining juices back into skillet, and keep warm.

In a jar, add together flour and water and vigorously shake, then stir into sauce, stirring constantly, until thickened. When sauce has thickened, add sour cream and serve.

PER SERVING:
388 Calories; 15g Fat (47.8% calories from fat); 33g Protein; 8g Carbohydrate; 1g Dietary Fiber; 106mg Cholesterol; 782mg Sodium. Exchanges: ½ Grain (Starch); 4½ Lean Meat; ½ Vegetable; 0 Non-Fat Milk; 2 Fat.

SERVING SUGGESTIONS: Serve with brown rice, sautéed yellow squash, and zucchini, and a salad.

GRILLED GINGER FISH

Serves 6

½ cup soy sauce (use low sodium, if available)
1 teaspoon fresh gingerroot, grated
¼ cup brown sugar
1 clove garlic, minced
1 teaspoon dry mustard
6 fish fillets

In a large zipper-topped plastic bag, mix everything except the fish. Add fish to mix and refrigerate 4–8 hours before serving. Turn often if you are able.

Heat grill to medium temperature. Grill fish until done, but not dry, basting with marinade frequently. Fish will flake easily with a fork when cooked.

PER SERVING:
213 Calories; 4g Fat (17.6% calories from fat); 36g Protein; 6g Carbohydrate; trace Dietary Fiber; 54mg Cholesterol; 123mg Sodium. Exchanges: 0 Grain (Starch); 5 Lean Meat; 0 Vegetable; 0 Fat; ½ Other Carbohydrates.

SERVING SUGGESTIONS: Couscous; sliced summer tomatoes, mozzarella, and fresh basil, drizzled with balsamic vinegar and olive oil.

INDIAN LENTILS AND RICE

Serves 6

6 tablespoons olive oil
1 onion, sliced into rings
2 cups lentils, uncooked
1 14½-ounce can chicken broth (plus a little more water)
1 teaspoon curry powder, divided
1 teaspoon garlic powder, divided
Salt and pepper, to taste
1½ cups brown rice
½ cup plain yogurt
Chopped cilantro

Heat olive oil in a large skillet over medium heat. Stir in the onion and cook about 10 minutes, until browned. Remove from heat and set aside.

In a medium saucepan, cover lentils with the chicken broth and a little more water as needed to cover them. Add half the curry, half the garlic, and salt and pepper to taste. Bring to a boil, reduce heat, and simmer about 5 minutes.

Now add brown rice and enough water to cover the lentils and rice together. Season with remaining spices and salt and pepper. Cover saucepan and continue to simmer about 30 minutes, or until rice and lentils are tender.

Mix half the onions into the lentil mixture. Top with plain yogurt, chopped cilantro, and remaining onions to serve.

PER SERVING:
301 Calories; 14g Fat (43.7% calories from fat); 4g Protein; 38g Carbohydrate; 1g Dietary Fiber; 3mg Cholesterol; 12mg Sodium. Exchanges: 2½ Grain (Starch); 0 Non-Fat Milk; 3 Fat; 0 Other Carbohydrates.

SERVING SUGGESTIONS: A big spinach salad and some baby carrots for the table.

PASTA SALAD PRIMAVERA

Serves 6

3 cups pasta shells, uncooked
3 carrots, sliced
3¾ cups broccoli florets
1 small red bell pepper, diced
1 small red onion, minced
1 7-ounce can whole kernel corn, drained
3 tablespoons olive oil
4 cloves garlic, pressed
2 teaspoons basil
Salt and pepper to taste
6 ounces chopped Provolone cheese

Prepare pasta according to package directions; drain and set aside.

Meanwhile, steam the carrots and broccoli just until tender, about 4–5 minutes. Place the vegetables in a large bowl, along with the bell pepper, onion, and corn.

Add remaining ingredients and mix well.

Add pasta to bowl and toss lightly.

PER SERVING:
203 Calories; 15g Fat (57.7% calories from fat); 2g Protein; 9g Carbohydrate; 3g Dietary Fiber; 0mg Cholesterol; 30mg Sodium. Exchanges: 0 Grain (Starch); 2 Vegetable; 1½ Fat.

SERVING SUGGESTION: Serve with a big green salad.

HUNGARIAN HAMBURGER STEAKS

Serves 6

1½ pounds extra-lean ground beef
1 large onion, chopped
6 cloves garlic, pressed
3 teaspoons paprika
1½ teaspoons dried marjoram
Salt and pepper to taste
1 cup low-fat sour cream

In a bowl, mix together ground beef, onion, garlic, paprika, marjoram, salt, and pepper until well combined.

Divide into 6 equal portions; with wet hands, form into patties.

Heat grill. Grill on medium, turning every 2 minutes, until well browned but still juicy and slightly pink inside, 8–10 minutes.

Serve with sour cream for dipping.

PER SERVING:
101 Calories; 8g Fat (70.8% calories from fat); 2g Protein; 6g Carbohydrate; 1g Dietary Fiber; 17mg Cholesterol; 733mg Sodium. Exchanges: 0 Grain (Starch); 0 Lean Meat; ½ Vegetable; 0 Non-Fat Milk; 1½ Fat.

SERVING SUGGESTIONS: Serve with pan sautéed potatoes, coleslaw, and some baby carrots.

DO AHEAD TIP: Cook cabbage for tomorrow's Crock-Pot Cabbage Rolls (see below for directions).

CROCK-POT CABBAGE ROLLS

Serves 6

1 cabbage
1 pound ground turkey
¼ cup brown rice, uncooked
1 egg, beaten
1 onion, minced
1 carrot, minced
1 teaspoon salt
½ teaspoon pepper
¼ cup cider vinegar
½ cup brown sugar
1 8-ounce can tomato sauce
Toothpicks

Drop cabbage in boiling water and simmer for 5–10 minutes; cool (unless you've done yesterday's Do Ahead Tip).

In the meantime, in a bowl, mix ground turkey, rice, egg, onion, carrot, salt, and pepper. In another bowl, mix together vinegar, brown sugar, and tomato sauce.

When cabbage has cooled sufficiently, remove 12 large leaves. Chop remaining cabbage and place in bottom of Crock-Pot. Place 2–4 tablespoons of meat mixture in center of each cabbage leaf. Roll up, envelope style, and secure with toothpick. Place seam side down in Crock-Pot. Pour tomato sauce mixture over all. Cover and cook on low for 8–10 hours.

PER SERVING:
272 Calories; 10g Fat (33.0% calories from fat); 5g Protein; 27g Carbohydrate; 1g Dietary Fiber; 65mg Cholesterol; 644mg Sodium. Exchanges: ½ Grain (Starch); 0 Lean Meat; 1 Vegetable; 0 Non-Fat Milk; 3 Fat; 1 Other Carbohydrates.

SERVING SUGGESTIONS: Serve with brown rice, sour cream, steamed broccoli, and a salad.

Week Two

DAY ONE: Restaurant-Style Chinese Chicken
DAY TWO: Poached Salmon with Creamy Horseradish Sauce
DAY THREE: Cincinnati Chili
DAY FOUR: Great Greek Salad
DAY FIVE: BBQ Beef Kabobs
DAY SIX: Lemon Roast Chicken

SHOPPING LIST

MEAT

1 pound chicken breast halves (skinned and boned)
6 salmon steaks or fillets
3 pounds round, flank, or chuck steak
1 whole chicken

CONDIMENTS

vegetable oil
soy sauce (I prefer low sodium)
low-fat mayonnaise
prepared horseradish (not creamed)
olive oil
dry sherry
balsamic vinegar

PRODUCE

3 pounds onions (keep on hand)
1 head garlic (keep on hand)
1 piece gingerroot (you'll need 3 teaspoons grated)
1 bunch green onions
4 lemons
1 bunch celery (you'll need 2 stalks)
1 bunch carrots (keep on hand)
1 bunch broccoli
3 tomatoes
2 green peppers

2 red bell peppers (**another red bell pepper if you follow
    Serving Suggestions)
1 red onion
1 English cucumber (seedless)
**baby carrots (2 meals)
**baby spinach (1 meal)
**baby red potatoes (1 meal)
**green beans (2 meals)
**yellow squash (1 meal)
**potatoes for mashed potatoes (1 meal)
**2–3 heads lettuce (*not* Iceberg)

CANNED GOODS
1 16-ounce can diced tomatoes
1 14½-ounce can chicken broth
1 16-ounce can tomato sauce
1 6-ounce can tomato paste
2 16-ounce cans red kidney beans
12 Greek olives (these may be in the deli section)

SPICES
ginger
chili powder
cinnamon
oregano

DAIRY/DAIRY CASE
low-fat sour cream (you'll need ½ cup)
12 ounces Feta cheese
low-fat shredded Cheddar cheese

DRY GOODS
4 ounces unsalted roasted peanuts
cornstarch
sugar
1 pound spaghetti

**brown rice (2 meals)
18 bamboo skewers

BAKERY
**corn muffins (1 meal)
**whole-grain rolls (1 meal)

RESTAURANT-STYLE CHINESE CHICKEN

Serves 6

6 tablespoons soy sauce (low sodium, if available)
6 tablespoons dry sherry, optional
3 cloves garlic, pressed
3 teaspoons gingerroot, grated
1 pound chicken breast halves, skinned, boned, and cubed
3 teaspoons vegetable oil
4 ounces unsalted roasted peanuts, shelled
1 red bell pepper, sliced in strips
¼ cup green onions, sliced diagonally
¾ cup chicken broth
3 teaspoons cornstarch

In a large zipper-topped plastic bag, combine soy sauce, sherry, garlic, and gingerroot. Mush the bag to blend well, then add chicken, turning several times to coat. Place bag of chicken in the fridge for at least 30 minutes.

In a skillet, heat oil over medium-high heat. Add peanuts and cook, stirring frequently, until nuts are lightly browned, about 1 minute. Transfer nuts to plate and set aside. Now cook chicken in the skillet (reserving marinade), until browned all over, about 2–3 minutes. Transfer chicken to the same plate with peanuts; set aside.

Add bell pepper and green onions to skillet and cook over medium-high heat, stirring frequently, until crisp-tender, 1–2 minutes. Mix broth, cornstarch, and reserved marinade, then add to the skillet. Use a wire whisk to dissolve cornstarch, then add chicken and peanuts.

Cook, stirring constantly, until mixture comes to a boil and thickens, 2–3 minutes.

PER SERVING:
188 Calories; 8g Fat (42.7% calories from fat); 15g Protein; 9g Carbohydrate; 1g Dietary Fiber; 39mg Cholesterol; 1169mg Sodium. Exchanges: 0 Grain (Starch); 2 Lean Meat; 1½ Vegetable; ½ Fat.

SERVING SUGGESTIONS: Serve over brown rice with a nice big spinach salad.

POACHED SALMON WITH CREAMY HORSERADISH SAUCE

Serves 6

6 cups water
2 lemons, sliced
2 carrots, sliced
2 stalks celery, sliced
6 salmon steaks or fillets
½ cup low-fat mayonnaise
½ cup low-fat sour cream
3 teaspoons prepared horseradish (not creamed)
2 teaspoons lemon juice
2 green onions, chopped

Combine first 4 ingredients in large skillet; cover and bring to a boil. Reduce heat and simmer for 10 minutes. Add salmon, cover, and simmer another 10 minutes. Remove skillet from heat and let stand for 8 minutes. Remove salmon to serving plate; set aside.

Prepare Creamy Horseradish Sauce: In a bowl, combine last 5 ingredients. Serve with salmon.

PER SERVING:
152 Calories; 16g Fat (83.3% calories from fat); 1g Protein; 6g Carbohydrate; 2g Dietary Fiber; 6mg Cholesterol; 133mg Sodium. Exchanges: 0 Grain (Starch); ½ Vegetable; 0 Fruit; 1½ Fat.

SERVING SUGGESTIONS: Serve with steamed baby red potatoes, green beans, and baby carrots.

CINCINNATI CHILI

Serves 6

1 tablespoon olive oil
½ small green pepper, chopped
1 onion, chopped and divided
2 cloves garlic, pressed
1 16-ounce can tomatoes, undrained and diced
1 16-ounce can tomato sauce
1 6-ounce can tomato paste
1 cup water
2 cans red kidney beans, rinsed and drained
1 tablespoon chili powder
1 teaspoon sugar
¼ teaspoon cinnamon
1 pound spaghetti
½ cup low-fat Cheddar cheese, shredded

In large pot, heat olive oil over medium-high heat and sauté green pepper and half the onion until golden. Add garlic and sauté a minute longer.

Stir in tomatoes with juice, tomato sauce, tomato paste, water, kidney beans, chili powder, sugar, and cinnamon. Bring to a boil, reduce heat, cover, and simmer for 30 minutes.

Meanwhile, cook pasta according to package directions. Drain and set aside, keeping warm.

Serve chili over spaghetti; sprinkle with Cheddar cheese and remaining onion.

PER SERVING:

711 Calories; 6g Fat (7.5% calories from fat); 36g Protein; 132g Carbohydrate; 20g Dietary Fiber; 10mg Cholesterol; 778mg Sodium. Exchanges: 7½ Grain (Starch); 2 Lean Meat; 3 Vegetable; ½ Fat; 0 Other Carbohydrates.

SERVING SUGGESTIONS: Serve with a big green salad and some corn muffins.

GREAT GREEK SALAD

Serves 6

¼ cup olive oil
3 tablespoons lemon juice
1 tablespoon balsamic vinegar
¾ teaspoon dried oregano
Salt and pepper to taste
1 red bell pepper, seeded and sliced
1 green bell pepper, seeded and sliced
1 red onion, sliced into thin rings
1 English cucumber, seedless
1 bunch broccoli, chopped
12 Greek olives, drained
3 tomatoes, sliced
12 ounces Feta cheese, crumbled

In a small bowl, whisk together the dressing ingredients (olive oil though pepper).

In a large bowl, toss remaining ingredients together. Pour dressing over the salad and toss again.

PER SERVING:

392 Calories; 18g Fat (25% calories from fat); 13g Protein; 15g Carbohydrate; 5g Dietary Fiber; 50mg Cholesterol; 740mg Sodium. Exchanges: 0 Grain (Starch); 1 Lean Meat; 2 Vegetable; 0 Fruit; 6 Fat; 0 Other Carbohydrates.

SERVING SUGGESTION: Serve with whole-grain rolls.

DO AHEAD TIP: Marinate the beef (see instructions in the BBQ Beef Kabob recipe on page 207).

BBQ BEEF KABOBS

Serves 6

¾ cup dry sherry
½ cup soy sauce
4 tablespoons vegetable oil
3 cloves garlic, pressed
1 large onion, minced
2½ teaspoons ground ginger
3 pounds round, flank, or chuck steak, cut in 1-inch cubes
18 bamboo skewers, soaked in water

Combine first 6 ingredients; mix well.

Put beef chunks in large zipper-topped plastic bag; add marinade, turning to make sure all meat is coated. Close bag and refrigerate for at least 3 hours, or overnight if desired.

Preheat the grill for 10–15 minutes, with all burners on high.

While grill is heating, drain the marinade from the bag and discard it. Thread the marinated beef onto the skewers, with sides of the pieces touching.

Once grill is hot, turn all burners to medium. Place skewers on grill and cook meat for about 8–12 minutes, turning once or twice.

PER SERVING:
129 Calories; 9g Fat (82.6% calories from fat); 1g Protein; 3g Carbohydrate; trace Dietary Fiber; 0mg Cholesterol; 1375mg Sodium. Exchanges: ½ Vegetable; 2 Fat.

SERVING SUGGESTIONS: Serve with brown rice, sautéed squash and red bell pepper, and a salad.

LEMON ROAST CHICKEN

1½ teaspoons oregano
3 cloves garlic, pressed
1 whole chicken, with skin removed
1 tablespoon olive oil
Salt and pepper to taste
¼ cup water
3 tablespoons lemon juice

Sprinkle half the oregano and garlic inside the cavity of the chicken.

In a skillet, heat olive oil over medium-high heat. Brown chicken on all sides, then place in Crock-Pot. Add remaining oregano and garlic, salt and pepper to taste.

Add water to skillet and use a wire whisk to loosen brown bits. Pour the skillet water into the Crock-Pot.

Cook on low for 8 hours. Add lemon juice in the last hour of cooking. When chicken is finished, pour cooking juices into a saucepan and heat over medium-high heat; allow it to simmer. The sauce needs to simmer for about 10 minutes to reduce, then serve.

PER SERVING:
413 Calories; 21g Fat (39% calories from fat); 48g Protein; 2g Carbohydrate; trace Dietary Fiber; 251mg Cholesterol; 242mg Sodium. Exchanges: 0 Grain (Starch); 6½ Lean Meat; 0 Vegetable; 0 Fruit; 5 Fat.

SERVING SUGGESTIONS: Serve with mashed potatoes, steamed green beans, and baby carrots.

Week Three

DAY ONE: Spicy Chicken with Pineapple Avocado Salsa
DAY TWO: Potato-Crusted Fish
DAY THREE: Black Bean Quesadillas
DAY FOUR: Mega-Layered Salad
DAY FIVE: Grilled Rosemary Chicken
DAY SIX: Crock-Pot Gingered Beef

SHOPPING LIST

MEAT
12 boneless, skinless chicken breast halves
6 fish fillets
2 pounds round roast
**chopped chicken (1 meal, if you use Optional Serving Idea)
**turkey bacon (1 meal, if you use Optional Serving Idea)

CONDIMENTS
olive oil
vegetable oil
ketchup
honey
dry red wine
vinegar
low-fat mayonnaise

PRODUCE
3 pounds onions (keep on hand)
1 head garlic (keep on hand)
1 avocado
1 bunch green onions
1 head romaine lettuce
1 bunch cilantro
1 lime
potatoes (you'll need 2 cups, shredded)
mushrooms (you'll need 1½ cups, sliced)
3 lemons (**additional lemons for 1 meal if you follow
   Serving Suggestions)

1 bunch celery (you'll need ½ cup, chopped)
2 tomatoes
1 green bell pepper
1 red bell pepper
**baby carrots (2 meals)
**tiny sugar tomatoes (1 meal)
**zucchini (1 meal)
**sweet potatoes (1 meal)
**spinach (2 meals)
**green beans (2 meals)
**yellow squash (1 meal)
**melon (1 meal)
**2–3 head lettuce (*not* Iceberg)

CANNED GOODS
1 14½-ounce can beef broth
1 7-ounce can pressed pineapple
1 15-ounce can black beans

SPICES
cayenne pepper
ginger
cumin
chili powder
garlic powder
curry powder
rosemary
fennel seeds
red pepper flakes
tarragon
whole black peppercorns

DAIRY/DAIRY CASE
low-fat shredded Cheddar cheese (you'll need 1 cup)
2 eggs
Romano cheese (you'll need 2 tablespoons)

DRY GOODS
light brown sugar
**couscous (1 meal)
**brown rice (2 meals)

FROZEN FOODS
1 10-ounce package corn
1 package peas (petite peas, if you can find them)

BAKERY
12 flour tortillas (whole wheat, if available)
**whole-grain rolls

SPICY CHICKEN WITH PINEAPPLE AVOCADO SALSA

Serves 6

1 7-ounce can pineapple, crushed and unsweetened
1 avocado, peeled, seeded, and chopped
3 tablespoons green onions, sliced
3 teaspoons lime juice
¼ teaspoon cayenne pepper, optional
1 teaspoon ground ginger
1 teaspoon cumin
2 tablespoons cilantro, chopped
2 tablespoons chili powder
2 cloves garlic, pressed
2 tablespoons olive oil, divided
6 boneless, skinless chicken breast halves
5 tablespoons honey

For Pineapple Avocado Salsa: combine first 8 ingredients in a bowl; set aside.

In a small bowl, combine chili powder and garlic. Stir in enough oil to make a thick paste and rub it on both sides of chicken breast halves.

In a large non-stick skillet on medium heat, heat remaining oil. Brown chicken on both sides, about 2–3 minutes per side. Drizzle with honey. Lower heat and cook, basting with pan juices, until chicken is no longer pink inside. Serve with salsa.

PER SERVING:
673 Calories; 12g Fat (19.2% calories from fat); 62g Protein; 23g Carbohydrate; 2g Dietary Fiber; 186mg Cholesterol; 215mg Sodium. Exchanges: 0 Grain (Starch); 8½ Lean Meat; ½ Vegetable; ½ Fruit; 2 Fat; 1 Other Carbohydrates.

SERVING SUGGESTIONS: Serve with brown rice and a big green salad.

POTATO-CRUSTED FISH

Serves 6

2 cups potatoes, shredded
1 onion, chopped
1 teaspoon tarragon
Salt and pepper to taste
6 fish fillets
3 teaspoons olive oil

In a bowl, combine potatoes, onion, tarragon, salt, and pepper.

Place fish on wax paper, pressing half the potato mixture evenly over fish. Carefully turn fish over and repeat with remaining potato mixture.

In large nonstick skillet, heat oil on medium-high heat and carefully place fish in skillet; cook 4 minutes on each side, or until potatoes are golden.

PER SERVING:
255 Calories; 4g Fat (14.2% calories from fat); 42g Protein; 10g Carbohydrate; 1g Dietary Fiber; 99mg Cholesterol; 306mg Sodium. Exchanges: ½ Grain (Starch); 5½ Lean Meat; ½ Fat.

SERVING SUGGESTIONS: Serve with lemon wedges, a big green salad, and some steamed green beans and baby carrots.

BLACK BEAN QUESADILLAS

Serves 6

1 tablespoon olive oil
1 onion, finely chopped
2 cloves garlic, pressed
1 15-ounce can black beans, rinsed and drained
1 red bell pepper, chopped
2 tomatoes, chopped
½ package frozen corn (5 ounces)
12 flour tortillas (whole wheat, if available)
1 cup low-fat Cheddar cheese, shredded

In a large skillet, add half the oil and sauté the onion and garlic until soft. Mix in beans, bell pepper, tomatoes, and corn. Cook until heated through.

Place a tortilla on a plate or flat surface, sprinkle some Cheddar cheese over the tortilla. Spoon some of the bean and vegetable mixture over the cheese. Top with another tortilla. Repeat until all of the tortillas are used.

Heat remaining oil in a large skillet over medium-high heat. Place quesadillas in the skillet and heat and flip until both sides are browned.

PER SERVING:
394 Calories; 7g Fat (26.8% calories from fat); 34g Protein; 131g Carbohydrate; 17g Dietary Fiber; 20mg Cholesterol; 814mg Sodium. Exchanges: 8½ Grain (Starch); 1½ Lean Meat; 1 Vegetable; 4 ½ Fat.

SERVING SUGGESTIONS: A big spinach salad and some sliced melon.

DO AHEAD TIP: Hardboil eggs for tomorrow's Mega-Layered Salad.

MEGA-LAYERED SALAD

1 head romaine lettuce, chopped

½ cup celery, chopped

½ cup green bell pepper, chopped

½ cup green onions, chopped

1½ cups fresh mushrooms, sliced

1½ cups frozen green peas (don't thaw, and use petite peas if you
   can)

2 eggs, cooked, peeled, and quartered

2 cups low-fat mayonnaise

2 tablespoons brown sugar

½ teaspoon garlic powder

½ teaspoon curry powder

2 tablespoons Romano cheese, grated

In a large bowl, layer ½ of the romaine lettuce. Follow with a layer of celery, bell pepper, green onion, mushrooms, peas and egg, then top with remaining romaine.

Prepare the dressing by whisking together the mayonnaise, brown sugar, garlic powder, and curry powder.

Spread evenly over top of the salad. Sprinkle with Romano cheese. Cover and refrigerate until ready to serve.

PER SERVING:
100 Calories; 2g Fat (20.8% calories from fat); 7g Protein; 14g Carbohydrate; 5g Dietary Fiber; 64mg Cholesterol; 113mg Sodium. Exchanges: ½ Grain (Starch); ½ Lean Meat; 1 Vegetable; 0 Fat; 0 Other Carbohydrates.

SERVING SUGGESTIONS: This salad is rich, and all you need are a bowl of baby carrots, some of those tiny sugar tomatoes, and some whole-grain rolls.

OPTIONAL SERVING IDEA: Add chopped chicken or crumbled turkey bacon, if desired, as one of the layers.

GRILLED ROSEMARY CHICKEN

Serves 6

6 cloves garlic
2 teaspoons whole black peppercorns
1 tablespoon rosemary
1 teaspoon fennel seeds
¼ teaspoon red pepper flakes
1 tablespoon lemon juice
4 tablespoons olive oil
6 boneless, skinless chicken breast halves
Lemon wedges

In a blender or food processor, place garlic, peppercorns, rosemary, fennel seeds, red pepper flakes, lemon juice, and oil and pulse into a coarse paste.

Crank up the barbecue. Rub the paste over both sides of the chicken and grill over medium-hot coals about 5–10 minutes per side, depending on size and thickness of the chicken. There should be no pink when you cut into the chicken. Serve with lemon wedges.

PER SERVING:
382 Calories; 14g Fat (32.4% calories from fat); 56g Protein; 8g Carbohydrate; 3g Dietary Fiber; 137mg Cholesterol; 159mg Sodium. Exchanges: ½ Grain (Starch); 7½ Lean Meat; 0 Vegetable; 0 Fruit; 2 Fat.

SERVING SUGGESTIONS: Serve with grilled zucchini and yellow squash, couscous, and a big green salad.

CROCK-POT GINGERED BEEF

Serves 6

2 tablespoons vegetable oil
2 pounds round roast, trimmed
2 onions, sliced
1 cup dry red wine
½ cup ketchup
6 tablespoons light brown sugar
3 tablespoons vinegar
½ teaspoon powdered ginger
4 cloves garlic, pressed
½ cup beef broth
Salt and pepper to taste

In a large skillet, heat oil over medium-high heat and brown roast on all sides.

In the bottom of your Crock-Pot, place the sliced onions first, then the browned roast.

Mix remaining ingredients in a bowl and pour over roast; cover and cook on low 6–8 hours or until meat is tender and can be shredded with a fork.

Pour cooking juices into a saucepan and simmer on the stove until reduced, about 10 minutes. Serve sauce over the top of the beef.

PER SERVING:
325 Calories; 12g Fat (33.6% calories from fat); 34g Protein; 20g Carbohydrate; 1g Dietary Fiber; 88mg Cholesterol; 564mg Sodium. Exchanges: 4½ Lean Meat; 1 Fat; 1½ Other Carbohydrates.

SERVING SUGGESTIONS: Serve with brown rice, sautéed green beans, steamed sweet potatos, and a spinach salad.

Week Four

DAY ONE: Skillet Lemon Chicken with Rosemary
DAY TWO: Fish Romano
DAY THREE: Tuscan Squash and Beans on Rice
DAY FOUR: Marinated Flank Steak
DAY FIVE: Warm Spinach Salad
DAY SIX: Crock-Pot BBQ Chicken

SHOPPING LIST

MEAT

6 boneless, skinless chicken breast halves
6 fish fillets
1½ pounds flank steak
½ pound turkey bacon
1 whole chicken

CONDIMENTS

olive oil
honey
soy sauce (I prefer low sodium)
balsamic vinegar
red wine
dry white wine
Dijon mustard
barbecue sauce

PRODUCE

3 pounds onions (keep on hand)
1 head garlic (keep on hand)
3 lemons
1½ 10-ounce packages spinach (**additional baby spinach
    for 1 meal if you follow Serving Suggestions)
zucchini (you'll need 3 cups, chopped)
1 red onion
3 large tomatoes
1 red bell pepper

**baby carrots (4 meals)
**red rose potatoes (1 meal)
**broccoli (1 meal)
**corn on the cob (1 meal)
**sugar tomatoes (2 meals)
**radishes (1 meal)
**yellow squash (1 meal)
**2–3 heads lettuce (*not* Iceberg)

CANNED GOODS
1 14½-ounce can chicken broth
1 15-ounce can cannellini beans (or substitute white beans,
   if unavailable)

SPICES
chili powder
rosemary
oregano
thyme
pressed red pepper, optional

DAIRY/DAIRY CASE
butter (I keep 1 pound unsalted in the freezer)
Romano cheese (you'll need ½ cup)
blue cheese

DRY GOODS
cornstarch
flour
sugar
brown rice (**additional brown rice for 2 meals if you follow
   Serving Suggestions)

FROZEN FOODS
1 10-ounce package corn

BAKERY
**whole-grain rolls (1 meal)

SKILLET LEMON CHICKEN WITH ROSEMARY

Serves 6

⅓ cup fresh lemon juice

¼ cup dry white wine, optional

3 tablespoons Dijon mustard

3 cloves garlic

¼ teaspoon dried rosemary, pressed

6 boneless, skinless chicken breast halves

1 cup chicken broth

1 tablespoon cornstarch

1 tablespoon olive oil

In a blender or food processor, blend lemon juice, wine, mustard, garlic, and rosemary until well combined. In a large zipper-topped plastic bag, throw the chicken in and add the lemon juice mixture. Keep in the fridge for at least an hour (or do this in the morning and have it well marinated that night).

In a small bowl, stir together 2 tablespoons of the chicken broth and the cornstarch until dissolved; set aside.

In a skillet, heat oil over medium-high heat. Cook chicken (reserving the marinade) on each side, about 4 minutes or until no longer pink. Remove chicken from skillet and cover to keep warm.

Now add reserved marinade to the skillet and, using a wire whisk, stir in the cornstarch mixture and the remaining broth. Bring to a boil, stirring constantly. Cook and stir for 2 minutes more. Return chicken to skillet, heat through, and serve with sauce.

PER SERVING:
300 Calories; 16g Fat (47.1% calories from fat); 32g Protein; 4g Carbohydrate; trace Dietary Fiber; 93mg Cholesterol; 315mg Sodium. Exchanges: 0 Grain (Starch); 4½ Lean Meat; 0 Vegetable; 0 Fruit; 0 Fat; 0 Other Carbohydrates.

SERVING SUGGESTIONS: Serve with steamed spinach, brown rice, and steamed baby carrots.

THE MAGIC OF MARVELOUS MARINADE

☀ Making marinades for grilling is as basic as putting butter on bread. Marinades are the perfect vehicle for transporting incredible flavor to most any food. It will positively make over a lackluster skinless breast of chicken.

The delightful way a marinade infuses itself into food has made it a popular choice for low-fat, healthy cooking—especially this time of year when outdoor grilling is just a part of life.

Marinades can tenderize and flavorize nearly anything into something exotic, delicious, and gourmet, even. Try it yourself. Even regular, right-out-of-the-bottle teriyaki sauce can make your chicken sizzle.

Here's the general breakdown for making your own marinades:

Oil: Any type from safflower to olive oil

Acid: Wine, citrus fruit, or vinegar

Seasonings: Whatever turns your key. From your secret blend of herbs and spices, to soy sauce and everything in between.

FISH ROMANO

Serves 6

¾ cup white wine
1 teaspoon thyme
¼ teaspoon pressed red pepper, optional
4 cloves garlic, pressed
6 fish fillets
½ cup flour
½ cup Romano cheese, grated
Salt and pepper to taste
1 tablespoon olive oil
Lemon wedges

In a large zipper-topped plastic bag, combine first 4 ingredients. Add fish, seal bag, and marinate in refrigerator for 30 minutes, turning bag occasionally.

Meanwhile, combine flour, Romano cheese, salt, and pepper in another large zipper-topped plastic bag. Remove fish fillets from marinade (discard marinade) and add them to the flour bag, close bag, and shake to coat evenly with flour mixture.

In a skillet, heat oil over medium-high heat. Add fish and cook 6 minutes on each side or until fish flakes easily when tested with a fork. Serve with lemon wedges.

PER SERVING:
283 Calories; 6g Fat (21.2% calories from fat); 45g Protein; 8g Carbohydrate; trace Dietary Fiber; 109mg Cholesterol; 237mg Sodium. Exchanges: ½ Grain (Starch); 6 Lean Meat; ½ Fat.

SERVING SUGGESTIONS: Serve with sautéed yellow squash, brown rice, and a big green salad.

TUSCAN SQUASH AND BEANS ON RICE

Serves 6

3 tablespoons olive oil
1 onion, chopped
1 red bell pepper, chopped
3 large tomatoes, diced
3 cups zucchini, chopped
½ teaspoon dried oregano
½ teaspoon thyme
3 cloves garlic, pressed
Salt and pepper to taste
1 15-ounce can cannellini beans, drained
1 cup brown rice, cooked

In a saucepan over medium heat, heat olive oil. Stir in onion and bell pepper and cook until tender. Mix in tomatoes and zucchini and season with oregano, thyme, garlic, salt, and pepper. Reduce heat, cover, and simmer 10 minutes, stirring occasionally.

Stir beans into zucchini mixture and continue cooking about 5 minutes.

Serve over the cooked rice.

PER SERVING:
307 Calories; 7g Fat (21.2% calories from fat); 17g Protein; 45g Carbohydrate; 14g Dietary Fiber; 0mg Cholesterol; 16mg Sodium. Exchanges: 3 Grain (Starch); 1 Lean Meat; ½ Vegetable; 1½ Fat.

SERVING SUGGESTIONS: A big green salad and a bowl of baby carrots will do it.

DO AHEAD TIP: Make marinade and marinate meat for tomorrow's Marinated Flank Steak.

* One of my very favorite parts of summer is the incessant use of the barbecue (at least at my house—I love that thing). In my opinion, being able to cook everything over an open flame would be wonderful for all seasons, but for all practical purposes and usage, I've limited the barbecue here to the summer menus and once a week at that.

When using a barbecue, whether it is gas or charcoal, it is imperative to preheat the grill. You cannot put the food on a cold grill and start that way for the same reasons you don't stick food in an oven that hasn't been preheated—it messes up the cooking time and the way it should cook. Don't do it!

And when you do preheat your grill and are enjoying the smoky flavor that only an outside barbecue can produce, you might want to try some new fun barbecue implements. There are some wonderful grilling accessories that you just cannot live without. One is a hole-y wok. That's right . . . big holes in a flat bottomed wok. I grilled the most incredible stir-fried squash in one of those things. It was easy—I tossed together sliced zucchini, summer squash, a little olive oil, and garlic in the bowl, then threw the mixture into the wok. Those vegetables were amazing. Think of the possibilities!

MARINATED FLANK STEAK

Serves 6

½ cup honey
½ cup soy sauce (low sodium, if available)
½ cup red wine
3 cloves garlic, pressed
¼ teaspoon dried rosemary, crumbled
¼ teaspoon chili powder
½ teaspoon pepper
1½ pounds flank steak

In a large zipper-topped plastic bag, mix together the honey, soy sauce, red wine, garlic, rosemary, chili powder, and pepper. Add the flank steak and marinate overnight in the fridge. Make sure you turn it at least once in the marinating process.

Light the barbecue and let the coals get medium hot. Grill the steak for 7 minutes per side for medium rare, or to desired doneness. Let stand 10 minutes before slicing very thin against the grain.

PER SERVING:
315 Calories; 12g Fat (35.1% calories from fat); 23g Protein; 26g Carbohydrate; trace Dietary Fiber; 58mg Cholesterol; 1465mg Sodium. Exchanges: 0 Grain (Starch); 3 Lean Meat; ½ Vegetable; ½ Fat; 1½ Other Carbohydrates.

SERVING SUGGESTIONS: Serve with steamed broccoli, corn on the cob, and a green salad.

WARM SPINACH SALAD

Serves 6

1½ 10-ounce packages spinach leaves, washed
½ pound turkey bacon, chopped
1 red onion, finely chopped
1 10-ounce package frozen corn
¾ cup balsamic vinegar
6 teaspoons sugar
¼ cup blue cheese, crumbled

Make a bed of spinach on each dinner plate.

In a large skillet, over medium-high heat, stir turkey bacon until browned and crisp, about 5 minutes. Spoon equal portions of the bacon over spinach.

In the same skillet, add onion, corn, vinegar, and sugar. Stir mixture until onion is limp, 3–4 minutes. With a slotted spoon, transfer onion and corn onto plates of spinach, then spoon cooking liquid over salads, and crumble blue cheese over the tops and serve.

PER SERVING:
215 Calories; 10g Fat (39.1% calories from fat); 10g Protein; 25g Carbohydrate; 2g Dietary Fiber; 39mg Cholesterol; 600mg Sodium. Exchanges: 1 Grain (Starch); 1 Lean Meat; ½ Vegetable; 1 Fat; ½ Other Carbohydrates.

SERVING SUGGESTIONS: Serve with whole-grain rolls and butter. Throw a few sugar tomatoes and baby carrots in a bowl and serve, too.

CROCK-POT BBQ CHICKEN

Serves 6

1 whole chicken
2 onions, sliced
2 cups barbecue sauce

Put chicken in Crock-Pot with onions on top and add the barbeque sauce; cook on low 6–8 hours. Drain off fat and serve.

PER SERVING:
385 Calories; 26g Fat (62.0% calories from fat); 32g Protein; 3g Carbohydrate; 1g Dietary Fiber; 157mg Cholesterol; 123mg Sodium. Exchanges: 4½ Lean Meat; ½ Vegetable; 2½ Fat.

SERVING SUGGESTIONS: Steamed red rose potatoes tossed with a little garlic butter, a big green salad, and a relish tray with baby carrots, sugar tomatoes, and radishes.

I also purchased a flat hole-y cookie sheet–looking thing. That's how I cook my fish without losing it through the grill slats.

The last things you need for the barbecue are grilling tools. I used to use my kitchen spatula till the day I burned the hair off my arm when I was turning chicken; that was enough to convince me.

Use real grilling tools and spend a few dollars on some nice ones. Lousy tools give you lousy results. Don't forget to get the wire brush, too. Keeping the grill immaculate will improve what you're eating immensely. "Burning off" the old food works only to a degree—you need the brush!

Week Five

DAY ONE: Chicken Lo Mein
DAY TWO: Steamed Citrus Ginger Fish
DAY THREE: Mexican Black Bean and Rice Salad
DAY FOUR: Chicken with Toasted Couscous Salad
DAY FIVE: Grilled Tuna Nicoise Salad
DAY SIX: Reyna's Crock-Pot Enchilada Casserole

SHOPPING LIST

MEAT

12 boneless, skinless chicken breast halves
6 fish fillets
4 tuna steaks (or other thick meaty fish)
1 pound extra-lean ground beef

CONDIMENTS

sesame oil
vegetable oil
olive oil
salsa
soy sauce (I prefer low sodium)
balsamic vinegar
Dijon mustard
1 3-ounce jar capers

PRODUCE

3 pounds onions (keep on hand)
1 head garlic (keep on hand)
1 head cabbage
6 cups lettuce greens
1 bunch carrots
mushrooms (you'll need 1½ cups, sliced)
2 lemons
4 limes (you'll need ¾ cup juice)
cherry tomatoes (you'll need 1 cup)
1 bunch cilantro
1 bunch parsley

1 bunch green onions
1½ pounds green beans
8 red potatoes
1 red onion
5 large tomatoes
1 red bell pepper
6 cups mixed lettuce greens
**baby carrots (1 meal)
**baby spinach (1 meal)
**sugar tomatoes (1 meal)
**radishes (1 meal)
**yellow squash (1 meal)
**2–3 heads lettuce (*not* Iceberg)

CANNED GOODS
1 14½-ounce can chicken broth
1 15-ounce can whole kernel corn
1 15-ounce can black beans
1 14½-ounce can whole tomatoes
1 6-ounce can tomato paste
1 can black olives
anchovy fillets, optional

SPICES
ginger
basil
pressed red pepper

DAIRY/DAIRY CASE
3 cups low-fat Cheddar cheese, shredded
orange juice
eggs

DRY GOODS
cornstarch
12 ounces angel hair pasta
couscous (whole wheat, if available)

brown rice (**additional brown rice for 1 meal if you follow
Serving Suggestions)

BAKERY
12 corn tortillas
**whole-grain rolls (2 meals)

CHICKEN LO MEIN

Serves 6

12 ounces angel hair pasta
3 teaspoons sesame oil
5 tablespoons chicken broth
5 tablespoons soy sauce (low sodium, if available)
1½ teaspoons cornstarch
⅛ teaspoon ground black pepper
1 tablespoon vegetable oil
2 cloves garlic, pressed
6 chicken breast halves, boneless, skinless, and cut into thin strips
3 cups cabbage, finely shredded
3 carrots, coarsely shredded
1½ cups fresh mushrooms, sliced
¾ cup onions, chopped

Cook pasta according to package directions. Transfer pasta to a large
bowl; add sesame oil and toss until coated. In a small bowl, stir together
the broth, soy sauce, cornstarch, and pepper; set aside.

In a skillet or a wok, heat oil over medium-high heat. Add garlic and
stir-fry for 30 seconds.

Add chicken strips and stir-fry about 3 minutes or until no longer
pink; remove from wok or skillet and cover to keep warm.

Add cabbage, carrots, mushrooms, and onions to the wok or skillet
and continue to stir-fry another 3 minutes. Add broth mixture to the
skillet. Stir-fry, mixing well, for 2 minutes more. Return chicken and
garlic to the skillet and heat through. Serve.

PER SERVING:
304 Calories; 14g Fat (41.3% calories from fat); 33g Protein; 11g Carbohydrate; 3g Dietary
Fiber; 93mg Cholesterol; 1012mg Sodium. Exchanges: 0 Grain (Starch); 4½ Lean Meat; 2 Vegetable; 0 Fat.

SERVING SUGGESTION: Serve with a salad.

STEAMED CITRUS GINGER FISH

Serves 6

4 cups orange juice
½ cup lime juice
3 tablespoons ground ginger
6 fish fillets
1½ tablespoons cornstarch
3 tablespoons water

In a saucepan, combine orange and lime juices and ginger. Place a vegetable steamer in the pot and bring to a boil. Place fish on the steamer and cover the pan. Lower heat and allow to simmer for about 8–10 minutes. (If you don't have a vegetable steamer, you can poach fish. Just place fish directly in the juice and proceed.)

Lift out steamer. With a spatula, carefully lift fish from steamer, place on a plate, and cover to keep warm. Increase heat to high and boil pan juices, uncovered, until reduced to about 1½ cups, about 10–12 minutes.

In a small bowl, combine cornstarch with 3 tablespoons water and mix well to blend. Add mixture to reduced pan juices; stir until boiling. Turn the heat down and allow sauce to thicken, still stirring as needed.

Top fish with sauce and serve.

PER SERVING:
223 Calories; 3g Fat (12.7% calories from fat); 25g Protein; 23g Carbohydrate; 1g Dietary Fiber;
36mg Cholesterol; 64mg Sodium. Exchanges: 0 Grain (Starch); 3½ Lean Meat; 1½ Fruit; 0 Fat.

SERVING SUGGESTIONS: Serve with brown rice, steamed squash, and a green salad.

DO AHEAD TIP: Make extra rice (3 cups, cooked) for tomorrow's recipe.

MEXICAN BLACK BEAN AND RICE SALAD

Serves 6

3 tomatoes, chopped
1 red bell pepper, chopped
½ cup lemon juice
1 cup cilantro, chopped
½ teaspoon basil
⅛ teaspoon red pepper flakes
1 15-ounce can whole kernel corn, drained
1 15-ounce can black beans, drained
1 tablespoon olive oil
1 onion, chopped
1 clove garlic, pressed
3 cups brown rice, cooked
Salt and pepper to taste
6 tablespoons salsa

In a large bowl, combine tomatoes, bell pepper, lemon juice, cilantro, basil, red pepper flakes, corn, and beans. Mix well and set aside.

In a medium saucepan, heat olive oil over medium-low heat. Add onion and sauté until translucent. Add garlic and sauté for another minute, then add to the tomato mixture. Now combine the rice and the vegetable mixtures, salt and pepper to taste. Top each portion with a tablespoon of salsa and serve.

PER SERVING:
571 Calories; 7g Fat (10.2% calories from fat); 23g Protein; 110g Carbohydrate; 15g Dietary Fiber; 0mg Cholesterol; 14mg Sodium. Exchanges: 6½ Grain (Starch); 1 Lean Meat; 1 Vegetable; 0 Fruit; 1 Fat.

SERVING SUGGESTION: Serve with whole-grain rolls.

✸ On a recent trip to one of my favorite stores, Trader Joe's, I discovered a couple of gems in the frozen-food section—little frozen cubes of pure, fresh garlic and little frozen cubes of pure, fresh basil. These little icy treasures contain nothing fake or phony so they don't taste icky like that jarred chopped garlic does or the way jarred pesto can taste. You get all the flavor of fresh without the hassle. The brand name is Dorot Vegetable Products. Trader Joe's is the only place I've seen them, but they could be in other stores.

Even if you can't find these handy products, no one says you can't make them yourself. It's fairly simple and well worth the time simply to chop some fresh basil leaves (use a food processor or blender—and just the leaves, no stems or buds) and a little water to make a thick paste and pack this flavorful goop into ice cube trays. When they're completely hard, transfer to a freezer-weight, zipper-topped plastic bag to avoid freezer burn.

Also, while perusing the frozen-food section, don't forget to check out the following products, all worthy of space in your freezer:

- chopped frozen onions. I much prefer to chop an onion fresh, but having these back-up onions in my freezer serves me well when in a total pinch.
- frozen chopped bell pepper. I bought a bag with yellow, red, and orange bell pepper strips. Again, another easy shortcut!
- frozen petite peas. Sometimes called baby peas. Either way, who cares as long as they make it into your freezer. The flavor, texture, and everything is ten times that of those bigger green gumballs. I accidentally purchased the big guys one time and tossed them because no one would touch them. The difference is that great.

CHICKEN WITH TOASTED COUSCOUS SALAD

Serves 6

¾ pound couscous (whole wheat, if available)
¼ cup fresh lemon juice
¼ cup fresh lime juice
¼ cup olive oil, divided
2 tablespoons fresh parsley, chopped
4 tablespoons fresh cilantro, chopped
½ cup red onion, chopped
1 cup cherry tomatoes, cut in half
Salt and pepper to taste
6 skinless, boneless chicken breast halves
½ cup green onions, chopped

Cook couscous according to package directions

In a large bowl, mix the lemon juice, lime juice and ¼ cup *less* 2 tablespoons of the olive oil together. Add couscous, parsley, cilantro, red onion, and tomatoes. Season with salt and pepper to taste. Chill while you prepare the chicken.

In a skillet, heat the reserved 2 tablespoons of olive oil over medium-high heat. Cook the chicken; add salt and pepper to taste. Cook the breasts until browned, 4 minutes or so on each side. Chicken needs to be cooked through.

Slice the cooked chicken breast halves into strips. Place strips over the couscous salad and sprinkle with chopped green onions.

PER SERVING:
298 Calories; 9g Fat; 10g Protein; 5g Carbohydrate; 1g Dietary Fiber; 0mg Cholesterol; 5mg Sodium. Exchanges: ½ Vegetable; 0 Fruit; 2 Fat.

SERVING SUGGESTIONS: A relish tray for the table is all you need. Include baby carrots, radishes, sugar tomatoes, and anything else you like.

DO AHEAD TIP: Cook potatoes, green beans, and eggs for tomorrow's Grilled Tuna Nicoise Salad.

GRILLED TUNA NICOISE SALAD

Serves 6

¾ cup olive oil

¼ cup balsamic vinegar

½ teaspoon Dijon mustard

1 tablespoon green onion, minced

2 tablespoons fresh parsley, chopped

Salt and pepper to taste

6 cups lettuce greens (your choice of what kind—use a mixture, but no Iceberg)

8 red potatoes, washed and halved

1½ pounds green beans, ends and strings removed

2 eggs, hard-cooked, peeled and quartered

4 tuna steaks (or other thick meaty fish)

2 large tomatoes, cut into wedges

12 black olives

⅛ cup capers

Mix first 7 ingredients (oil through pepper) well with a wire whisk and refrigerate. Wash and dry lettuce greens and refrigerate. Cook potatoes, beans, and eggs and refrigerate (unless you used the Do Ahead Tip). Grill tuna over medium-hot coals until cooked to your liking.

To assemble, arrange the lettuce greens as a base on the bottom of each dinner plate. Place potatoes, green beans, tomato wedges, and egg quarters evenly around the plate. Break up grilled tuna into big chunks and pile them in the center. Scatter the black olives and capers on top. Then pour dressing over the top and serve. Or do what I do—put everything into a big mixing bowl, toss together, and serve evenly on six dinner plates.

PER SERVING:

471 Calories; 20g Fat (38.9% calories from fat); 7g Protein; 17g Carbohydrate; 7g Dietary Fiber; 10mg Cholesterol; 702mg Sodium. Exchanges: ½ Lean Meat; 3 Vegetable; 0 Fruit; 8½ Fat; 0 Other Carbohydrates.

SERVING SUGGESTION: Some whole-grain rolls, and you're set.

REYNA'S CROCK-POT ENCHILADA CASSEROLE

Serves 6

1 14½-ounce can whole tomatoes
1 onion, cut into fourths
2 cloves garlic, pressed
½ teaspoon ground red pepper
½ teaspoon salt
1 6-ounce can tomato paste
12 corn tortillas
1 pound extra-lean ground beef, browned and drained
3 cups low-fat Cheddar cheese, shredded

In a blender or food processor, blend tomatoes and their liquid with onion and garlic. Pour into medium-size saucepan. Add ground red pepper, salt, and tomato paste and blend again.

Place 4 tortillas in bottom of Crock-Pot. Add one-third of the ground beef, one-third of the tomato sauce, and one-third of the Cheddar cheese. Repeat each layer two more times.

Cover Crock-Pot and cook on low for 6–8 hours.

PER SERVING:
384 Calories; 14g Fat (29.3% calories from fat); 19g Protein; 34g Carbohydrate; 5g Dietary Fiber; 59mg Cholesterol; 840mg Sodium. Exchanges: 1½ Grain (Starch); 2 Lean Meat; 2 Vegetable; 2½ Fat.

SERVING SUGGESTION: Serve with a spinach salad to round things off.

Week Six

DAY ONE: Chinese Stir-Fried Chicken and Rice
DAY TWO: Orange-Poached Fish with Rosemary
DAY THREE: Texas Caviar Salad with Lone Star Vinaigrette
DAY FOUR: Vietnamese-Style Chicken Salad
DAY FIVE: Honey Mustard Chicken Drumsticks
DAY SIX: Crock-Pot Stuffed Peppers

SHOPPING LIST

MEAT
6 boneless, skinless chicken breast halves
6 fish fillets
¾ pound extra-lean ground beef
12 chicken drumsticks, skin removed

CONDIMENTS
dark sesame oil
vegetable oil
dry sherry
balsamic vinegar
olive oil
Tabasco sauce
honey
ketchup
Worcestershire sauce
soy sauce (I prefer low sodium)
rice vinegar
Dijon mustard
low-fat mayonnaise

PRODUCE
3 pounds onions (keep on hand)
2 heads garlic (keep on hand)
1 head green cabbage (**additional cabbage for coleslaw for
    1 meal if you follow Serving Suggestions)

1 head red cabbage
6 cups mixed salad greens
1 bunch carrots
mushrooms (you'll need 1½ cups sliced)
1 lemon
1 bunch cilantro
1 bunch green onions
1 red onion
3 tomatoes
6 red bell peppers
1 green bell pepper
**baby carrots (3 meals)
**baby spinach (1 meal)
**zucchini (1 meal)
**green beans (1 meal)
**cherry tomatoes (3 meals)
**potatoes (1 meal)
**radishes (1 meal)

CANNED GOODS
1 4-ounce can diced green chilies
1 8-ounce can tomato sauce

SPICES
rosemary
cumin
mint flakes
garlic powder

DAIRY/DAIRY CASE
orange juice
1 cup low-fat Cheddar cheese, shredded
**low-fat sour cream (1 meal)

DRY GOODS
4 ounces angel hair pasta

brown rice (**additional brown rice for 1 meal of you follow
    Serving Suggestions)
**couscous (whole wheat, if available) (1 meal)

FROZEN FOODS
black-eyed peas (you'll need 3¾ cups)
1 10-ounce package corn
1 10-ounce package peas (petite or baby peas are best)

BAKERY
**whole-grain rolls (1 meal)

CHINESE STIR-FRIED CHICKEN AND RICE

Serves 6

3 tablespoons vegetable oil, divided
3 boneless, skinless chicken breast halves, cut into strips
1 onion, chopped
1½ cups mushrooms, sliced
¼ cup dry sherry
4 tablespoons soy sauce
3 cloves garlic, pressed
6 cups cooked brown rice
1 cup green onions, chopped
1½ cups green peas, frozen (petite or baby are best)
2 tablespoons dark sesame oil

In a skillet, heat 1 tablespoon of the oil in a skillet over medium-high heat. Add chicken and cook, stirring occasionally. Add chopped onion and cook another minute. Add remaining oil, then add mushrooms, sherry, soy sauce, and garlic and cook about 1 minute. Then add rice and cook about 3 minutes, stirring frequently.

Slice the green onions, using the white and green tops. Add to skillet and stir well. Add peas and sesame oil and cook, stirring, 1 minute more to heat through.

PER SERVING:
464 Calories; 12g Fat (24.3% calories from fat); 23g Protein; 61g Carbohydrate; 3g Dietary Fiber; 46mg Cholesterol; 742mg Sodium. Exchanges: 3½ Grain (Starch); 2 Lean Meat; ½ Vegetable; 1 Fat.

SERVING SUGGESTIONS: Serve with a big spinach salad and some baby carrots.

ORANGE-POACHED FISH WITH ROSEMARY

Serves 6

1 tablespoon cooking oil
3 tablespoons red onion, *diced*
Salt and pepper to taste
⅓ cup fresh orange juice
½ teaspoon dried rosemary, *pressed*
6 fish fillets

In a large skillet, heat the oil over medium heat and cook the onion until translucent.

Sprinkle with salt and pepper and add orange juice and rosemary; stir and cook for 1 minute.

Add fish and lower heat to a simmer. Cover and cook 8–10 minutes, or until fish flakes easily with a fork. Serve fish and spoon sauce over the top.

PER SERVING:
218 Calories; 4g Fat (16.7% calories from fat); 41g Protein; 2g Carbohydrate; trace Dietary Fiber; 99mg Cholesterol; 303mg Sodium. Exchanges: 0 Grain (Starch); 5½ Lean Meat; 0 Vegetable; 0 Fruit; ½ Fat.

SERVING SUGGESTIONS: Couscous and sautéed zucchini with halved cherry tomatoes.

TEXAS CAVIAR SALAD WITH LONE STAR VINAIGRETTE

Serves 6

3¾ *cups frozen black-eyed peas*
2¼ *cups tomatoes, chopped*
1 *small green bell pepper, chopped*
1 *onion, chopped*
3 *tablespoons canned mild green chilies, chopped*
3 *cloves garlic, pressed*
3 *tablespoons balsamic vinegar*
3 *tablespoons olive oil*
6 *tablespoons cilantro, chopped*
1 *teaspoon cumin*
Salt and pepper to taste
6 *cups mixed salad greens*

In a saucepan, cook black-eyed peas according to package instructions; drain, cool, and set aside.

In a large bowl, mix together black-eyed peas, tomatoes, bell pepper, onion, green chilies, and garlic. Cover and refrigerate. In a small bowl, whisk together the vinegar and olive oil, half the cilantro, cumin, and salt and pepper to taste. Next add the dressing to the bean mixture and mix well. Serve on individual plates on a bed of 1 cup mixed salad greens and top with remaining cilantro.

PER SERVING:
198 Calories; 7g Fat (32.1% calories from fat); 5g Protein; 11g Carbohydrate; 4g Dietary Fiber; 0mg Cholesterol; 11mg Sodium. Exchanges: ½ Grain (Starch); ½ Lean Meat; 1 Vegetable; 3 Fat; 0 Other Carbohydrates.

SERVING SUGGESTIONS: Serve with whole-grain rolls.

DO AHEAD TIP: Cook chicken for tomorrow's Vietnamese-Style Chicken Salad.

VIETNAMESE-STYLE CHICKEN SALAD

Serves 6

⅓ cup rice vinegar
2 tablespoons vegetable oil
½ teaspoon salt
½ teaspoon Tabasco sauce
4 ounces angel hair pasta
3 chicken breast halves, cooked and chopped
3 cups shredded green cabbage
3 cups shredded red cabbage
1½ cups shredded carrots
3 green onions, sliced diagonally
½ cup chopped cilantro
1 teaspoon dried mint flakes

In a small bowl, combine the first 4 ingredients and set aside. In the meantime, cook pasta according to package directions; drain, rinse, and place in a large bowl.

Combine chicken, remaining salad ingredients, and dressing; toss and serve.

PER SERVING:
125 Calories; 5g Fat (32.4% calories from fat); 2g Protein; 21g Carbohydrate; 3g Dietary Fiber; 0mg Cholesterol; 215mg Sodium. Exchanges: 1½ Vegetable; 1 Fat; 1 Other Carbohydrates.

SERVING SUGGESTIONS: A relish tray of cherry tomatoes, baby carrots, and radishes would be nice.

DO AHEAD TIP: Make marinade and marinate chicken for tomorrow's Honey Mustard Chicken Drumsticks.

HONEY MUSTARD CHICKEN DRUMSTICKS

Serves 6

12 chicken drumsticks, skin removed
9 cloves garlic, pressed
4 tablespoons honey
3 tablespoons Dijon mustard
3 tablespoons soy sauce
1 tablespoon lemon juice
½ teaspoon pepper

Using a knife, slash two separate, parallel gashes in the thick part of the drumstick. This will improve both penetration of the marinade and the cooking time.

In a large zipper-topped plastic bag, combine garlic, honey, mustard, soy sauce, lemon juice, and pepper. Add slashed drumsticks and toss to coat evenly. Cover and refrigerate overnight.

Light the barbecue and grill over medium-hot coals, turning every 3 minutes until chicken is cooked through.

PER SERVING:
177 Calories; 4g Fat (19.9% calories from fat); 19g Protein; 16g Carbohydrate; 1g Dietary Fiber; 58mg Cholesterol; 670mg Sodium. Exchanges: 0 Grain (Starch); 2½ Lean Meat; ¼ Vegetable; 0 Fruit; 0 Fat; 1 Other Carbohydrates.

SERVING SUGGESTIONS: Coleslaw (shredded cabbage mixed with a little mayo), steamed potatoes, and some baby carrots.

CROCK-POT STUFFED PEPPERS

Serves 6

1 10-ounce package frozen corn
¾ pound extra-lean ground beef
1 8-ounce can tomato sauce
Salt and pepper to taste
½ teaspoon garlic powder
1 cup Cheddar cheese, shredded
½ teaspoon Worcestershire sauce
¼ cup onion, chopped
6 red bell peppers
2 tablespoons ketchup
3 tablespoons water

In a large bowl, combine all ingredients *except* bell peppers, ketchup, and water. Stir well.

Stuff peppers two-thirds full and place carefully in Crock-Pot. Pour 3 tablespoons of water into the Crock-Pot and pour ketchup over tops of peppers.

Cover and cook on low 7–9 hours or on high 3–4 hours.

PER SERVING:
315 Calories; 17g Fat; 21g Protein; 15g Carbohydrate; 2g Dietary Fiber; 72mg Cholesterol; 546mg Sodium. Exchanges: ½ Grain (Starch); 2½ Lean Meat; ½ Vegetable; 2 Fat; 0 Other Carbohydrates.

SERVING SUGGESTIONS: Serve with brown rice, steamed green beans, and a dollop of low-fat sour cream.

Week Seven

DAY ONE: Garbanzo Bean Salad
DAY TWO: Tuna Tarragon
DAY THREE: Grilled Asian Chicken
DAY FOUR: Summer Pasta Primavera
DAY FIVE: BBQ Gyros
DAY SIX: Crock-Nutty Chicken

SHOPPING LIST

MEAT
12 boneless, skinless chicken breast halves
6 tuna fillets (or other firm-fleshed fish)
1 pound extra-lean ground beef

CONDIMENTS
vegetable oil
white wine
olive oil
Tabasco sauce
honey
soy sauce (I prefer low sodium)
tahini salad dressing (in the dressing section; also called
   sesame dressing)
Italian salad dressing
peanut butter

PRODUCE
3 pounds onions (keep on hand)
1 head garlic (keep on hand)
2 lemons
1 bunch green onions
2 red onions
2 cucumbers
2 tomatoes
1 cup fresh corn (or use frozen, if fresh not available)

1 zucchini (**additional zucchini for 1 meal if you follow
     Serving Suggestions)
cherry tomatoes (**additional cherry tomatoes for 1 meal
     if you follow Serving Suggestions)
**corn on the cob (1 meal)
**celery (1 meal)
**sugar tomatoes (1 meal)
**baby carrots (2 meals)
**baby spinach (1 meal)
**yellow squash (1 meal)
**red potatoes (1 meal)
**green beans (1 meal)
**radishes (1 meal)
**2–3 heads lettuce (*not* Iceberg)

CANNED GOODS
2 15-ounce cans garbanzo beans
1 15-ounce can black olives, pitted
1 15-ounce can chicken broth

SPICES
curry powder
chili powder
garlic powder
tarragon
oregano
onion powder
thyme
red pepper flakes
ginger
white pepper

DAIRY/DAIRY CASE
orange juice
butter (I keep 1 pound unsalted in the freezer)
Feta cheese (you'll need 1 ounce)
milk

Romano cheese
plain yogurt (you'll need 1 cup)

DRY GOODS
flour
1 pound ziti pasta
cornstarch
brown rice (**additional brown rice for 2 meals if you follow
    Serving Suggestions)

FROZEN FOODS
1 10-ounce package corn, if fresh not available

BAKERY
6 whole-wheat pitas

GARBANZO BEAN SALAD

Serves 6

2 15-ounce cans garbanzo beans, drained
1 cucumber, sliced
12 cherry tomatoes, halved
½ red onion, chopped
2 cloves garlic, pressed
1 15-ounce can black olives, pitted, drained, and chopped
1 ounce Feta cheese, crumbled
¼ cup Italian salad dressing
½ lemon, juiced
Salt and pepper to taste

In a large bowl, combine beans, cucumber, tomatoes, red onion, garlic, olives, and cheese and toss together lightly.

In another bowl, whisk together salad dressing, lemon juice, and salt and pepper to taste. Pour over bean mixture and lightly toss again. If you can, refrigerate for an hour or two before serving. If not, no big deal!

PER SERVING:
417 Calories; 7g Fat (15.4% calories from fat); 22g Protein; 69g Carbohydrate; 20g Dietary Fiber; 3mg Cholesterol; 203mg Sodium. Exchanges: 4½ Grain (Starch); 1 Lean Meat; 1 Vegetable; 0 Fruit; ½ Fat.

SERVING SUGGESTIONS: A nice relish tray with veggies you like: baby carrots, celery sticks, sugar tomatoes, radishes, etc.

TUNA TARRAGON

Serves 6

> 6 *tuna fillets (or other firm-fleshed fish)*
> 2 *cups white wine*
> 4 *teaspoons dried tarragon, crumbled*
> *Flour*
> *Salt and pepper to taste*
> 2 *tablespoons butter*
> 2 *tablespoons olive oil*

In a large zipper-topped plastic bag, marinate tuna in white wine and tarragon for 2 hours; drain, reserving wine marinade.

To cook, rinse tuna steaks and pat dry; dust lightly with flour, sprinkle with salt and pepper, and sauté in butter and oil on both sides until brown and fish flakes with a fork when cooked. Remove fish and keep warm.

Add the reserved marinade to the skillet and cook on medium-high heat until the wine is reduced to half.

Serve with sauce spooned over the fish.

PER SERVING:
403 Calories; 18g Fat (46.6% calories from fat); 44g Protein; 1g Carbohydrate; trace Dietary Fiber; 82mg Cholesterol; 117mg Sodium. Exchanges: 0 Grain (Starch); 6 Lean Meat; 1½ Fat.

SERVING SUGGESTIONS: Steamed red potatoes, sautéed green beans with cherry tomatoes, and a big salad.

DO AHEAD TIP: Marinate chicken for tomorrow's Grilled Asian Chicken.

GRILLED ASIAN CHICKEN

Serves 6

½ cup soy sauce
¼ cup lemon juice
¼ cup orange juice
¼ cup vegetable oil
3 green onions, minced
1 tablespoon curry powder
1 tablespoon tahini salad dressing
2 teaspoons chili powder
1 teaspoon garlic powder
6 boneless, skinless chicken breast halves

In a large zipper-topped plastic bag, combine all ingredients except the chicken and squish it around to mix. Next add the chicken, seal the bag, and squish it around again, this time to completely coat the chicken. Allow chicken to marinate 8 hours or so. Turn it as you can, but don't lose sleep if you can't.

Light the barbecue and allow grill to heat to medium-low heat. Remove chicken from marinade and place on grill. Grill chicken, turning and basting with marinade frequently. Cook about 10 minutes or until done.

PER SERVING:
181 Calories; 8g Fat (12% calories from fat); 21g Protein; 6g Carbohydrate; 1g Dietary Fiber; 0mg Cholesterol; 1407mg Sodium. Exchanges: 0 Grain (Starch); ½ Vegetable; 0 Fruit; ½ Fat; 0 Other Carbohydrates.

SERVING SUGGESTIONS: Brown rice, corn on the cob (do on the grill!), and steamed yellow squash and zucchini.

Serves 6

1 pound ziti pasta
1 tablespoon olive oil
1 medium red onion, chopped
2 cups chopped zucchini
1 clove garlic, minced
2 cups chopped fresh tomato
1 cup fresh corn (if available) or 1 cup frozen corn, thawed
¼ teaspoon hot red pepper flakes, optional; or add more if you like it hot
1 cup non-fat milk
½ cup freshly grated Romano cheese
Salt and pepper to taste

Prepare pasta according to package directions; drain and set aside.

In a skillet, heat the oil over medium heat. Add the red onion and zucchini and cook until the onion is golden. Reduce heat to medium and add the garlic, tomato, corn, red pepper flakes, milk, and Romano cheese. Stir until the cheese is melted and the vegetables are hot. Add the pasta and mix thoroughly. Season with salt and pepper to taste.

PER SERVING:
398 Calories; 6g Fat (13.8% calories from fat); 16g Protein; 70g Carbohydrate; 4g Dietary Fiber; 6mg Cholesterol; 163mg Sodium. Exchanges: 4 Grain (Starch); ½ Lean Meat; 1 Vegetable; 0 Non-Fat Milk; 1 Fat.

SERVING SUGGESTIONS: Serve with a big green salad and a sprinkling of Romano over the top of your pasta, if desired.

BBQ GYROS

1 pound extra-lean ground beef
2 tablespoons oregano
1 tablespoon onion powder
2½ teaspoons thyme
1 cup plain yogurt
¼ cup cucumber, seeded and finely chopped
1 onion, finely chopped
2 teaspoons olive oil
2½ teaspoons garlic powder
Salt and white pepper to taste
6 whole-wheat pitas, cut in half

Light the barbecue so it can preheat. In a large bowl, combine first 4 ingredients thoroughly. Wet your hands and shape into 12 thin patties and grill, turning once, until done as desired.

In a small bowl, make the sauce by combining the yogurt, cucumber, onion, and olive oil. Add garlic powder, salt and white pepper to taste. Assemble gyro sandwiches by placing 1 meat patty in each pita half and topping with yogurt sauce.

PER SERVING:
108 Calories; 7g Fat (61.7% calories from fat); 6g Protein; 4g Carbohydrate; 1g Dietary Fiber; 24mg Cholesterol; 130mg Sodium. Exchanges: 0 Grain (Starch); ½ Lean Meat; ½ Vegetable; 0 Non-Fat Milk; 1 Fat; 0 Other Carbohydrates.

SERVING SUGGESTION: A great big green salad is all you need.

CROCK-NUTTY CHICKEN

Serves 6

½ cup peanut butter
6 tablespoons soy sauce, divided
3½ teaspoons onion, minced
2 cloves garlic, pressed
Several drops Tabasco sauce
¼ teaspoon ground ginger
6 boneless, skinless chicken breast halves
3 tablespoons honey
1 tablespoon butter, melted
2 cups chicken broth
2 tablespoons cornstarch

Mix peanut butter, 3 tablespoons of the soy sauce, onion, garlic, Tabasco, and ginger.

Spread peanut butter mixture on one side of each chicken breast half. Fold in half; close with small skewer or toothpick. Place in Crock-Pot. In a bowl, mix remaining 3 tablespoons soy sauce with honey, butter, and broth and pour over chicken. Cover and cook on low for 4–5 hours.

Remove chicken from Crock-Pot and keep warm. Transfer remaining cooking liquid to a saucepan and heat to a boil. In a small bowl, dissolve cornstarch in small amount of cold water and stir into sauce. Cook for about 5 minutes or until sauce thickens nicely. Serve with sauce spooned over the top of chicken. Don't forget to remove toothpicks before serving!

PER SERVING:
478 Calories; 20g Fat (42% calories from fat); 40g Protein; 16g Carbohydrate; 2g Dietary Fiber; 98mg Cholesterol; 1497mg Sodium. Exchanges: ½ Grain (Starch); 5½ Lean Meat; ½ Vegetable; 2½ Fat; ½ Other Carbohydrates.

SERVING SUGGESTIONS: Brown rice, a spinach salad, and some baby carrots.

Week Eight

DAY ONE: Chicken Diane
DAY TWO: Poor Guy's Lobster
DAY THREE: Cajun Chicken Caesar Sandwiches
DAY FOUR: Summer Bean Salad
DAY FIVE: Mega Cheesyburgers
DAY SIX: Swedish Beef Crock-Pot

SHOPPING LIST

MEAT

12 boneless, skinless chicken breast halves
6 frozen cod fillets (*frozen is a must*)
12 strips turkey bacon
1 pound round steak
1½ pounds extra-lean ground beef

CONDIMENTS

white vinegar
olive oil
Dijon mustard
balsamic vinegar
low-fat Caesar salad dressing
**mustard (1 meal)
**mayonnaise (1 meal)
**ketchup (1 meal)
**pickles (1 meal)

PRODUCE

3 pounds onions (keep on hand)
1 head garlic (keep on hand)
3 lemons, or 2 lemons and 1 lime
1 bunch green onions
2 heads romaine lettuce
1 green bell pepper
4 scallions
**tomatoes (3 meals)
**baby carrots (1 meal)

**sugar tomatoes (1 meal)
**fresh basil (1 meal)
**broccoli (1 meal)
**patty pan squash (1 meal)
**red potatoes (1 meal)
**green beans (1 meal)
**radishes (1 meal)
**2–3 heads lettuce (*not* Iceberg)

CANNED GOODS
1 15-ounce can black beans
1 14½-ounce can Italian tomatoes
2 15-ounce cans chicken broth

SPICES
Cajun seasoning
dill weed

DAIRY/DAIRY CASE
Swiss cheese, grated
butter (I keep 1 pound unsalted in the freezer)
low-fat sour cream (you'll need 1 cup)
Parmesan cheese
Romano cheese

DRY GOODS
flour
**egg noodles (1 meal)
**brown rice (1 meal)

FROZEN FOODS
1 package peas (petite or baby peas are best)
1 package corn

BAKERY
6 whole-wheat sandwich rolls
**6 whole-wheat buns (1 meal)

CHICKEN DIANE

Serves 6

6 boneless, skinless chicken breast halves
Salt and pepper to taste
2 tablespoons olive oil
2 tablespoons butter
4 tablespoons green onions, chopped
Juice of ½ lemon or lime
3 teaspoons Dijon mustard
⅓ cup chicken broth

Place chicken breast halves 2 at a time in a freezer-quality, gallon-size zipper-topped plastic bag. Sprinkle with salt and pepper. Take a rolling pin and roll to flatten slightly.

In a skillet, heat 1 tablespoon each of the oil and butter over medium-high heat. Add chicken and cook for 4 minutes on each side till completely cooked through. Remove and keep warm.

Add green onions, lemon juice, and mustard to pan. Cook for 15 seconds, whisking constantly. Whisk in broth and stir until sauce is smooth. Whisk in remaining butter and oil.

Spoon sauce over chicken and serve immediately.

PER SERVING.
363 Calories; 16g Fat (53% calories from fat); 31g Protein; trace Carbohydrate; trace Dietary Fiber; 108mg Cholesterol; 371mg Sodium. Exchanges: 0 Grain (Starch); 4 ½ Lean Meat; 0 Vegetable; 2½ Fat.

SERVING SUGGESTIONS: Brown rice, sautéed patty pan squash and tomatoes, and a nice green salad.

POOR GUY'S LOBSTER

Serves 6

6 frozen cod fillets (frozen is a must!)
water to cover
3 tablespoons salt
3 tablespoons white vinegar
melted butter
lemon juice

In a saucepan, place frozen fillets and cold water just to cover; add the salt. Bring to a boil; lower heat, and cook for 10 minutes. Drain.

Cover again with cold water, and this time add the white vinegar. Bring to boil; lower heat, and cook 10 minutes more. Drain.

Serve, dipping each bite into melted butter and lemon juice.

PER SERVING:
92 Calories; trace Fat (doesn't include dipping butter); 9g Protein; 3g Carbohydrate; 0g Dietary Fiber; 0mg Cholesterol; 3339mg Sodium. Exchanges: 0 Other Carbohydrates.

SERVING SUGGESTIONS: Steamed red potatoes, steamed green beans, and a big salad.

CAJUN CHICKEN CAESAR SANDWICHES

Serves 6

12 strips turkey bacon
2 tablespoons olive oil
6 chicken breast halves, boneless, skinless, and cut into strips
1½ teaspoons Cajun seasoning mix
½ head romaine lettuce, rinsed, dried, and chopped
¼ cup Caesar salad dressing (low fat)
¼ cup Romano cheese, grated
6 whole-wheat sandwich rolls

In skillet over medium-high heat, cook bacon until evenly brown. Crumble and set aside.

In the same skillet, heat the oil over medium-high heat and add the chicken and seasoning mix. Cook chicken about 4 minutes on each side, or until cooked through. Remove from heat and set aside.

In a small bowl, combine romaine lettuce, enough dressing to coat, Romano cheese, and bacon. Toast buns and place chicken on one side of the bun, then the salad mixture; close and serve.

PER SERVING:
673 Calories; 51g Fat (69.9% calories from fat); 41g Protein; 9g Carbohydrate; 2g Dietary Fiber; 133mg Cholesterol; 1424mg Sodium. Exchanges: 5½ Lean Meat; ½ Vegetable; ½ Fruit; 6½ Fat; 0 Other Carbohydrates.

SERVING SUGGESTION: Serve with sliced tomatoes drizzled with balsamic vinegar and little olive oil. Add fresh basil if available!

DO AHEAD TIP: Make marinade and marinate beans overnight or start the marinating in the morning.

THE FROZEN CHOSEN

There are many recipes in this book that are well worth their weight in gold—or maybe we should make that ice. Doubling a favorite recipe is a good way to a get a jump on stocking your freezer for a rainy day. If you use a freezer-quality zipper-topped plastic bag and mark it with the contents and date, you can keep your freezer organized and functional. (Sharpie pens work the best—keep your Sharpie in the box of freezer bags if you know what's good for you; otherwise it will never be heard from again.)

But knowing what to freeze is crucial. Here's a few rules of thumb for deciding on what to freeze:

- cooked chicken and turkey in casseroles
- stews, soups, and noodle dishes generally work well (the exception would be stir-fries that rely on fresh vegetables, and foods with large amounts of potatoes)
- meat loaves and burger-type meals
- most anything with cooked dried beans, rice, or pasta.

What doesn't freeze well:

- egg dishes—especially egg whites
- russet potatoes—a waxier type of potato is okay, like red rose, but still not great when defrosted
- any salad type of meal with fresh lettuce, tomatoes, etc. Mayonnaise is also iffy and will usually separate once thawed.

To use a frozen casserole or other frozen food:

First, allow food to thaw overnight in the refrigerator. When you're ready to reheat it, preheat the oven to the temperature the recipe called for in the first place. Then bake the food for one-third to one-half again as long as the recipe called for. Most frozen food combinations (like casseroles) will take more time to cook than a freshly prepared one.

SUMMER BEAN SALAD

1 16-ounce can black beans, rinsed and drained

1 14½-ounce can Italian tomatoes, drained

2 cups frozen peas (petite or baby peas are best)

1 cup frozen corn

1 small onion, chopped

⅓ cup green bell pepper, chopped

2 tablespoons balsamic vinegar

2 tablespoons olive oil

1 clove garlic, pressed

Salt and pepper to taste

1 head romaine lettuce, chopped

In a large bowl, combine the first 6 ingredients (beans through bell pepper).

In a small bowl, combine the vinegar, oil, garlic, salt, and pepper to make the dressing. Pour over bean mixture.

Toss gently to coat. Cover and refrigerate for at least 8 hours (make in the morning or the night before). Serve beans on a bed of chopped romaine lettuce.

PER SERVING:
354 Calories; 2g Fat (4.7% calories from fat); 22g Protein; 66g Carbohydrates; 18g Dietary Fiber; 0mg Cholesterol; 249mg Sodium. Exchanges: 4 Grain (Starch); 1 Lean Meat; 1½ Vegetable; 0 Fat.

SERVING SUGGESTIONS: Serve with a relish tray of baby carrots, sugar tomatoes, radishes, and whatever else you would like.

MEGA CHEESYBURGERS

Serves 6

1½ *pounds extra-lean ground beef*
¾ *cup Swiss cheese, grated*
½ *cup Parmesan cheese, grated*
1 *clove garlic, pressed*
4 *scallions, minced*
1 *tablespoon Dijon mustard*

In a bowl, mix all ingredients together. Wet your hands and press firmly into patties.

Light the barbecue. Cook patties over medium-high heat until done to your liking.

PER SERVING:
275 Calories; 18g Fat (28% calories from fat); 21g Protein; 2g Carbohydrate; 1g Dietary Fiber; 18mg Cholesterol; 200mg Sodium. Exchanges: 1 Lean Meat; ½ Vegetable; ½ Fat; 0 Other Carbohydrates.

SERVING SUGGESTIONS: Serve on whole-wheat buns with all the condiments; we like mustard, mayo, ketchup, tomato, onions, and pickles. A big salad would round out the rest of the meal.

SWEDISH BEEF CROCK-POT

Serves 6

1 *pound round steak, cut into 2-inch cubes*
1 *onion, sliced*
Salt and pepper to taste
¾ *cup chicken broth*
¼ *cup flour*
¼ *cup cold water*
1 *teaspoon dill weed*
1 *cup low-fat sour cream*

In the Crock-Pot, place the beef, onion, and salt and pepper to taste. Add the broth and cook on low for 6–8 hours.

Remove meat from Crock-Pot. Pour remaining juices in a saucepan, heat on medium-high heat, and thicken with flour dissolved in ¼ cup cold water and mixed well (or use a jar and shake for a lumpless blend). When sauce is thickened, remove from heat and stir in sour cream. Serve with sauce spooned over the top of the meat.

PER SERVING:
469 Calories; 15g Fat (31.2% calories from fat); 38g Protein; 7g Carbohydrate; 1g Dietary Fiber; 129mg Cholesterol; 117mg Sodium. Exchanges: ½ Grain (Starch); 5 Lean Meat; ½ Vegetable; 0 Non-Fat Milk; 3 Fat.

SERVING SUGGESTIONS: Serve on egg noodles with steamed broccoli and a salad.

ON THE SIDE: NICE AND EASY

Getting dinner on the table sometime before nine P.M. is one of the reasons why I consider side dishes to be unnecessary "recipes." It's a no-brainer to steam two vegetables at once, or throw some squash and potatoes in the oven at the same time that your dinner is cooking. You can fling together a green salad in the time it takes to set the table. Who needs a recipe for doing that?

Keeping it simple is the key to making successful family dinners a reality. I am adamant about that. I even debated if I should write this chapter—I don't want people to get hung up on "side dishes" in everyday cooking. With today's busy families, being able to sit down together for dinner is often done in between activities—like Junior's baseball practice and Suzie's ballet lesson. Simplicity is critical for making it all happen.

With that caveat, I have some mostly non-recipe-type recipes (if you can wrap your mind around that one, we speak the same language) to consider for side dishes with your weekly meals. This is sort of a bonus. As you'll notice in the weekly menus, the Serving Suggestions I make include very simple side dishes and rarely go with something requiring more than one step. However, there are always exceptions!

ROASTED RED POTATOES

Serves 6

1 pound red potatoes, quartered or halved, depending on size
2 tablespoons olive oil
Salt and pepper, to taste

Preheat oven to 400 degrees F. Toss potatoes in olive oil, salt and pepper to taste, place on a cookie sheet, and bake for about 20 minutes or so. Turn over once and continue cooking till golden brown.

PER SERVING:
64 Calories; trace Fat (1.0% calories from fat); 2g Protein; 15g Carbohydrate; 1g Dietary Fiber; 0mg Cholesterol; 68mg Sodium. Exchanges: 1 Grain (Starch); 0 Other Carbohydrates.

VARIATIONS: You can use a variety of different potatoes for the same effect. Use big russets and call them Oven Fries (same idea). Add Parmesan cheese (2 tablespoons) and call them Roasted Cheese Potatoes. Add some garlic powder (1 teaspoon), and you have Garlic Roasted Potatoes.

GOOD OLD-FASHIONED MASHED POTATOES

Serves 6

4 large russet potatoes, peeled and quartered
3 tablespoons unsalted butter
¼ cup milk
Salt and pepper to taste

In a large saucepan, boil potatoes for 15–20 minutes or until potatoes are tender when pierced with a fork. Drain.

Add butter and milk and mash with a potato masher until smooth. Add salt and pepper to taste.

PER SERVING:
121 Calories; 6g Fat (44.7% calories from fat); 2g Protein; 15g Carbohydrate; 1g Dietary Fiber; 17mg Cholesterol; 11mg Sodium. Exchanges: 1 Grain (Starch); 0 Non-Fat Milk; 1 Fat.

VARIATIONS: To make these taters a little lower in fat, skip the butter and use ¼ cup Neufchatel cheese and skim milk. Still creamy and rich, but with only 1 gram of fat.

Quick Garlic Mashed Potatoes. Add 1 teaspoon garlic powder at the same time as the salt and pepper.

Roasted Garlic Mashed Potatoes. Add one head of roasted garlic. To roast garlic, trim a small portion off the top of the head to expose cloves. Place trimmed garlic head on a square of aluminum foil. Drizzle with the olive oil. Seal package and place in a 400 degree F oven for 40 minutes. Remove from oven and let cool. When cool enough to handle, hold the whole head and squish the whole thing into your potatoes, as if you're squeezing a tube of toothpaste (trust me, it'll be fabulous!). Use the potato masher to mash it in. Throw away the papery outside of the garlic head.

SO-EASY, YOU-DON'T-NEED-A-RECIPE COLESLAW

I love a good coleslaw with the right dish. The crunch and tangy sweetness of the flavors are perfect with certain spicy foods.

Anyway, this is how to make it really, really fast—no recipe, no measurements. You're just gonna have to trust me on this, but I know you'll like it.

1 bag of already shredded, ready-to-go coleslaw from the grocery store
Mayonnaise (low-fat, if you're trying to watch fat grams)
Rice vinegar

In a bowl, pour in as much coleslaw as you need. Now add a little mayonnaise (go easy), stir, and if it looks dry, add some more; if it looks about right, leave it. You don't want it swimming in mayo. Now add a touch of rice vinegar. The ratio I use is about 1 teaspoon vinegar to 1 tablespoon mayo—that should help you in your measuring. The rice vinegar is slightly sweet, so it gives the coleslaw that hint of sweetness without being over the top.

That's it! Now serve or refrigerate for later.

VARIATION: Use half mayo and half sesame oil, the same rice vinegar, a handful of chopped cilantro, and some dry roasted peanuts for a to-die-for Asian coleslaw. You can make this a main course just by adding some sliced grilled chicken. Oops, I'm getting way ahead of myself here!

SO-EASY, YOU-DON'T-NEED-A-RECIPE POTATO SALAD

Potatoes
Apple cider vinegar
Mayonnaise
Celery
Onion
Hard-boiled egg, optional
Salt and pepper to taste

Believe it or not, potato salad can be made very similarly to coleslaw. After you have boiled the potatoes and drained them, toss them in a large bowl with a little vinegar (apple cider is what I use for this task) while they're still warm. This will make them permeable to the dressing—it's a great hint that will give you better-tasting potato salad.

Next, add mayo and chopped whatever you want. I like celery and onion in mine (about a 1:1 ratio) and sometimes a hard-boiled egg, but not always. Salt and pepper to taste, and there you go. Perfect with many of the summer menus and easy to make—this is potato salad, not an event.

FAST AND EASY CORN MUFFINS

I really prefer corn muffins over corn bread—they're just easier. Less mess and the leftovers are easily frozen (if you even have leftovers, that is!) for another time.

Use those little cupcake liners for even less clean-up, too.

BUTTERMILK CORN MUFFINS

Makes 1 dozen

1 cup cornmeal
1 cup flour, or whole-wheat pastry flour (my choice)
2 teaspoons baking powder
1 teaspoon baking soda
2 eggs, beaten
¾ cup buttermilk, or add 1 tablespoon vinegar to plain milk
½ cup honey
4 tablespoons vegetable oil

Preheat oven to 375 degrees F. Line muffin pan with cupcake liners.

In a large bowl, combine dry ingredients. Add the rest of the ingredients and mix until blended. Pour batter into muffin tins, two-thirds full.

Bake for 15–25 minutes or until a light golden color. Let cool for a minute in the tin; then pull the muffins out to cool on a rack.

PER SERVING:
181 Calories; 6g Fat (28.0% calories from fat); 4g Protein; 30g Carbohydrate; 1g Dietary Fiber; 32mg Cholesterol; 213mg Sodium. Exchanges: 1 Grain (Starch); 0 Lean Meat; 0 Non-Fat Milk; 1 Fat; 1 Other Carbohydrates.

SALAD DRESSINGS

Heck, the easiest thing to do is make a basic vinaigrette salad dressing—less than a minute, if all your ingredients are already out. I really prefer a jar to make dressing rather than a bowl because it's easier to keep the dressing emulsified before you pour it on the salad, so that's the way I'm going to give the directions.

Here's my favorite vinaigrette dressing. Now, I've given measurements here, but train yourself to "see" what 1 tablespoon of balsamic vinegar looks like and what ¼ cup of olive oil looks like, too. Then you can dispense with the extra clean-up measuring requires and eyeball it enough to make your dressing sans measuring cups.

BASIC VINAIGRETTE

Makes 1 cup

1 tablespoon Dijon mustard
4 tablespoons balsamic vinegar
1 teaspoon sugar
¾ cup olive oil
Salt and pepper to taste

Throw it all in a jar and shake it hard enough to feel your eyeballs banging around in their sockets.

VARIATION: Like garlic? We must be related. Throw a clove of pressed garlic (or two, if you need to ward off vampires) in there for good measure. Keep shaking!

RANCH DRESSING

Makes 2 cups

This recipe is really for my son Peter, who thinks everything tastes better with ranch dressing.

½ cup mayonnaise
½ cup low-fat sour cream
½ cup buttermilk
1 teaspoon dried chives
½ teaspoon dried parsley
¼ teaspoon dried dill
½ teaspoon garlic powder
¼ teaspoon onion powder
Salt and pepper to taste

In a large bowl, whisk everything together well and pour into a jar. Keep refrigerated.

PER SERVING:
71 Calories; 7g Fat (86.8% calories from fat); 1g Protein; 2g Carbohydrate; trace Dietary Fiber; 5mg Cholesterol; 64mg Sodium. Exchanges: 0 Grain (Starch); 0 Lean Meat; 0 Vegetable; 0 Non-Fat Milk; ½ Fat; 0 Other Carbohydrates.

FREEZER MEALS

Success in any form relies intrinsically on the ability to be flexible. Blessed are the flexible, for they will not be broken—if you'll allow me this turn on an old truth. Life changes, circumstances vary, and it becomes necessary to rework your plan. This is particularly true when dinnertime starts to look more like a commercial for a drive-thru, red flag! It's time to change it up.

This is how our whole freezer menu concept on SavingDinner.com was born; out of the need to get dinner done even faster, nearly instantaneously, in fact. Could we do it? our subscribers asked. Could we do it like those new dinner-assembly franchise places people were finding sprouting up like wildflowers all over their suburban countrysides? And could we do it without sacrificing flavor, nutrition, and dinnertime communion?

We were up for the challenge. After a lot of contemplation and kitchen experimentation, yes, we could definitely do it. Not only that, but we could do it better and we did. We now have almost a cult following for our freezer menu products, from the Mega Menu-Mailer, offering twenty meals all assembled at one time, to the more manageable Five for the Freezer, where five meals are assembled in one mini-session using one meat at a time (great for those buy-one/get-one scenarios at the grocery store).

We've got a taste of those menus here, in our four mini-sessions of chicken, beef, pork, and shrimp. Just follow the directions—it's easy,

Five for the Freezer is a bargain
shopper's dream! Have you ever
walked past the meat department and seen huge packages of
meat on sale, but you just didn't
quite know what to do with all
that meat?

Now, you can watch for sales,
and with a minimal number of
ingredients (most of which can
be stored on hand!), you can
bring home the fish and whip up
a few meals for the freezer in no
time at all!

and when you're all done, you'll have twenty meals (we call them Dinner Kits) in your freezer that you, too, can nearly instantaneously enjoy
with your family. That's a whole month's worth of weeknight dinners!
Let's get started . . .

Are you ready? Get on your mark, get set, *go*!!! We're going to do
our first mini-session! Off we go to the grocery store with the Dinner
Kit Shopping List! But *wait*—not just yet.

Take a deep cleansing breath, exhale, and relax. This can be a lot of
fun, but there are some things you have to do before heading out the
door. First, you need to check our prepared shopping list against what's
in your pantry, fridge, and freezer. Cross off anything you already have.
See? You're already saving time and money!

Next, you must read through *all* the recipes before shopping with
your edited grocery list. There are times when it is perfectly acceptable
to make substitutions, but you won't know what will work as a substi-
tution if you haven't read through the recipes, now will you? For example, say you had a box of ziti in your pantry, but not the rotini that the
grocery list calls for. Substitute the ziti by all means! The recipe will still
work just fine, and you will know that because you've read the recipe. I
wouldn't advise making any overly creative substitutes, like trying to
use sausage for chicken, for example. That's just wrong.

Okay, so you've read through the recipes. The next thing is to read
through the assembly instructions. Why? I knew you'd ask me that. For
the same reason you read through the recipes. When it comes to actually setting up your own assembly line for putting together your Dinner
Kits, you'll know how you want it instead of just guessing. And I made
it painless for you—the assembly instructions are sitting right next to
the actual recipe. Isn't that easy?

After that, we're off to the grocery store, for real this time! Don't forget to put on your working shoes—yes, the lace-ups. This isn't time for
a fashion show—we've got work to do.

SHOP TILL YOU DROP

The freezer meal portion of *Saving Dinner* is slightly different than the regular weekly menus. We've tried not to color too much out of the lines that make up the *Saving Dinner* formula, but we do have a few things that need to be changed up, necessarily.

First off, you'll notice there are two different shopping lists; one is an assembly-day shopping list, the other a mealtime shopping list. You need to remember that these are meals you are assembling and then placing in your freezer for another day. You may use them up quickly or they may sit there in the freezer for a month or two. Therefore, the mealtime shopping list needs to be used when you've planned to use your meals; otherwise, those items could get a little too much age on them. Obviously, there are some things that are staples that you'll most likely have, like olive oil, etc. However, there are some things you may not necessarily have on hand, so make sure you double-check the mealtime shopping lists on each section before pulling one of your Dinner Kits from the freezer.

Secondly, although I have Serving Suggestions for all of the Dinner Kits to help you plan nutritionally balanced meals, I have not put any of these items on either shopping list; these items are definitely perishable, and when you use your Dinner Kits is totally up to you. If you do want to use my Serving Suggestions, I suggest you just jot those items down on your shopping list for the week so you'll be set!

SUBSTITUTIONS ANYONE?

You may not like chicken and prefer to enjoy other meats; maybe turkey was on sale this week instead of chicken . . . Many of these recipes are very flexible and could easily be made up with another meat of your choice.

ONCE BEGUN, HALF DONE

The thought of preparing five dinners all at once may seem daunting! Hang in there, we'll get you through it painlessly. Remember, foods taste better if they are frozen fresh (as opposed to cooking, thawing, and reheating them). For this reason, you should plan your meal preparations as soon as you get home from shopping, or shop the night before and start assembling in the morning.

Grocery shopping shouldn't take you too long and many of the ingredients can be bought ahead of time to have on hand, waiting for those periodic meat specials. Be sure to use the handy preassembly prep list to zip through the meal-assembly process.

STATIONS, EVERYONE!

To make sure you have plenty of room for your assembly stations once you bring home the goods, you need to clear off your counters, big-time. Canisters, small appliances, and other kitschy kitchen knickknacks must go. Wipe down your counters so they're ready. If you don't have enough room with just the counters, feel free to use the kitchen and even dining room tables—that's what they're there for.

Begin by setting up your assembly line the same way your grocery list is set up—condiments all together, the canned goods all together, the produce in another section. Then the work begins—chop the onion, celery, and whatever else needs chopping, placing them in containers you can measure or grab from. Measure the spices and other ingredients as well, labeling if necessary. In other words, get everything ready to go (including making labels for your bags or marking your freezer bags—use a black Sharpie pen for best nonrunning results). This is called *mis en place*, a culinary term (French) meaning "everything in its place." Using a *mis en place* when you start assembling these meals ensures

BAG LADIES

The type of bag you use is incredibly important. You cannot use a standard-issue zipper-topped bag unless you really don't care about the quality of your food. Pay the extra money and buy freezer-quality bags. This is how you'll ensure against freezer burn (if it's used within a few months) and have a fresh-tasting meal!

And while we're on the subject of quality, let's talk about what *not* to freeze in: that would include margarine, ricotta cheese, yogurt, or whipped-topping containers (or anything else that is used to house something you bought from the grocery store), produce bags, bread bags, and any type of glass jar. This is not the time to be green and recycle. We heartily recommend using brand-name freezer-quality zipper-topped bags; they close well, freeze well, and are designed to keep your food fresh in the freezer.

Remember, the biggest enemies of frozen food are air and moisture. Freezer burn is caused by both of these culprits, and this is why we so staunchly warn against using containers and/or bags that won't hold up in the freezer. Why go to all this trouble only to defrost a freezer-burned meal?

It's also important to properly label your bags. Do you prefer a label or do you like to go label-free and use a Sharpie pen? (Personal preference: I like my Sharpie and just mark the bags!) If you do decide to use a label, it's wise to place it *inside* the bag with the writing facing out so the label is readable and won't fall off in the freezer.

speedy delivery on the cooking side of things and helps you get it done with minimum fuss, especially when you're assembling five recipes at a time!

There are three stages to getting these Dinner Kits put together: preassembly (where you do all the important prepping), assembly, and, finally, freezing. Keep that in mind when you're making the magic happen for all these meals, and you'll breeze through it all in no time flat!

Here are the first five recipes (your first session), all using chicken. Using one meat at a time to assemble five recipes all at once prevents any cross contamination and makes your assembly go much faster. Obviously, you won't be eating all five chicken recipes one after the other! However, once you have all of your sessions assembled and frozen, you'll be able to use your Dinner Kits night after night if you want, with plenty of variety.

You will notice that after the shopping lists there is a prep list for your session's *mis en place*. Follow those directions implicitly, and you'll throw this session together in no time flat. Listen, we've been there/done that and gotten our freezers full doing this! We have laid it out as simply as possible to make getting it done Easy Button easy . . . just follow the directions!

CHICKEN

THE RECIPES

Dijon Rosemary Chicken Breasts
Chicken Supreme
Spicy Chinese Chicken
Chicken Breasts with Artichoke Sauce
Stuffed Chicken Breasts

Dinner Kit Shopping Lists

ASSEMBLY-TIME SHOPPING LIST

MEAT

30 boneless, skinless chicken breast halves

CONDIMENTS

olive oil
splash of cider vinegar (if not using dry white wine)
Dijon mustard (you'll need 3 tablespoons)
low sodium soy sauce (you'll need 2¼ cups)
molasses (you'll need 3 tablespoons)
sherry (you'll need ⅓ cup or use additional chicken broth)
dry white wine (you'll need ¾ cup if not using white grape juice)

PRODUCE

9 cloves garlic (or use the minced, jarred kind)
3 teaspoons grated fresh gingerroot
½ cup chopped fresh parsley
6 fresh basil leaves
1 lemon

CANNED GOODS

24.5 ounces low sodium chicken broth (plus ⅓ cup if not using sherry)
1 9-ounce can marinated artichoke hearts
1 12-ounce jar roasted red peppers

1 7-ounce jar sun-dried tomatoes
¾ cup white grape juice (if not using dry white wine)

SPICES
dried rosemary leaves, crushed (you'll need 1½ teaspoons)
white pepper (you'll need ¼ teaspoon)
dried thyme (you'll need ½ teaspoon)
lemon pepper (you'll need 1½ teaspoons)
fennel seeds (you'll need ½ teaspoon)
cinnamon stick (you'll need 1)
paprika (you'll need 1½ teaspoons)
ground red pepper (you'll need ¼ teaspoon)
oregano (you'll need ½ teaspoon)

DAIRY
low-fat sour cream (you'll need 3 tablespoons)
butter (you'll need 3 tablespoons)
shredded low-fat mozzarella cheese (you'll need 14 ounces)

DRY GOODS
whole-wheat flour (you'll need ¼ cup)
brown sugar (you'll need 3 tablespoons)

OTHER
aluminum foil wrap
disposable aluminum baking pan (optional)
toothpicks (optional)
freezer bags:
    1-quart 2
    1-gallon 8
    2-gallon 1

MEALTIME SHOPPING LIST
CONDIMENTS
olive oil

Preassembly Prep List

When it's time to get our meals assembled, that's exactly what we're going to do—put them together. To that end, it's important you get a lot of preassembly work done before you start the whole assembly process, such as chopping, slicing, dicing, measuring, grating, etc. I like to use little ramekins for the measured spices, larger bowls or mixing bowls even for the larger chopped stuff, and simply open cans or open bags as necessary.

An important component to getting your preassembly accomplished is, of course, reading through each of the recipes. When you do, you'll be well aware of what it is you need to do and how you need to get it done. This will save you gobs of time.

A couple of safety tips: keep all meats/poultry and fish refrigerated until it's time to use them in a Dinner Kit. As a matter of fact, keep everything refrigerated that should be until its assembly time. Don't forget, all produce should be washed before using. Better to be safe than sorry!

Let's get busy!

MEAT

Rinse chicken in cold water; pat dry.

Pound 6 chicken breast halves flat (I do this by putting thawed chicken into a large plastic bag and pounding flat with a rolling pin—like I'm making a piecrust. Works!)

Refrigerate chicken until ready to place in freezer kit.

CONDIMENTS

Set out:

olive oil

cider vinegar (if not using dry white wine)

Dijon mustard

olive oil

low sodium soy sauce

molasses

sherry (optional)

dry white wine (if not using white grape juice)

PRODUCE

GARLIC

Press 9 cloves of garlic (or use the minced, jarred kind).

GINGERROOT

Peel gingerroot or not (I don't).

Using the small grid on your grater, grate 3 teaspoons gingerroot.

PARSLEY

Rinse parsley in cold water; chop ½ cup parsley.

BASIL

Remove stems from basil leaves; rinse in cold water; pat dry.

LEMON

Using your palm, press and roll the lemon on your countertop a few times to help release the juice from the pulp. (Tip: Lemons stored at room temperature release more juice than lemons stored in your refrigerator.)

Cut lemon in half and juice.

If you don't have a juicer, squeeze the lemon over a bowl by hand. Be sure to remove any seeds from the juice.

CANNED GOODS

LOW SODIUM CHICKEN BROTH

Open 1 14.5-ounce can.

Measure out ⅓ cup low sodium chicken broth if you're not using sherry

ARTICHOKE HEARTS

Drain artichoke hearts and save the liquid.

ROASTED RED PEPPERS
Drain roasted red peppers.
    Chop roasted red peppers.

SUN-DRIED TOMATOES
Drain sun-dried tomatoes.
    Chop sun-dried tomatoes.

WHITE GRAPE JUICE (IF NOT USING DRY WHITE WINE)
Measure out ¾ cup.

SPICES
Set out:
    dried rosemary leaves
    white pepper
    dried thyme
    lemon pepper
    fennel seeds
    cinnamon stick
    paprika
    ground red pepper
    oregano

DAIRY
Measure 3 tablespoons of low-fat sour cream.
    Measure 2 teaspoons of butter.
    Shred 14 ounces of low-fat mozzarella cheese.

DRY GOODS
Measure ¼ cup whole-wheat flour.
    Measure 3 tablespoons brown sugar.

DIJON ROSEMARY CHICKEN BREASTS

Serves 6

Assembly Guidelines

In a 1-gallon freezer bag, place:

3 tablespoons low-fat sour cream
3 tablespoons Dijon mustard
1 teaspoon dried rosemary leaves, crushed
¼ teaspoon white pepper
6 boneless, skinless chicken breast halves

Seal bag and gently massage it to blend ingredients well. Open bag and carefully squeeze it to remove excess air. Seal the bag.

To prevent freezer burn, place the filled bag in a second 1-gallon freezer bag. Seal the bag and place your label on it or write the recipe name and preparation date on the bag with your Sharpie marking pen (it's the only brand that doesn't run in the freezer!); place bag in your freezer.

DIJON ROSEMARY CHICKEN BREASTS

Serves 6

Cooking Instructions

Preassembled Ingredients
3 tablespoons low-fat sour cream
3 tablespoons Dijon mustard
1 teaspoon dried rosemary leaves, crushed
¼ teaspoon white pepper
6 boneless, skinless chicken breast halves

Cooking Instructions

Thaw contents of freezer bag.
Preheat oven to 375 degrees. Lightly grease a baking pan.

Place chicken in the pan and bake, uncovered, for 30 minutes or until chicken is no longer pink when centers of thickest pieces are cut.

PER SERVING:
145 Calories; 2g Fat; 28g Protein; 2g Carbohydrate; trace Dietary Fiber; 70mg Cholesterol; 179mg Sodium. Exchanges: 0 Grain (Starch); 4 Lean Meat.

SERVING SUGGESTION: Steamed red-skinned potatoes and steamed carrots with petite green peas.

CHICKEN SUPREME

Serves 6

Assembly Guidelines
In a 1-gallon freezer bag, place:

> *6 boneless, skinless chicken breast halves*
> *¼ cup whole-wheat flour*
> *Salt and pepper, to taste*

Seal bag and gently shake to coat chicken. Open the bag and carefully squeeze it to remove excess air. Seal the bag.
In a 1-quart freezer bag, add:

> *1½ tablespoons olive oil*
> *2 teaspoons butter, melted*
> *½ teaspoon dried thyme*
> *1 lemon, juiced*
> *½ cup low sodium chicken broth*
> *½ cup chopped fresh parsley*

Carefully squeeze the bag to remove excess air. Seal the bag.
To prevent freezer burn, place the filled bags in a 1-gallon freezer bag. Seal the bag and place your label on it or write the recipe name and preparation date on the bag with your Sharpie marking pen; place bag in your freezer.

CHICKEN SUPREME

Cooking Instructions

Preassembled Ingredients
6 boneless, skinless chicken breast halves
¼ cup whole-wheat flour
Salt and pepper, to taste
1½ tablespoons olive oil
2 teaspoons butter, melted
½ teaspoon dried thyme
1 lemon, juiced
½ cup low sodium chicken broth
½ cup chopped fresh parsley

At-Time-of-Cooking Ingredients
1 tablespoon olive oil

Cooking Instructions

Thaw contents of both freezer bags.

Heat the olive oil in a large skillet over medium heat; brown chicken on both sides until cooked through; remove from skillet and keep warm.

Add contents of sauce bag to skillet; bring to a boil and whisk up all of the browned bits from the bottom of the pan. Pour sauce over chicken and serve.

PER SERVING:
216 Calories; 9g Fat; 29g Protein; 5g Carbohydrate; 1g Dietary Fiber; 72mg Cholesterol; 136mg Sodium. Exchanges: 0 Grain (Starch); 4 Lean Meat; 1½ Fat.

SERVING SUGGESTION: Brown rice, steamed broccoli, and a green salad.

SPICY CHINESE CHICKEN

Assembly Guidelines
In a 1-gallon freezer bag, place:

2¼ cups low sodium soy sauce
3 tablespoons molasses
¾ cup low sodium chicken broth
⅓ cup sherry (or use additional chicken broth)
3 tablespoons brown sugar
3 teaspoons grated fresh gingerroot
1½ teaspoons lemon pepper
½ teaspoon fennel seeds
1 cinnamon stick
6 boneless, skinless chicken breast halves

Seal bag and gently massage to coat chicken. Open bag and carefully squeeze it to remove excess air. Seal the bag.

To prevent freezer burn, place the filled bag in a second 1-gallon freezer bag. Seal the bag and place your label on it or write the recipe name and preparation date on the bag with your Sharpie marking pen; place bag in your freezer.

SPICY CHINESE CHICKEN

Serves 6

Cooking Instructions

Preassembled Ingredients
2¼ cups low sodium soy sauce
3 tablespoons molasses
¾ cup low sodium chicken broth
⅓ cup sherry (or use additional chicken broth)
3 tablespoons brown sugar
3 tablespoons grated fresh gingerroot
1½ teaspoons lemon pepper

½ teaspoon fennel seeds
1 cinnamon stick
6 boneless, skinless chicken breast halves

Cooking Instructions

Thaw ingredients of freezer bag.

Lightly grease the inside of a slow cooker; add ingredients of freezer bag.

Cover and cook on low for about 6 hours.

Remove cinnamon stick and serve.

PER SERVING:
263 Calories; 2g Fat; 34g Protein; 24g Carbohydrate; 2g Dietary Fiber; 68mg Cholesterol; 633mg Sodium. Exchanges: 0 Grain (Starch); 4 Lean Meat; 2 Vegetable; 0 Fat; 1 Other Carbohydrates.

SERVING SUGGESTION: Brown rice with stir-fried zucchini, yellow squash, and snow peas.

CHICKEN BREASTS WITH ARTICHOKE SAUCE

Serves 6

Assembly Guidelines

In a 1-gallon freezer bag, place:

6 boneless, skinless chicken breast halves
½ teaspoon salt
Reserved liquid from a 9-ounce can artichoke hearts

Seal bag and gently massage it to coat chicken. Open bag and carefully squeeze it to remove excess air. Seal the bag.

In a 1-quart freezer bag, place:

1 9-ounce can artichoke hearts, drained
¾ cup roasted red peppers, drained and coarsely chopped
9 cloves garlic, pressed (or use minced, jarred)

¾ cup dry white wine (or use white grape juice with a splash of cider vinegar)

1½ teaspoons paprika

¼ teaspoon ground red pepper (more or less to taste)

Seal bag and gently toss to blend ingredients. Open bag and carefully squeeze it to remove excess air. Seal the bag.

To prevent freezer burn, place both bags in a second 1-gallon freezer bag. Seal the bag and place your label on it or write the recipe name and preparation date on the bag with your Sharpie marking pen; place bag in your freezer.

CHICKEN BREASTS WITH ARTICHOKE HEARTS

Serves 6

Cooking Instructions

Preassembled Ingredients

6 boneless, skinless chicken breast halves

½ teaspoon salt

9 ounces marinated artichoke hearts, drained and liquid reserved

¾ cup roasted red peppers, drained and coarsely chopped

9 cloves garlic, pressed

¾ cup dry white wine (or use white grape juice with a splash of cider vinegar)

1½ teaspoons paprika

¼ teaspoon ground red pepper (more or less to taste)

At-Time-of-Cooking Ingredients

1 tablespoon olive oil

Cooking Instructions

Thaw chicken and sauce mixture.

Heat the oil in a large skillet over medium heat. Remove chicken from bag, reserving artichoke liquid. Brown chicken in oil on both sides until cooked through; remove from skillet and keep warm.

Add contents of sauce bag and artichoke liquid to skillet; bring to a boil and whisk up all of the browned bits from the bottom of the pan. Return chicken to skillet for a minute or so to heat through. Serve chicken with sauce.

PER SERVING:
198 Calories; 4g Fat; 29g Protein; 6g Carbohydrate; 2g Dietary Fiber; 68mg Cholesterol; 394mg Sodium. Exchanges: 0 Grain(Starch); 4 Lean Meat; 1 Vegetable; ½ Fat.

SERVING SUGGESTION: Baked sweet potatoes and sautéed spinach.

STUFFED CHICKEN BREASTS

Serves 6

Assembly Guidelines

> *6 boneless, skinless chicken breast halves, pounded flat*
> *3 tablespoons olive oil, divided*
> *6 fresh basil leaves*

Place flattened chicken breast halves on a work surface; coat 1 side of each piece with 1½ tablespoons of olive oil; place 1 basil leaf on top of each chicken piece.

In a small bowl, combine:

> *1 7-ounce jar sun-dried tomatoes, drained and chopped*
> *6 ounces shredded low-fat mozzarella cheese*
> *½ teaspoon dried rosemary, crushed*
> *½ teaspoon oregano*
> *Salt and pepper, to taste*

Spoon an equal amount of this mixture on top of each basil leaf; carefully roll each chicken piece around the basil leaf and filling; secure with toothpicks if necessary.

Place chicken rolls in a casserole dish or disposable aluminum baking pan, seam side down; drizzle with remaining olive oil.

Cover dish or aluminum pan with aluminum foil wrap and seal well.

To prevent freezer burn, place foil-wrapped dish/pan in a 2-gallon freezer bag. Seal the bag and place your label on it or write the recipe name and preparation date on the bag with your Sharpie marking pen; place bag in your freezer.

STUFFED CHICKEN BREASTS

Serves 6

Cooking Instructions

Preassembled Ingredients
6 boneless, skinless chicken breast halves, pounded flat
3 tablespoons olive oil, divided
6 fresh basil leaves
1 7-ounce jar sun-dried tomatoes, drained and chopped
6 ounces shredded low-fat mozzarella cheese
½ teaspoon dried rosemary, crushed
½ teaspoon oregano
Salt and pepper, to taste

Cooking Instructions
Thaw chicken rolls.
Preheat oven to 375 degrees.
Cover baking dish/pan with aluminum foil wrap and bake for 20–25 minutes. Uncover and continue to bake until golden brown.

PER SERVING:
271 Calories; 13g Fat; 35g Protein; 1g Carbohydrate; trace Dietary Fiber; 84mg Cholesterol; 233mg Sodium. Exchanges: 0 Grain(Starch); 5 Lean Meat; 1½ Fat.

SERVING SUGGESTION: Fettuccine pasta tossed with olive oil and grated Parmesan cheese. Add steamed asparagus.

BEEF

Dinner Kit Shopping Lists

ASSEMBLY-TIME SHOPPING LIST

MEAT
5 pounds extra-lean ground beef

CONDIMENTS
vegetable oil
non-aerosol cooking spray
mild or medium chunky salsa (you'll need 2 11-ounce jars)
ketchup (you'll need 6 tablespoons)
taco sauce (optional)
Dijon mustard (you'll need 2 tablespoons)
sliced ripe olives (you'll need ⅓ cup)

PRODUCE
3 medium onions
1 clove garlic
6 green onions (plus additional, optional)
6 portabella mushroom caps, 4 to 5 inches wide
romaine lettuce (optional)
½ cup chopped parsley

CANNED GOODS
1 14.5-ounce can diced tomatoes
1 14.5-ounce can Mexican-style tomatoes
3 16-ounce cans pinto beans
1 11-ounce can whole kernel corn

SPICES
chili powder (you'll need 2 teaspoons)
cumin (you'll need ½ teaspoon)
onion powder (you'll need 2 teaspoons)
oregano (you'll need 1 teaspoon)
Italian seasoning (you'll need 1 teaspoon)

DAIRY
2 eggs
3 tablespoons Neufchatel cheese (or low-fat cream cheese)
1 8-ounce package shredded low-fat Cheddar cheese
4 ounces Monterey Jack cheese (plus optional garnish)
4 ounces part-skim mozzarella cheese
5 tablespoons grated Parmesan cheese

DRY GOODS
Italian-style bread crumbs (you'll need 2½ cups)
taco seasoning mix (you'll need 3 tablespoons)
1 small package corn-bread mix

FROZEN
1 26-ounce package frozen shredded potatoes

BAKERY
6 flour tortillas

OTHER
aluminum foil wrap
plastic freezer bags:
    1-gallon 6
    2-gallon 4

MEALTIME SHOPPING LIST
CONDIMENTS
vegetable oil
non-aerosol cooking spray
sliced ripe olives, for optional garnish

PRODUCE
6 portabella mushroom caps, 4 to 5 inches wide
shredded romaine lettuce, for optional garnish
chopped green onions, for optional garnish

DAIRY
4 ounces Monterey Jack cheese plus optional garnish
1 egg (for corn-bread mix)
milk (for corn-bread mix)

DRY GOODS
1 small package corn-bread mix

BAKERY
6 flour tortillas

Preassembly Prep List

MEAT (GROUND BEEF)
Cook and crumble 2 pounds; drain and blot off excess grease;
allow beef to cool until safe to handle, then separate in half.

Divide remaining 3 pounds as follows: ½ pound, 1 pound,
1½ pounds.

Refrigerate all meat until ready to assemble in kit.

CONDIMENTS
Set out:
    vegetable oil
    non-aerosol cooking spray
    salsa
    ketchup
    Dijon mustard

PRODUCE

ONIONS
White or yellow onions: Cut off both ends and peel first layer.
    Chop 3 onions.
    Saute ½ cup of chopped onion.

GREEN ONIONS
Rinse green onions under running water and trim the ends.
   Chop 6 green onions plus optional garnish.

PARSLEY
Rinse parsley under running water.
   Chop ½ cup of parsley.

CANNED GOODS
Open all cans; rinse/drain contents where necessary.

SPICES
Set out:
   chili powder
   cumin
   onion powder
   oregano
   salt
   black pepper

EGGS
Lightly beat 2 eggs, each in a separate bowl or cup.

DAIRY
CHEESES
Shred:
   4 ounces low-fat Cheddar
   4 ounces mozzarella
   4 ounces (plus optional) Monterey Jack
Grate 5 tablespoons Parmesan.
Soften Neufchatel cheese (or low-fat cream cheese).

DRY GOODS
Set out:
   Italian-style bread crumbs
   taco seasoning mix

CAMPFIRE CASSEROLE

Serves 6

Assembly Guidelines

In a 1-gallon freezer bag, place:

1 pound extra-lean ground beef, cooked and crumbled

½ cup chopped onion, sautéed

3 tablespoons dry taco seasoning mix

*1 14.5-ounce can Mexican-style tomatoes, chopped (discard
    2 tablespoons of liquid)*

2 16-ounce cans pinto beans, drained and rinsed

⅓ cup sliced ripe olives

3 tablespoons chopped fresh parsley

Seal bag and gently massage it to blend ingredients well. Open bag and carefully squeeze it to remove excess air. Seal the bag.

To prevent freezer burn, place the filled bag in a second 1-gallon freezer bag. Seal the bag and place your label on it or write the recipe name and preparation date on the bag with your Sharpie marking pen; place bag in your freezer.

CAMPFIRE CASSEROLE

Serves 6

Cooking Instructions

Preassembled Ingredients

1 pound extra-lean ground beef, cooked and crumbled

½ cup chopped onion, sautéed

3 tablespoons dry taco seasoning mix

*1 14.5-ounce can Mexican-style tomatoes, chopped (discard
    2 tablespoons of liquid)*

2 16-ounce cans pinto beans, drained and rinsed

⅓ cup sliced ripe olives

3 tablespoons chopped fresh parsley

At-Time-of-Cooking Ingredients
non-aerosol cooking spray
4 ounces Monterey Jack cheese, shredded
1 small package corn-bread mix, prepared according to package
  directions

Cooking Instructions
Preheat oven to 350 degrees.

Thaw contents of freezer bag and place in a baking dish that has been lightly coated with non-aerosol cooking spray; sprinkle with cheese and top with prepared corn-bread mixture.

Bake for 15 to 20 minutes or until lightly browned on top.

PER SERVING:
397 Calories; 18g Fat; 27g Protein; 32g Carbohydrate; 7g Dietary Fiber; 64mg Cholesterol; 114mg Sodium. Exchanges: 1½ Grain (Starch); 3 Lean Meat; 1 Vegetable; 0 Fruit; 2 Fat; 0 Other Carbohydrates.

SERVING SUGGESTION: A big salad.

CONFETTI BURRITOS

Serves 6

Assembly Guidelines
In a 1-gallon freezer bag, place:

½ pound extra-lean ground beef
2 teaspoons chili powder
½ teaspoon cumin
1 cup mild or medium chunky salsa
1 11-ounce can whole kernel corn, drained
1 16-ounce can pinto beans, drained and rinsed

Seal bag and gently massage it to blend ingredients well. Open bag and carefully squeeze it to remove excess air. Seal bag.

To prevent freezer burn, place the filled bag in a second 1-gallon freezer bag. Seal the bag and place your label on it or write the recipe name and preparation date on the bag with your Sharpie marking pen; place bag in your freezer.

CONFETTI BURRITOS

Serves 6

Cooking Instructions

Preassembled Ingredients
½ pound extra-lean ground beef
2 teaspoons chili powder
½ teaspoon cumin
1 cup mild or medium chunky salsa
1 11-ounce can whole kernel corn, drained
1 16-ounce can pinto beans, drained and rinsed

At-Time-of-Cooking Ingredients
6 flour tortillas

Optional Toppings:
shredded Monterey Jack cheese
shredded romaine lettuce
sliced ripe olives
chopped green onions

Cooking Instructions

Thaw contents of freezer bag and place in a large nonstick skillet over medium heat; heat through. Meanwhile, in a separate nonstick skillet, warm tortillas.

To assemble: Spoon approximately ⅓ cup of beef mixture into each tortilla and garnish as desired.

PER SERVING:
426 Calories; 12g Fat; 18g Protein; 62g Carbohydrate; 7g Dietary Fiber; 26mg Cholesterol; 971mg Sodium. Exchanges: 4 Grain (Starch); 1 Lean Meat; ½ Vegetable; 1½ Fat.

SERVING SUGGESTION: Serve a big bowl of broccoli slaw on the side (use a ready-made mix and toss with mayo and a little rice vinegar). Add a bowl of raw baby carrots to the table.

DOUBLE-CHEESE MEAT LOAF

Serves 6

Assembly Guidelines

Non-aerosol cooking spray
6 tablespoons ketchup, divided
2 tablespoons Dijon mustard, divided
4 ounces part-skim mozzarella cheese, shredded
½ cup Italian-seasoned bread crumbs
¼ cup chopped fresh parsley
2 tablespoons grated Parmesan cheese
2 teaspoons onion powder
1 teaspoon oregano
¼ teaspoon black pepper
1 egg, lightly beaten
1½ pounds extra-lean ground beef

Lightly coat a loaf pan with cooking spray.

In a large bowl, combine 4 tablespoons of ketchup, 1 tablespoon of mustard, and next 8 ingredients (mozzarella through egg); crumble ground beef over cheese mixture and blend well with your very clean hands. Pack mixture into prepared loaf pan. In a small bowl or cup, combine remaining ketchup and mustard; spread over the top of the loaf.

Wrap and seal loaf pan with aluminum foil wrap, then place it in a 2-gallon freezer bag. Carefully squeeze the bag to remove excess air. Seal the bag.

To prevent freezer burn, place the bag in a second 2-gallon freezer bag. Seal the bag and place your label on it or write the recipe name and preparation date on the bag with your Sharpie marking pen; place bag in your freezer.

DOUBLE-CHEESE MEAT LOAF

Serves 6

Cooking Instructions

Preassembled Ingredients

Non-aerosol cooking spray

6 tablespoons ketchup, divided

2 tablespoons Dijon mustard, divided

4 ounces part-skim mozzarella cheese, shredded

½ cup Italian-seasoned bread crumbs

¼ cup chopped parsley

2 tablespoons grated Parmesan cheese

2 teaspoons onion powder

1 teaspoon oregano

¼ teaspoon black pepper

1 egg, lightly beaten

1½ pounds extra-lean ground beef

Cooking Instructions

Thaw meat loaf.

Preheat oven to 375 degrees.

Bake meat loaf, uncovered, for 1 hour or until a meat thermometer inserted in the center registers 160 degrees. Let meat loaf stand for 10 minutes before serving.

PER SERVING:
439 Calories, 29g Fat; 29g Protein; 15g Carbohydrate; 1g Dietary Fiber; 128mg Cholesterol; 726mg Sodium. Exchanges: ½ Grain (Starch); 4 Lean Meat; ½ Vegetable; 3½ Fat; ½ Other Carbohydrates.

SERVING SUGGESTION: Mashed potatoes, steamed broccoli, and steamed baby carrots.

BEEFY POTATO CHEESE PIE

Serves 6

Assembly Guidelines
In a large bowl, place:

> *1 pound extra-lean ground beef*
> *2 cups Italian-style bread crumbs*
> *1 cup chopped onion*
> *1 egg, lightly beaten*
> *Salt and pepper, to taste*

Blend well with your very clean hands; press into the bottom and up the sides of an aluminum pie pan or an 8 x 8–inch baking dish.

In another large bowl, combine:

> *2 cups chopped onion*
> *1 (26-ounce) package frozen shredded potatoes*

Place mixture on top of beef mixture; top with:

> *4 ounces low-fat Cheddar cheese, shredded*

Wrap and seal pie pan or baking dish with aluminum foil wrap, then place it in a 2-gallon freezer bag. Carefully squeeze the bag to remove excess air. Seal the bag.

To prevent freezer burn, place the filled bag in a second 2-gallon freezer bag. Seal the bag and place your label on it or write the recipe name and preparation date on the bag with your Sharpie marking pen; place bag in your freezer.

BEEFY POTATO CHEESE PIE

Serves 6

Cooking Instructions

> Preassembled Ingredients
> *1 pound extra-lean ground beef*
> *2 cups Italian-style bread crumbs*

3 cups chopped onion
1 egg, lightly beaten
Salt and pepper, to taste
1 26-ounce package frozen shredded potatoes
4 ounces low-fat Cheddar cheese, shredded

Cooking Instructions

Thaw casserole.

Preheat oven to 325 degrees.

Bake for 25 to 30 minutes or until cooked through and lightly browned on top.

PER SERVING:
410 Calories; 18g Fat; 22g Protein; 41g Carbohydrate; 3g Dietary Fiber; 78mg Cholesterol; 951mg Sodium. Exchanges: 2½ Grain (Starch); 2 Lean Meat; ½ Vegetable; 2 Fat.

SERVING SUGGESTION: A big spinach salad.

BEEF-STUFFED PORTABELLAS

Serves 6

Assembly Guidelines

In a 1 gallon freezer bag, place:

1 pound extra-lean ground beef, cooked, drained, and crumbled
½ of a 14.5-ounce can diced tomatoes, drained
6 green onions, chopped
3 tablespoons grated Parmesan cheese
3 tablespoons Neufchatel cheese (or low-fat cream cheese), softened
1 teaspoon Italian seasoning
Salt and pepper, to taste
1 clove garlic, pressed

Seal the bag and gently massage it to blend ingredients well. Open the bag and carefully squeeze it to remove excess air. Seal the bag.

To prevent freezer burn, place the filled bag in a second 1-gallon freezer bag. Seal the bag and place your label on it or write the recipe name and preparation date on the bag with your Sharpie marking pen; place bag in your freezer.

BEEF-STUFFED PORTABELLAS

Serves 6

Cooking Instructions

Preassembled Ingredients
1 pound extra-lean ground beef, cooked, drained, and crumbled
½ of a 14.5-ounce can diced tomatoes, drained
6 green onions, chopped
3 tablespoons grated Parmesan cheese
3 tablespoons Neufchatel cheese (or low-fat cream cheese), softened
1 teaspoon Italian seasoning
Salt and pepper, to taste
1 clove garlic, pressed

At-Time-of-Cooking Ingredients
Vegetable oil
6 portabella mushroom caps, 4 to 5 inches wide

Cooking Instructions
Thaw beef filling.

Preheat oven to 325 degrees. Lightly coat a baking sheet with vegetable oil.

Remove gills (and stems, if necessary) from mushroom caps and place them on the baking sheet, top side down; fill with beef mixture and lightly drizzle with oil; bake for 30 minutes or until lightly browned.

PER SERVING:
242 Calories; 15g Fat; 19g Protein; 9g Carbohydrate; 2g Dietary Fiber; 57mg Cholesterol; 121mg Sodium. Exchanges: 0 Grain (Starch); 2 Lean Meat; 2 Vegetable; 1½ Fat.

SERVING SUGGESTION: A big salad and garlic toast.

Shrimp

Dinner Kit Shopping Lists

ASSEMBLY-TIME SHOPPING LIST

MEAT

10 pounds large raw shrimp, peeled, deveined, and tails removed

NOTE: Be sure to use either fresh shrimp or frozen shrimp that have not been thawed. Work quickly to make sure your shrimp does not thaw while putting your Dinner Kits together.

CONDIMENTS

olive oil (you'll need ¼ cup)

vegetable oil (you'll need ¼ cup plus 1½ teaspoons)

rice wine vinegar (you'll need 1½ tablespoons)

hoisin sauce (in ethnic section of grocery store) (you'll need 3 tablespoons)

low sodium soy sauce (you'll need 1½ tablespoons)

PRODUCE

2 onions

9 large cloves garlic (or use minced, jarred)

9 green onions, cut into 1-inch pieces

¾ cup chopped celery

5 teaspoons grated fresh gingerroot

¾ cup chopped green bell pepper

4½ tablespoons parsley, chopped

½ cup lemon juice

CANNED GOODS
1 14.5-ounce can crushed tomatoes
1 14.5-ounce can low sodium chicken broth

SPICES
Cajun seasoning (you'll need 1½ teaspoons)
ground red pepper (you'll need ½ teaspoon)
1 bay leaf
crushed red pepper flakes

DRY GOODS
sugar (you'll need 3 teaspoons)
flour (you'll need 4½ tablespoons)

FROZEN
2 cups frozen chopped tricolored bell peppers

OTHER
Freezer bags:
    1-quart 1
    1-gallon 8
    2-gallon 1

MEALTIME SHOPPING LIST
SPICES
basil (you'll need 2 teaspoons)

DAIRY
3 tablespoons grated Romano cheese

DRY GOODS
fettuccine pasta (you'll need 12 ounces)

Preassembly Prep List

MEAT
See note in Shopping List.

CONDIMENTS
Set out:
   olive oil
   vegetable oil
   rice wine vinegar
   hoisin sauce
   low sodium soy sauce

PRODUCE

ONIONS
Chop 2 cups onions.

GARLIC
Press 9 cloves garlic (if not using minced, jarred kind).

GREEN ONIONS
Rinse green onions under running water to wash; trim the ends.
   Chop 9 green onions into 1-inch pieces.

GINGERROOT
Peel gingerroot, or not (I don't).
   Grate 5 teaspoons gingerroot.

PARSLEY
Rinse parsley under running water to wash.
   Chop 4½ tablespoons parsley.

CANNED GOODS
Open all cans.

SPICES
Set out:
   Cajun seasoning
   ground red pepper
   bay leaves
   crushed red pepper flakes

HOISIN SHRIMP

Serves 6

Assembly Guidelines
In a 1-quart freezer bag, place

> *3 tablespoons hoisin sauce*
> *1½ tablespoons rice wine vinegar*
> *3 teaspoons sugar*
> *¼ teaspoon salt*

Carefully squeeze the bag to remove excess air. Seal bag.
In a 1-gallon freezer bag, place:

> *¼ cup vegetable oil*
> *2½ pounds shrimp*
> *9 green onions, cut into 1-inch pieces*
> *2 teaspoons grated gingerroot*

Carefully squeeze the bag to remove excess air. Seal bag.

To prevent freezer burn, place the filled bags in a second 1-gallon freezer bag. Seal the bag and place your label on it or write the recipe name and preparation date on the bag with your Sharpie marking pen; place in your freezer.

HOISIN SHRIMP

Serves 6

Cooking Instructions

Preassembled Ingredients

3 tablespoons hoisin sauce

1½ tablespoons rice wine vinegar

3 teaspoons sugar

¼ teaspoon salt

¼ cup vegetable oil

2½ pounds shrimp

9 green onions, cut into 1-inch pieces

2 teaspoons grated fresh gingerroot

Cooking Instructions

Thaw shrimp bag and sauce mixture bag.

In a large wok or skillet, place contents of shrimp bag; stir-fry for
about 2 minutes; add contents of sauce bag and stir-fry for another 2 to
3 minutes or until shrimp are pink.

PER SERVING:
311 Calories; 13g Fat; 39g Protein; 8g Carbohydrate; 1g Dietary Fiber; 288mg Cholesterol;
502mg Sodium. Exchanges: 5½ Lean Meat; ½ Vegetable; 2 Fat; ½ Other Carbohydrates.

SERVING SUGGESTION: Brown rice with sautéed bok choy and snow peas.

SIMPLE SHRIMP CREOLE

Serves 6

Assembly Guidelines

In a 1-gallon freezer bag, place:

4½ tablespoons olive oil

1 cup chopped onion

¾ cup chopped green bell pepper

¾ cup chopped celery

2 cloves garlic, pressed (or used minced, jarred kind)

4½ tablespoons flour

1 14.5-ounce can crushed tomatoes, undrained

¾ cup low sodium chicken broth

1½ teaspoons Cajun seasoning

Salt, to taste

½ teaspoon ground red pepper (more or less to taste)

1 bay leaf

Seal the bag and turn to combine and blend ingredients. Open bag and carefully squeeze it to remove excess air. Seal bag.

In a 1-quart freezer bag, add:

1½ pounds shrimp

Carefully squeeze the bag to remove excess air. Seal bag.

To prevent freezer burn, place the filled bags in a 2-gallon freezer bag. Seal the bag and place your label on it or write the recipe name and preparation date on the bag with your Sharpie marking pen; place bag in your freezer.

SIMPLE SHRIMP CREOLE

Serves 6

Cooking Instructions

Preassembled Ingredients

4½ tablespoons olive oil

1 cup chopped onion

¾ cup chopped green bell pepper

¾ cup chopped celery

2 cloves garlic, pressed (or use minced, jarred kind)

4½ tablespoons flour

1 14.5-ounce can crushed tomatoes, undrained

¾ cup low sodium chicken broth

1½ teaspoons Cajun seasoning

Salt, to taste

½ teaspoon ground red pepper (more or less to taste)

1 bay leaf
1½ pounds shrimp

Cooking Instructions

Thaw shrimp bag and sauce mixture bag.

Heat contents of sauce bag in a large skillet with a tight-fitting lid over medium heat; stir until well combined. Cover skillet, reduce heat, and simmer for 20 minutes, stirring occasionally.

Stir in shrimp and cook for 5 minutes or until shrimp turn pink. Remove and discard bay leaves.

PER SERVING:

484 Calories; 14g Fat; 32g Protein; 59g Carbohydrate; 8g Dietary Fiber; 173mg Cholesterol; 505mg Sodium. Exchanges: 2½ Grain (Starch); 3½ Lean Meat; 3½ Vegetable; 2 Fat; 0 Other Carbohydrates.

SERVING SUGGESTION: Brown rice, steamed asparagus, and a big salad.

SHRIMP PEPPER SKILLET

Serves 6

Assembly Guidelines

In a 1-gallon freezer bag, place:

2 tablespoons olive oil
1 cup chopped onion
2 cups frozen chopped tricolored bell peppers
3 cloves garlic, pressed (or use minced, jarred kind)
Salt and pepper, to taste
1¼ pounds shrimp

Seal bag and gently toss to coat shrimp. Open the bag and carefully squeeze it to remove excess air. Seal the bag.

To prevent freezer burn, place the filled bag in a second 1-gallon freezer bag. Seal the bag and place your label on it or write the recipe name and preparation date on the bag with your Sharpie marking pen; place bag in your freezer.

SHRIMP PEPPER SKILLET

Serves 6

Cooking Instructions

Preassembled Ingredients
2 tablespoons olive oil
1 cup chopped onion
2 cups frozen chopped tricolored bell peppers
3 cloves garlic, pressed (or use minced, jarred kind)
Salt and pepper, to taste
1¼ pounds shrimp

At-time-of-Cooking Ingredients
12 ounces fettuccine pasta
2 teaspoons dried basil
3 tablespoons grated Romano cheese

Cooking Instructions

Thaw shrimp and sauce mixture.

Cook fettuccine pasta according to package directions; drain and set aside.

Meanwhile, pour shrimp and sauce mixture into a large skillet over medium heat. Cook until shrimp turn pink, stirring frequently.

Toss cooked pasta into shrimp mixture; add basil and toss again; serve with a sprinkling of Romano cheese on top.

PER SERVING:
166 Calories; 6g Fat; 20g Protein; 7g Carbohydrate; 1g Dietary Fiber; 144mg Cholesterol; 142mg Sodium. Exchanges: 2½ Lean Meat; 1 Vegetable; 1 Fat.

SERVING SUGGESTION: Serve a big salad on the side.

BROILED SHRIMP SCAMPI

Serves 6

Assembly Guidelines
In a 1-gallon freezer bag, place:

⅓ cup olive oil
⅓ cup lemon juice
4½ tablespoons chopped parsley
4 large cloves garlic, pressed (or use minced, jarred kind)
Salt and pepper, to taste
⅓ teaspoon crushed red pepper flakes
2¼ pounds shrimp

Seal the bag and gently shake to coat shrimp. Open the bag and carefully squeeze it to remove excess air. Seal the bag.

To prevent freezer burn, place the filled bag in a second 1-gallon freezer bag. Seal the bag and place your label on it or write the recipe name and preparation date on the bag with your Sharpie marking pen; place bag in your freezer.

BROILED SHRIMP SCAMPI

Serves 6

Cooking Instructions

Preassembled Ingredients
⅓ cup olive oil
⅓ cup lemon juice
4½ tablespoons chopped parsley
4 large cloves garlic, pressed (or use minced, jarred kind)
Salt and pepper, to taste
⅓ teaspoon crushed red pepper flakes
2¼ pounds shrimp

Cooking Instructions
Thaw shrimp bag.

Preheat oven broiler or outdoor or indoor grill. Lightly grease broiler pan or nonstick grid.

Drain shrimp, discarding marinade and bag. Arrange on prepared broiler pan/grid and cook for 4–5 minutes or until shrimp turn pink.

PER SERVING:
248 Calories; 10g Fat; 35g Protein; 4g Carbohydrate; trace Dietary Fiber; 259mg Cholesterol; 254mg Sodium. Exchanges: 0 Grain (Starch); 5 Lean Meat; 0 Vegetable; 0 Fruit; 1½ Fat.

SERVING SUGGESTION: Serve with fettuccine pasta tossed with olive oil and grated Parmesan cheese. Add steamed broccoli.

BROILED GINGER SHRIMP

Serves 6

Assembly Guidelines
In a 1-gallon freezer bag, place:

2½ pounds shrimp
1½ tablespoons low sodium soy sauce
1½ tablespoons lemon juice
1½ teaspoons vegetable oil
3 teaspoons grated fresh gingerroot

Seal the bag and gently shake to coat shrimp. Open the bag and carefully squeeze it to remove excess air. Seal the bag.

To prevent freezer burn, place the filled bag in a second 1-gallon freezer bag. Seal the bag and place your label on it or write the recipe name and preparation date on the bag with your Sharpie marking pen; place bag in your freezer.

BROILED GINGER SHRIMP

Cooking Instructions

Preassembled Ingredients
2½ pounds shrimp
1½ tablespoons low sodium soy sauce
1½ tablespoons lemon juice
1½ teaspoons vegetable oil
3 teaspoons grated fresh gingerroot

Cooking Instructions

Thaw shrimp bag.

Preheat oven broiler or outdoor or indoor grill. Lightly grease broiler pan or nonstick grill pan.

Drain shrimp, discarding marinade and bag. Arrange on prepared broiler pan or nonstick grid. Cook for 4–5 minutes or until shrimp turn pink.

PER SERVING:
373 Calories; 7g Fat; 69g Protein; 3g Carbohydrate; trace Dietary Fiber; 518mg Cholesterol; 512mg Sodium. Exchanges: 9½ Lean Meat; 0 Vegetable; 0 Fruit; 0 Fat.

SERVING SUGGESTION: Brown rice and steamed sugar snap peas and baby carrots.

PORK

THE RECIPES

Pork with Pears
Pork Fajitas
Tomato Pork Chops
Baked Sweet Potato Pork Chops
Sage Pork Chops

Dinner Kit Shopping Lists

ASSEMBLY-TIME SHOPPING LIST

MEAT

27 boneless loin pork chops

CONDIMENTS

olive oil (you'll need 1 tablespoon)
vegetable oil (you'll need 4 teaspoons)
balsamic vinegar (you'll need 1½ tablespoons)
Salsa, for garnish (optional)
pure maple syrup (you'll need 3 tablespoons)

PRODUCE

2 medium onions
1–2 cloves garlic
green onions (optional)
2 cups cooked, mashed sweet potatoes
1 large tomato
cilantro, for garnish (optional)
juice of one lemon

CANNED GOODS

3 cups low sodium chicken broth
3 cups low sodium tomato juice
1 15-ounce can sliced pears in juice
1 8-ounce can crushed pineapple

SPICES

chili powder (you'll need ¾ teaspoon)
dried oregano (you'll need ¾ teaspoon)
cinnamon (you'll need ¼ teaspoon)
sage (you'll need 1⅛ teaspoons)

DAIRY

butter (⅓ cup plus 5 tablespoons)
sour cream, for optional garnish

DRY GOODS

brown sugar (you'll need 1½ teaspoons)

FROZEN

1 16-ounce package frozen bell peppers stir-fry

BAKERY

6 whole-wheat flour tortillas

OTHER

aluminum foil wrap
freezer bags:
    1-quart 1
    1-gallon 9
    2-gallon 1

MEALTIME SHOPPING LIST

CONDIMENTS

olive oil (you'll need 1 tablespoon)
salsa, for optional garnish

PRODUCE

1 large tomato
green onions, chopped for optional garnish
cilantro, chopped for optional garnish

DAIRY

sour cream, for optional garnish

BAKERY

6 whole-wheat flour tortillas

Preassembly Prep List

MEAT

Rinse pork chops and pat dry.

Cut 3 pork chops into strips.

Refrigerate all pork until ready to assemble in kit.

CONDIMENTS

Set out:

vegetable oil

balsamic vinegar

maple syrup

PRODUCE

SWEET POTATOES

Rinse sweet potatoes under running water to wash.

Peel sweet potatoes.

Boil sweet potatoes until fork-tender; drain and mash with a potato masher.

ONIONS

White or yellow onions: Cut off both ends and peel first layer.

Thinly slice 2 onions.

GARLIC

Press 1–2 cloves of garlic.

LEMON

Rinse lemon under running water to wash.

Using your palm, press and roll the lemon on your countertop a few times to help release the juice from the pulp.

(Tip: Lemons stored at room temperature release more juice than lemons stored in your refrigerator.)

Cut lemon in half and juice.

If you don't have a juicer, squeeze the lemon over a bowl by hand. Be sure to remove any seeds from the juice.

CANNED GOODS

Open all cans; rinse/drain contents where necessary.

Measure out 2–3 cups low sodium tomato juice.

SPICES

Set out:

chili powder

oregano

cinnamon

sage

salt

black pepper

DRY GOODS

Measure 1½ teaspoons brown sugar.

PORK WITH PEARS

Serves 6

Assembly Guidelines

In a 1-gallon freezer bag, place:

4 tablespoons butter, melted

1 15-ounce can sliced pears in juice, drained

1½ teaspoons brown sugar

6 boneless loin pork chops

1½ cups low sodium chicken broth

1½ tablespoons balsamic vinegar

Seal the bag and gently massage it to coat pork. Open the bag and carefully squeeze it to remove excess air. Seal the bag.

To prevent freezer burn, place the filled bag in a second 1-gallon freezer bag. Seal the bag and place your label on it or write the recipe name and preparation date on the bag with your Sharpie marking pen; place bag in your freezer.

PORK WITH PEARS

Serves 6

Cooking Instructions

Preassembled Ingredients
4 tablespoons butter, melted
1 15-ounce can sliced pears in juice, drained
1½ teaspoons brown sugar
6 boneless loin pork chops
1½ cups low sodium chicken broth
1½ tablespoons balsamic vinegar

At-Time-of-Cooking Ingredients
1 tablespoon olive oil

Cooking Instructions

Thaw and remove pork chops from freezer bag; reseal bag and set aside.

Heat the olive oil in a large skillet with a tight-fitting lid over medium heat; add pork chops and sauté for 5 minutes or until lightly browned; remove from skillet and set aside.

Pour remaining ingredients from the freezer bag into the skillet and whisk up all of the browned bits from the bottom of the pan. Return pork chops to the skillet; bring to a boil, then reduce heat, cover, and simmer till cooked through.

PER SERVING:
348 Calories; 17g Fat; 26g Protein; 8g Carbohydrate; 1g Dietary Fiber; 97mg Cholesterol; 276mg Sodium. Exchanges: 3½ Lean Meat; ½ Fruit; 2½ Fat; 0 Other Carbohydrates.

SERVING SUGGESTION: Steamed red potatoes and steamed green beans.

PORK FAJITAS

Assembly Guidelines

In a 1-gallon freezer bag, place:

3 boneless loin pork chops, sliced into thin strips
4 teaspoons vegetable oil
1 lemon, juiced
1–2 cloves garlic, pressed
¾ teaspoon chili powder
¾ teaspoon dried oregano
1 medium onion, thinly sliced
1 16-ounce package frozen bell peppers stir-fry

Seal the bag and gently massage it to coat the pork. Open the bag and carefully squeeze it to remove excess air. Seal the bag.

To prevent freezer burn, place the filled bag in a second 1-gallon freezer bag. Seal the bag and place your label on it or write the recipe name and preparation date on the bag with your Sharpie marking pen; place bag in your freezer.

PORK FAJITAS

Serves 6

Cooking Instructions

Preassembled Ingredients
3 boneless loin pork chops, sliced into thin strips
4 teaspoons vegetable oil
1 lemon, juiced
1–2 cloves garlic, pressed
¾ teaspoon chili powder
¾ teaspoon dried oregano
1 medium onion, thinly sliced
1 16-ounce package frozen bell peppers stir-fry

At-Time-of-Cooking Ingredients
1 large tomato, cut into wedges
6 whole-wheat flour tortillas, warmed

Optional garnishes:
salsa
sour cream
chopped cilantro
chopped green onions

Cooking Instructions

Thaw contents of freezer bag and place in a wok or large skillet; stir-fry for 3–7 minutes or until pork is almost done. Add tomato and continue to stir-fry for about 1 minute.

Serve with tortillas and desired garnishes.

PER SERVING:
344 Calories; 11g Fat; 17g Protein; 44g Carbohydrate; 3g Dietary Fiber; 26mg Cholesterol; 371mg Sodium. Exchanges: 2½ Grain (Starch); 1½ Lean Meat; ½ Vegetable; 0 Fruit; 1½ Fat.

SERVING SUGGESTION: A big salad.

TOMATO PORK CHOPS

Serves 6

Assembly Guidelines

In a 1-gallon freezer bag, place:

6 boneless loin pork chops
2–3 cups low sodium tomato juice
Salt and pepper, to taste
1 medium onion, thinly sliced

Seal the bag and gently massage it to coat pork. Open the bag and carefully squeeze it to remove excess air. Seal the bag.

To prevent freezer burn, place the filled bag in a second 1-gallon freezer bag. Seal the bag and place your label on it or write the recipe name and preparation date on the bag with your Sharpie marking pen; place bag in your freezer.

TOMATO PORK CHOPS

Serves 6

Cooking Instructions

Preassembled Ingredients
6 boneless loin pork chops
2–3 cups low sodium tomato juice
Salt and pepper, to taste
1 medium onion, thinly sliced

Cooking Instructions

Preheat oven to 325 degrees.

Thaw contents of freezer bag, then place in an 8-inch baking dish, arranging so that onions are on the top; cover with aluminum foil wrap; bake for 30 minutes or until cooked through.

PER SERVING:
179 Calories; 7g Fat; 23g Protein; 7g Carbohydrate; 1g Dietary Fiber; 67mg Cholesterol; 65mg Sodium. Exchanges: 3 Lean Meat; 1 Vegetable.

SERVING SUGGESTION: Brown rice topped with a dollop of sour cream and chopped green onions. Add steamed broccoli.

BAKED SWEET POTATOES
AND PORK CHOPS

Serves 6

Assembly Guidelines
In a 1-quart freezer bag, place:

2 cups cooked, mashed fresh sweet potatoes

Carefully squeeze the bag to remove excess air. Seal the bag.
In a 1-gallon freezer bag, place:

6 boneless loin pork chops
1 tablespoon butter, melted
1 tablespoon olive oil
Salt and pepper, to taste
1 8-ounce can crushed pineapple
3 tablespoons pure maple syrup
¼ teaspoon cinnamon

Seal the bag and gently massage it to coat pork chops. Open the bag and carefully squeeze it to remove excess air. Seal the bag.

To prevent freezer burn, place both of the filled freezer bags in a 2-gallon freezer bag. Seal the bag and place your label on it or write the recipe name and preparation date on the bag with your Sharpie marking pen; place bag in your freezer.

BAKED SWEET POTATOES
AND PORK CHOPS

Serves 6

Cooking Instructions

Preassembled Ingredients
2 cups cooked, mashed fresh sweet potatoes
6 boneless loin pork chops
1 tablespoon butter, melted
1 tablespoon olive oil
Salt and pepper, to taste

1 8-ounce can crushed pineapple
3 tablespoons pure maple syrup
¼ teaspoon cinnamon

Cooking Instructions

Preheat oven to 350 degrees.

Thaw contents of freezer bags. Place contents of the 1-gallon freezer bag in a 9 x 13–inch baking dish; top with mashed sweet potatoes. Bake for 30 minutes or until pork chops are cooked through.

PER SERVING:
339 Calories; 13g Fat; 23g Protein; 33g Carbohydrate; 2g Dietary Fiber; 58mg Cholesterol; 187mg Sodium. Exchanges: 1½ Grain (Starch); 3 Lean Meat; ½ Fruit; 1½ Fat; ½ Other Carbohydrates.

SERVING SUGGESTION: Add steamed broccoli.

SAGE PORK CHOPS

Serves 6

Assembly Guidelines

In a 1-gallon freezer bag, place:

Salt and pepper, to taste
1⅛ teaspoons sage
6 boneless loin pork chops
⅓ cup butter
1½ cups low sodium chicken broth

Seal the bag and gently massage it to coat pork chops. Open the bag and carefully squeeze it to remove excess air. Seal the bag.

To prevent freezer burn, place the filled bag in a second 1-gallon freezer bag. Seal the bag and place your label on it or write the recipe name and preparation date on the bag with your Sharpie marking pen; place bag in your freezer.

SAGE PORK CHOPS

Cooking Instructions

Preassembled Ingredients
Salt and pepper, to taste
1⅛ teaspoons sage
6 boneless loin pork chops
⅓ cup butter
1½ cups low sodium chicken broth

Cooking Instructions
Preheat oven to 350 degrees.

Thaw contents of freezer bag; place in a 9 x 13–inch baking dish; bake, uncovered, for 30 minutes or until pork chops are fork-tender and cooked through.

PER SERVING:
199 Calories; 11g Fat; 24g Protein; 1g Carbohydrate; trace Dietary Fiber; 77mg Cholesterol; 221mg Sodium. Exchanges: 0 Grain (Starch); 3 Lean Meat; 1 Fat.

SERVING SUGGESTION: Mashed potatoes, steamed cauliflower, and steamed baby carrots.

INDEX

LEANNE ELY is considered *the* expert on family cooking and healthy eating. She is a certified nutritionist and the host of SavingDinner.com. Her syndicated newspaper column, The Dinner Diva, appears in 225 newspapers nationwide. She has a weekly Food for Thought column on the ever-popular FlyLady.net website, as well as her own e-zine, *Healthy Foods*. Along with Marla Cilley, she cohosts *The FLY Show: FlyLady, Leanne, and You* on World Talk Radio.

Ely has appeared on numerous television shows and has made contributions to such magazines as *Woman's Day, Women's Health and Fitness*, and to websites, including eDiets.com, where she is the family columnist, drlaura.com, FamilyNetwork.com, and iparenting.com. She is the author of several books, including the New York Times bestseller *Body Clutter*. She lives in North Carolina with her two teenage children.